Abortion and Moral Theory

L. W. SUMNER

Abortion and Moral Theory

PRINCETON UNIVERSITY PRESS
PRINCETON, NEW JERSEY

For Sue

Contents

Preface

This book has both a practical and a theoretical aim. On the one hand it joins the continuing public debate concerning the morality of abortion and the choice of an abortion policy. That debate has become polarized around two equally prominent and extreme positions: the liberal view advanced by most feminist organizations and the conservative view promoted by "prolife" groups. When these established views are subjected to careful critical analysis, both are revealed as indefensible. The ways in which they fail, however, point us toward a more moderate alternative that retains their strengths while avoiding their defects. This middle way in turn defines the outlines of a sound abortion policy.

On the other hand it joins the philosophical debate. Although philosophers have in recent years made indispensable contributions to our understanding of the abortion question, their discussions have too often lacked theoretical depth. Both the rejection of the established views and the defense of a moderate position must ultimately be grounded in a moral theory. Having identified the main types of ethical theory, this book defends classical utilitarianism against its traditional rivals. When this theory has been properly formulated, and when its implications for questions of killing and reproduction have been examined, it can be seen to provide the needed foundation for a moderate view of abortion. That view is strengthened by being grounded in a viable moral theory, and the theory is in turn confirmed by generating an independently attractive answer to the abortion question. The book's practical and theoretical aims are thus mutually supporting.

The order of presentation moves from the practical to the theoretical. The first chapter deploys resources that will be exploited in the discussion to follow. The next two chapters criticize the liberal/feminist and conservative/"prolife" positions. Once these have been discarded, the way is clear for constructing a more persuasive view to replace them. The fourth chapter defends this view on an intuitive level. The more theoretical work is done in the remaining two chapters. The classical version of utilitarianism is described and defended in chapter five, and in the last chapter utilitarianism is shown to be the deep structure of a moderate view of abortion.

Nonphilosophical readers should have little difficulty with the first four chapters, which can be understood without further, theoretical support. The last two chapters are addressed to issues with which philosophers will be more familiar, and they may therefore be somewhat more difficult for the general reader. They have, however, been written so as to avoid needless jargon and to make complex philosophical questions as plain and accessible as possible. All readers are urged to continue through them, since only then is a complete view possible of the way in which an abortion position can be given a philosophical justification.

April 1980

Acknowledgments

Work on this book was supported principally by a Canada Council Leave Fellowship for the academic year 1977–1978, but also by a University of Toronto Research Leave Grant (1977–1978) and a University of Toronto Humanities and Social Sciences Grant (1979–1980). To all of these sources I here record my gratitude.

All or part of an earlier draft was read by Derek Parfit and G. A. Cohen, both of whom made many valuable suggestions and raised many important criticisms. Derek Allen and the Princeton University Press readers Joel Feinberg and Judith Tormey contributed helpful comments on the final draft. I am also grateful to Susan Strawson and Esther Tameanko for their patient work on the unfamiliar task of typing the manuscript.

Finally, I owe a special debt to Colonel and Mrs. W. E. Brooks for their hospitality during my stay in England in the spring of 1978. Whatever merits this book may possess are due in no small measure to the peace and seclusion of their Sussex cottage.

Abortion and Moral Theory

CHAPTER ONE

The Abortion Debate

As late as two decades ago abortion was nowhere a prominent public issue. In virtually every nation of the world, performing an abortion was, under all but the rarest of circumstances, a criminal act. Abortions were done none the less, whether in the penumbra of the law where they could be disguised as orthodox medical procedures or in the backstreets, but transactions in the abortion market were shrouded in secrecy. Abortionists, qualified and unqualified alike, risked prosecution for practicing their trade. Their patients were liable to subtler but surer pressures from a public that regarded abortion, like sex itself, as dark and shameful. Few voices were raised against this conspiracy of silence and guilt. An organized women's movement was nonexistent in the fifties. Although the control of reproduction had been an issue for decades, the energies of reform groups were largely directed to securing legal access to contraceptives. Most such groups, whether out of principle or pragmatism, took pains to distinguish the availability of contraception from that of abortion. The consensus on all sides was that abortion was a further and much more troubled question, one that it was premature to place on the public agenda.

Once introduced onto that agenda, the revision of traditional abortion laws was accomplished with astonishing swiftness. In many countries the prohibition of abortion was weakened by broadening the grounds on which the procedure would be permitted. Other jurisdictions went even further by decriminalizing the act altogether, except for the requirement (common to all medical procedures) that it be performed by a licensed physician in appropriate facilities. Today the policies in force in Canada, the United States, Great Britain, Eastern Europe, the Soviet

Union, China, India, Japan, and most of the countries of Western Europe permit millions of abortions to be carried out legally every year. The old prohibitions are now the nearly exclusive property of Latin America, Africa, and parts of Asia. The tide continues to run in the direction of liberalization. Once the former controls have been loosened or removed they are seldom restored, and nearly every year new jurisdictions introduce reforms. These changes of law have been grounded in equally dramatic shifts in public opinion. In most countries only a small minority continues to favor the old restrictions; the majority appears to support at least a moderate policy permitting a significant number of legal abortions.[1]

The period of reform has also been the period of public debate concerning the status of abortion. In the democracies of the West that debate has been dominated by two parties: "prolife" organizations advocating the traditional restrictive policies, and feminists lobbying for the reform or repeal of abortion laws. The political goals of these parties are quite obviously incompatible: any policy acceptable to one side must of necessity offend the other. Neither group is lacking in commitment, energy, or resources. Since the rate of unwanted pregnancies, and hence the demand for abortion, shows no sign of declining, the practical problem that elicits these conflicting responses is unlikely to resolve itself spontaneously. Further, these opposed views on the specific question of abortion are embedded within equally opposed ideologies concerning the status of women, the significance of marriage and the nuclear family, and the morality of sex and reproduction. On these larger issues the principal parties to the abortion debate simply inhabit different worlds. For each there is too much at stake for any accommodation of the other to be acceptable. Although legislative compromises can be im-

---

1. Badgley (1977), pp. 459–460, gives the results of an opinion survey in Canada. For similar results in Britain, see Lane (1974), vol. 2, pp. 20–23.

posed upon the parties, there is a deeper sense in which the political issue of abortion is insoluble. No policy, however judiciously drafted, can fail to violate principles held dear by at least one of these groups.

For most of us the important question is not how this political conflict will actually be resolved, but how it *ought* to be resolved. Answering this question requires deciding what to think about abortion. Since each of the two main parties to the public debate is telling us what to think about abortion, it is natural to begin with a critique of their positions, a critique whose objective will be to discover which, if either, of them merits the allegiance of thoughtful and conscientious persons. Conducting this critique requires that we bring into sharper focus the issues on which the established views are so deeply divided.

1. *The Elements of Conflict*

Abortion is a moral problem. The existence of a moral problem presupposes some conflict of values or goals or interests. A solution to a moral problem is a resolution of such conflict; the purpose of moral principles is to tell us how to resolve moral conflicts. Where the conflict is genuine, any resolution will require some degree of sacrifice of at least one of the competing elements, and our moral principles will therefore direct us to the proper balance or trade-off among them. The paradigm of moral conflict is a collision between the good or well-being of different persons. If abortion is a moral problem, we should expect it to display this dimension of interpersonal conflict.

Pregnancy in our species consists in a special relation between a sexually mature member of the species (so far at least, invariably a woman) and an immature member (a child). The relation is, roughly, that the child is resident within the woman's body and dependent upon her body for life support. If we describe the child throughout the duration of pregnancy as a fetus, then pregnancy consists in a special relation between a woman and a fetus.[2] This condition normally begins with conception and ends when the fetus has emerged from the woman's body and the life-support connection between the two has been broken. The normal outcome of pregnancy is live birth. In general a process or sequence of events has aborted when it has been interrupted before issuing in its normal or natural outcome. In the broadest sense, therefore, a pregnancy has aborted when it has terminated before issuing in live birth. Usually, however, the term "abortion" is reserved for two special cases. Spontaneous abortion is the expulsion of a previable fetus by natural causes, that is, where the expulsion has not been intentionally brought about by any agent. Induced abortion is the intentional termination of a pregnancy before the fetus is viable.[3] In the discussion to follow, "abortion" will mean induced abortion.

Before viability the fetus is dependent for survival on the maternal life-support system. By definition, abortion deprives the fetus of the life support that has nurtured it up to the time at which the abortion is performed. Most techniques for inducing abortion involve killing the fetus while it is still lodged within

2. Technically a fetus is "the product of conception from the end of the eighth week to the moment of birth" (*Stedman's Medical Dictionary*). The fetal stage is preceded by those of the zygote (conception to three weeks) and embryo (four to seven weeks). But the usual practice in the abortion debate is to refer to the unborn child at any stage of development as a fetus.

3. Fetal viability is the capacity of the fetus to survive outside the uterus. Conventionally a fetus is assumed to be viable sometime during the sixth month of gestation. Thus defined, viability is a weak statistical notion: a fetus is viable if it has some chance of survival, however small. The survival rate for sixth-month fetuses is low, and the rate escalates steadily until the ninth month. Abortion is to be distinguished from premature birth and stillbirth, both of which involve fetuses that are (statistically) viable. However, the statistical definition of viability and the somewhat arbitrary location of a "point" of viability ensure that there will be borderline cases in which it is unclear whether to describe a procedure as abortion or premature delivery.

the uterus. There is thus a close causal connection between induced abortion and the death of the fetus, a connection close enough to tempt one to suppose that abortion necessarily (by definition) brings about fetal death. If this were so, abortion would necessarily be an act of killing. But it is not so. This is suggested by the fact that one abortion technique—hysterotomy—does not involve killing the fetus before it is separated from its mother.[4] Since hysterotomy is usually performed close to the stage of viability, it can produce a live fetus with some chance of extrauterine survival—a premature birth. Technically, this may no longer count as an abortion since the fetus, as it turned out, was not previable. But there is no *point* in pregnancy at which a fetus becomes viable; the probability of extrauterine survival becomes more than negligible sometime after the midpoint of pregnancy and increases steadily until the normal term of forty weeks. Any cutoff point distinguishing abortions from stillbirths or premature births is thus highly arbitrary. Certainly in cases like the one mentioned, hysterotomy is *intended* as abortion.

But we do not need the rare case in which a fetus survives abortion in order to show that abortion does not necessarily include killing, or otherwise causing the death of, the fetus. Abortion does necessarily deprive the fetus of the life-support system on which it has hitherto depended, but it does not preclude substituting another such system. Imagine that we develop a technology of fetal transfer enabling us to relocate a previable fetus from its natural mother either to another woman or to an artificial placenta. For the woman whose pregnancy is thereby terminated such a transfer has precisely the same effect as an abortion—indeed, it is an abortion. The abortion technology that we

4. Hysterotomy involves removing the fetus through an abdominal incision of the uterus. It is generally performed only when the fetus is too large to permit the use of other techniques, thus at or near the conventional point of viability.

now employ generally precludes the possibility of such transfers by killing the fetus in the uterus. But abortion is not to be identified with any particular abortion technique; if techniques are possible (at least in principle) that preserve the life of the fetus, then abortion need not (logically) bring about the death of the fetus. It is a necessary truth that abortion interrupts pregnancy, not that it is fatal to the fetus.

The relation between abortion and fetal death is therefore not logical but causal. This conceptual fact notwithstanding, it remains the case that the three abortion techniques now in commonest use—dilatation and curettage, vacuum aspiration, and saline injection—all invariably kill the fetus. The fourth and least common—hysterotomy—nearly always results in fetal death. Until we develop an abortion technology compatible with fetal survival, the practice of abortion will continue to present us with a moral conflict.

The principal parties to the conflict are the two individuals whose special relation constitutes pregnancy. What is at stake for the fetus is life itself. In the normal case in which the fetus is healthy we assume that its life, were it to continue, would be one worth living. To abort the fetus is to deprive it (or the individual into whom it will develop) of that life. What is at stake for the woman is autonomy—control of the uses to be made of her body. Pregnancy is a parasitic relation: whereas the mother supplies essential nutrients to the fetus and disposes of its wastes, the fetus makes no comparable contribution to her well-being.[5] For nine months of a normal gestation another creature lives off a woman's body. Not only does pregnancy violate a woman's physical integrity, but it also produces side effects ranging from the merely disagreeable (weight gain, damage to muscle tone, nausea, fatigue, depression) through the positively painful (giv-

5. A parasite is "an organism that lives on or in another and draws its nourishment therefrom" (*Stedman's Medical Dictionary*). Host and parasite need not be members of different species.

ing birth) to the downright dangerous (complications). Some of these side effects, moreover, are permanent and irreversible. As one feminist has put it, "Childbirth *hurts*. And it isn't good for you."[6]

In a mammalian species pregnancy is the (so far) indispensable means of producing offspring. If its normal end is wanted or valued, being pregnant may have its own unique rewards. These rewards, however, are dependent upon the bond created with the infant. It would be strange to encounter someone who valued pregnancy as an experience while caring not at all whether it culminated in the birth of a child. If a woman does not want a baby (or does not want one now), prolonging a pregnancy will understandably have little appeal for her. Once an unwanted pregnancy is under way, abortion is the only means available of preventing it from continuing through its normal duration. If a woman seeks an abortion, then denying her access to it imposes upon her the costs of pregnancy; more importantly, it also erodes her ability to control the disposition of her body.[7]

Once an unwanted pregnancy is under way, therefore, the life of the fetus may conflict with the autonomy of the woman who is carrying it. In such cases, given our present technology, one good must inevitably be sacrificed to the other: thus the moral dilemma of abortion. The dilemma can be avoided only by avoiding unwanted pregnancies. Although research continues on contraceptive techniques, every method developed to date has serious drawbacks. Unless women either decrease their sexual activity or increase their desire to bear children (neither tendency being currently visible), the frequency of unwanted pregnancies will remain at least constant. In that case we need moral princi-

6. Firestone (1972), p. 198.

7. Completing any unwanted pregnancy will be costly for a woman. The additional burden of losing control over the use of her body arises only if she chooses abortion and is prevented from carrying out that choice.

ples that will tell us how to weigh the lives of fetuses against the autonomy of women.

The conflict that generates the moral problem of abortion is particularly perplexing because it has two special features. The first is the unique relation between mother and fetus. In no other human context is one person's body necessary over a lengthy period as life support for the body of another. The mother/fetus relation resembles in some respects the relation between blood or organ donor and recipient, but the disanalogies are highly significant. In these latter cases the burden upon the donor is typically of brief duration, voluntarily assumed, and transferable to others. An unwanted pregnancy is continuous through nine months, unsought, and nontransferable. Perhaps a closer parallel is with the task of caring for an aged or chronically ill member of the family. But even here the fit is imperfect since this burden can often be shared with or turned over to others. Further, all these other cases feature individuals with previous histories and perhaps a previous relationship with one another. A woman can have no acquaintance with her fetus before she finds herself serving as its host. The mother/fetus relation lacks an exact, or even a near, analogue elsewhere in human life. We thus have no model available to guide our moral reflection upon it.

The second special feature of the abortion conflict is the unique nature of the fetus. Interpersonal conflict is conflict among persons. Our paradigm of a person is a mature human being; although the mother fits this paradigm nicely the fetus does not. Again we have no exact analogue to which to turn. A human fetus is not a nonhuman animal; it is a stage of a human being. But it is not quite like any other stage, although it is closer to some (infants) than to others (adults). Further, the term "fetus" masks the fact that we are here dealing with a being who undergoes enormous changes over a period of nine months. Are we to think of a fertilized ovum, an embryo, and a nine-month fetus in the same way? To what extent can we apply notions like interest, good, or well-being to such creatures? Indeed, should we think of abortion as containing an interpersonal conflict at all (perhaps only *one* person is involved)?

The moral problem of abortion is uncommonly perplexing because it turns on this special relation between a woman and a special sort of thing. A view of the morality of abortion will tell us what to think of both of these features by offering us models to which they may be assimilated. In doing so, it will explain the moral significance of each feature and show how each bears upon the proper resolution of the abortion conflict.

2. *Contexts of Decision*

Abortion is not one moral problem but two. Better, it is two sets of problems, each arising in its own context. The primary context is that in which a woman decides whether or not to have an abortion, and a physician decides whether or not to perform it. Here the focus is on the moral status of abortion itself. In what moral category does abortion belong? Is having an abortion, or performing one, right or wrong, moral or immoral, good or evil? What *sort* of act is an abortion? With what other acts should we associate it? Is it more like murder or unplugging a life-support system or removing an appendix? How should we compare it to the two acts that lie, so to speak, just on either side of it—contraception and infanticide? Is it worse than the former but not so bad as the latter? Which is it more like? Is completing an unwanted pregnancy obligatory? Can abortion ever be obligatory? Does abortion violate the rights of the fetus?

Because all of these questions arise in the first instance when a woman is deciding whether or not to seek an abortion, we may call them collectively the *personal* problem of abortion. On some views the personal problem receives a simple answer: either abortion is always wrong or it is never wrong. On any such view abortion is a kind of act with a uniform moral quality that is utterly unaffected by its circumstances. Simple treatments of the

problem avoid awkward further questions about the moral significance of circumstances. What are the conditions under which
an abortion is justified? What role is played by the burden that
the continuation of pregnancy will impose upon a woman—the
risk to her life, or health, or career, or economic position, or ability to meet other obligations? What role is played by her responsibility for being pregnant? Is the situation altered if she was
raped, or her contraceptive failed, or she was deceived by a man
who claimed to be sterile? Is it altered if she made no effort to
avoid conception, while fully aware of the risks she was taking?
What if she was ignorant of the mechanics of conception or had
been misled concerning the efficacy of her contraceptive
method? What role is played by her ability to understand what
she was doing? Is the moral status of abortion affected by the
fact that the "woman" is a mentally retarded adolescent? What
role is played by the age or condition of the fetus? Should we
think of early abortions as significantly different from later ones?
Is an intrauterine device (IUD) significantly different from a saline injection? Is abortion justified when the fetus is defective? If
so, how defective must it be? What if we cannot be certain
about the defect? If a number of these factors are relevant in determining the moral status of abortion, how are they to be combined and balanced in a particular case? How can we ever be certain whether a particular abortion is justified?

The other, and secondary, context is that in which a society
chooses a policy concerning abortion. Is a special policy necessary, or should abortion simply be regulated as any other medical
procedure? Should abortion be treated as a criminal offense? If
so, what should count as a defense? Should the woman be
charged as well as the abortionist? Should publicly funded institutions be required to allocate facilities for abortions? Should
abortions be funded by public medical insurance schemes?
Should abortions be permitted in specialized clinics as well as
hospitals? Should agencies be permitted to realize a profit from

abortion referrals? Because all of these questions require social policy decisions concerning abortion, we may call them collectively the *political* problem. Again, simple solutions are conceivable: either abortion ought to be entirely prohibited or it ought to be entirely unregulated. More complex views will need both to distinguish between those abortions that are to be permitted and those that are not and to select some mechanism for deciding particular cases.

The personal problem and the political problem are both moral problems. Each is rooted in the conflict that makes abortion a moral issue. Solving either problem requires stipulating how that conflict ought to be resolved. In both cases the questions we ask are moral ones, calling for answers from the moral point of view. In the one case the subject of moral assessment is abortion itself; in the other it is abortion policies. The personal problem is primary because we should expect an abortion policy to be adjusted at least in part to the kind of act that abortion is: if it is the moral equivalent of murder, that calls for one sort of policy; if it is no more serious than pulling a tooth, then quite another policy, or none at all, will be in order. The views advanced by the principal parties to the abortion debate offer connected solutions to the two problems. Those who regard abortion as virtually always evil tend also to advocate that it be illegal. Those who think abortion entirely innocent tend to oppose any special legal regulation of the act. The public debate thus wanders freely back and forth over the frontier between the two problems.

Each side to the debate provides an ordered pair of solutions to the personal and political problems of abortion. Each ordered pair appears to be a coherent grouping—it is intelligible that abortion should be illegal because it is immoral, or that it should be legal because it is not immoral. However, the connections between the two problems are not as straightforward as these packages suggest. Most accounts of the relations between law and morality leave room for acts that are immoral but should not be illegal (e.g., petty breaches of promise), and also for acts that should be illegal but are not immoral (e.g., swimming on unsafe beaches).[8] Though there is bound to be a large area of overlap between law and morality, the fit is far from perfect. In order to make a case for strict legal regulation of abortion, it is neither necessary nor sufficient to show that the act itself is wrong or evil; likewise, in order to make a case for little or no regulation, it is neither necessary nor sufficient to show that the act violates no moral rules. For both sides two further ingredients are required: an explanation of what makes abortion right or wrong and an account of the proper scope and function of the law. In order to be complete and well grounded a view of abortion must support its conclusions with both a moral and a political theory.

Every society has an abortion policy. The available options divide roughly into three groups.[9] A policy is *restrictive* if it either prohibits abortion altogether or confines its performance to those rare cases in which the continuation of pregnancy would threaten the woman's life. A policy is *moderate* if it stipulates a wider range of grounds for performing abortions—risk of impairment of the mother's health, fetal deformity, pregnancy due to rape, and so forth. A policy is *permissive* if it provides for abortion whenever the procedure has been agreed upon by a woman and her physician. A permissive policy could be accomplished by the simple absence of any legal treatment of abortion, so that it is governed by the same rules that apply to all other medical procedures. In practice, however, permissive policies invariably take the form of some explicit statutory or judicial provision for abortion. The distinctions among the three sorts of policy are obviously ones of degree. It is particularly easy to transform moderate policies into permissive ones by broadening the "indi-

8. See, for example, Gross (1979), pp. 13–18.
9. These categories are borrowed from Callahan (1970), p. 124.

cations" for abortion; a policy may thus be moderate on paper
and permissive in practice. However, the lines of division will be
clear enough for our purposes.

3. *The Established Views*

The liberal view of abortion is advanced chiefly by the women's
movement in the democracies of the West, although one need
not be a feminist in order to espouse it. Of the two features that
render the abortion conflict particularly perplexing, the liberal
view addresses only the special nature of the fetus. The claim
that is the heart of this view, and on which all of its further components depend, is that a fetus is not the kind of entity whose
rights or interests are properly taken into consideration in determining the morality of abortion. Although abortion results in
the death of the fetus, it does no harm or injury because the
fetus is not the sort of thing that can be harmed or injured.
Abortion therefore lacks a victim. In the liberal's opinion the appearance of interpersonal conflict in the case of abortion is an il-
lusion. The only party whose rights or interests are at stake is the
pregnant woman; because the fetus is granted no standing in the
question, there can be no genuine conflict. As long as an abortion is consented to and carried out competently, then it is a private matter between a woman and her physician. There is simply
no issue concerning the moral status of abortion—or at any rate
no issue that does not equally arise for all other surgical procedures.

On the liberal view abortion is morally on a par with appendectomy. If this is so, there is no ground for state regulation of
abortion that is not also a ground for state regulation of appendectomy. Any law that stipulates permissible grounds for performing abortions, or that prohibits their performance altogether, is an unwarranted invasion of the contractual
relationship between a woman and her physician. For abortion,
the only permissible policy is a permissive policy.

The link between the innocence of abortion and a permissive abortion policy is a liberal social theory. Such a theory divides the acts performed by responsible human agents into two categories: those that cause harm to others (public acts) and those that do not (private acts).[10] It is permissible for the state to use coercion against the performance of (at least some) public acts, by passing laws backed by sanctions prohibiting such acts. But it is absolutely impermissible for it to employ coercion against private acts. Any law regulating private activities is an illegitimate intrusion into the realm of personal liberty. Although abortion ostensibly displays this dimension of interpersonal injury, since causing a person's death is normally counted as causing injury, in fact the fetus does not possess the capacity to be injured. Abortion therefore belongs in the private realm, along with other medical procedures undertaken with the informed consent of the patient. Restrictive or moderate abortion laws protect no one against the use of force or fraud; therefore, they lack moral justification.

Such laws possess some special features that are particularly offensive to liberals. In the first place, they deny women equal opportunity. If women are to compete for social positions and rewards on an equal footing with men, it is essential that they have some control over any burdens that specially disadvantage them in such competitions. Certain cancers, for example, can occur only in women. It would clearly be discriminatory to permit men treatment for prostate cancer and to deny women treatment for cervical cancer. Likewise, only women can become pregnant. Pregnancy can be a significant interference in a woman's pursuit of social and economic goods. It is therefore essential that women be able to control their fertility. Such control requires access to both contraception and abortion. Denial of access to either impedes the ability of women to compete as

---

10. The classic source for such a theory is of course Mill (1977).

equals with their male counterparts and is therefore discriminatory.

Further, legal control of abortion is of a piece with legal control of sex. Until relatively recently most legal jurisdictions simply assumed their right to enforce standards of "normal" or acceptable sexual behavior. Virtually all jurisdictions still practice some such controls, whether of adultery, "deviant" sexual acts, incest, prostitution, or whatever. Historically, restrictions on access to contraceptives have been motivated by the belief that sex without procreative intent, or sex outside matrimony, was morally questionable. For the liberal, sexual activities among consenting, competent adults are private acts. They cannot be immoral and there is no justification for making them illegal. As governments relax their controls on sexual activities and life styles, and as they permit ready access to contraceptives, the influence of a liberal social theory becomes more and more deeply embedded in our legal systems. The continued existence of restrictive (or even moderate) abortion policies is, in the liberal's view, a relic of an earlier and more repressive age.

Finally, restrictive abortion laws are often the products of pressure exerted upon governments by religious groups who believe abortion to be immoral. In a free society such groups are entitled to hold and act upon this belief; they are even entitled to enforce their belief among their members, as long as membership itself is genuinely voluntary. But they are not entitled to enforce their belief among those who dissent from it. The enforcement by public law of the moral creed of some religious sect is out of place in a pluralistic and secular state.

In denying that the fetus is a party injured by an abortion, the liberal view makes short work of both the personal and political problems of abortion. The conservative view is almost as economical. Its principal advocate is the Catholic Church, although one need not be a Christian to espouse it. The claim at the heart of the conservative view is that abortion is a case of interpersonal conflict and that the fetus is a full party to this conflict, having essentially the same moral status as an adult. The fetus is an entity capable of being harmed, being killed is being harmed, abortion kills the fetus—thus abortion has a victim. The conservative sees an unwanted pregnancy as a genuine collision between the good of the mother (autonomy) and that of the fetus (life). Although the importance of autonomy must not be understated, life is the condition of possessing any goods at all. Life is more basic than, and therefore morally prior to, autonomy. When values conflict, the lesser should be sacrificed. Abortion sacrifices an entire life for a short-range gain in autonomy. It also employs violence against the fetus, thus transgressing traditional moral constraints on the use of violence even to secure a good end. Not only is abortion a public and not a private act, in the absence of some special justification it is immoral. There may be exceptional cases in which abortion is not immoral (where pregnancy, say, is a threat to the woman's life), but it is always the sort of act that requires moral justification, and for most abortions no such justification will be available.

On the conservative view abortion is morally on a par with (other forms of) homicide. If this is so, then there is an obvious ground for state regulation of the activity. Such regulation ought to confine the occasions on which abortion will be permissible as narrowly as possible; an abortion policy must therefore be restrictive. The link for the conservative between the evil of abortion and a restrictive abortion policy may be precisely the same social theory of which liberals make their own use. That theory includes protection of individuals against violence among the legitimate functions of the state. The fetus is an individual and abortion is an act of violence. Restrictive abortion laws are thus justifiable; indeed, it would be unjustifiable *not* to have such laws, for some members of society would then lack security against attack.

Conservatives may (though they need not) concede the liberal treatment of genuinely private acts. Their point is simply that abortion, since it causes fetal death, is not such an act. It is this dimension which distinguishes it from both private sexual activities and contraception. Although it may be true that women need access to abortion in order to compete on equal terms with men, no one has the right to kill in order to maintain a competitive position. Further, restrictive abortion laws do not simply reflect the moral opinions of some particular religious groups. Abortion is not a matter of private morality or taste at all, since it is not a private matter. When activities are private, no one's standards may be enforced against others. Restrictive abortion laws simply extend to fetuses the basic protection of life that is everyone's right. If abortion is not a private act, restrictive laws invade no one's privacy.

The liberal view has the simplest structure possible for a moral treatment of abortion. Since the stake that the fetus has in the decision is entirely discounted, abortions require no special justification. The liberal thus makes a clean sweep of all moral complications concerning abortion. It is the unique nature of the fetus that excludes it from consideration. No further attention need be given to the unique relation between the fetus and the mother, nor to grounds that will justify abortion. The conservative view is essentially simple as well. Whatever its circumstances, abortion brings about the death of a human being. If there are no circumstances in which killing is justified, then the conservative, too, makes a clean sweep of all moral complications concerning abortion. But if killing is sometimes justifiable, the conservative must decide whether the available justifications apply to any cases of abortion. Deciding this question may require attention to the special relation between the fetus and its host. Conservatives may therefore need to puzzle over a dimension of the problem that liberals enjoy the luxury of avoiding. They may also need to advocate a somewhat more complex abortion policy—one that, while remaining restrictive, permits some limited number of abortions.

The deep issue on which liberals and conservatives divide is the moral status of the fetus. They may share a background social theory, they may even share a background moral theory, but the data that they feed into these theories include very different ideas on the extent to which the fetus counts as a party to the abortion conflict. The views that liberals and conservatives hold on this issue are similar in two important respects. Each side attributes the same status to *all* fetuses regardless of such natural characteristics as gestational age, normality, level of development, and the circumstances of pregnancy. Each side, that is, holds a *uniform* view of the moral status of the fetus. Further, among possible uniform views the two sides have settled upon the two polar opposites: either the fetus counts for nothing at all or it counts for as much as anyone does. Each side thus holds an *extreme* view of the moral status of the fetus. It is this union of a uniform and an extreme view of the fetus that generates a simple treatment of the morality of abortion: either (voluntary) abortion is always innocent or it is (nearly) always wrong. Neither side can provide any rationale for a moderate view of the morality of abortion or for a moderate abortion policy. In order to move to some middle ground it would be necessary to abandon either a uniform view or an extreme view of the moral status of the fetus.

The conflict that has generated our moral quandary about abortion is between fetal life and the autonomy of women. Each of the established views in effect discounts one of these elements entirely—the liberal view because it counts the fetus for nothing, the conservative view because it ranks life as prior to autonomy. If either of the established views is correct, then the moral problems of abortion admit of a simple solution. If those problems do not seem simple, then we have some initial reason to suspect both views.

4. Side Issues

The central issue for both liberals and conservatives is the moral status of the fetus. For each side the view it takes of the fetus determines the moral category in which it places abortion. That category in turn determines the moral relevence of the relation between fetus and mother, and of the circumstances in which an abortion is performed. There is no shortage of further issues in the abortion debate, but it follows from the logic of both of the established views that the central issue must dominate all others. Resolving these further issues may not be entirely redundant, for they may affect the fine tuning of an abortion policy. However, they can have little weight, even collectively, against the implications of a uniform and extreme view of the fetus. Thus the established views are simple also in the manner in which they order the moral dimensions of abortion. Further issues are all side issues.

Given this convergence on the dominance of the question of the fetus, it is surprising how much of the abortion debate is nonetheless given to quarreling over side issues. Contention on such issues, though not trivial in its own right, is a diversion. A brief glance at some of the more common side issues will enable us to clear them away and avoid further treatment of them.

A. THE PHYSICAL HAZARDS OF ABORTION

Conservatives sometimes suggest that abortion is sufficiently risky that it ought to be regulated on that ground alone. The issue is secondary for conservatives since their defense of restrictive abortion laws depends on the injury that abortion does to fetuses, not to women. Women undergo abortions voluntarily, fetuses do not. It is also secondary for liberals, since, even if abortion does prove to be hazardous, their view is that women ought to be permitted to prefer its risks to the burden of completing an unwanted pregnancy.

The available facts give conservatives little comfort.[11] Abor-

---

11. See Callahan (1970), chaps. 2 and 8; Lane (1974), vol. 1, sections D and E; Sarvis and Rodman (1974); Badgley (1977), chap. 13; Cates (1977); Potts (1977), chaps. 4, 6, and 7.

tion usually requires (minor) surgery, and for any form of surgery there is some risk of complications. The short-run risks of abortion include hemorrhage, infection, and perforation of the uterus. Long-run risks include sterility, subsequent ectopic pregnancy, and subsequent premature delivery. We have reliable data for the short-run risks but not for the long-run, since a statistical study of the latter requires lengthy follow-up studies of women who have had abortions and then attempted further pregnancies. In evaluating any of these data we must decide on a comparison class. If we compare abortion with other forms of minor surgery, we find it is safer than many of them, including both tonsillectomy and appendectomy. Perhaps a more meaningful alternative is the only one open to a woman who seeks an abortion, namely, the completion of pregnancy. Abortion is safer than childbirth, and thus is the less hazardous option when an unwanted pregnancy is already under way. Contraception, on the other hand, is safer than both.

It is not clear that a conservative can plead the hazards of abortion in good faith. Statistics show not only that abortion is safer than childbirth, but also that early abortion (using menstrual extraction, dilatation and curettage, or vacuum aspiration) is safer than late abortion (using saline injection or hysterotomy), and that legal abortion is safer than illegal. Restrictive abortion policies force women into childbirth, delay abortions (if they are available at all), and raise the illegal abortion rate. Conservative concern for the safety of women is thus at odds with a conservative abortion policy.

B. THE PSYCHOLOGICAL HAZARDS OF ABORTION

Again a conservative preoccupation, this issue is in most respects an analogue of the previous one. The chief difference lies in the fact that what are here alleged to be common consequences of abortion (depression, regret, remorse, guilt) are less clearly harms than are the physical hazards. Psychological categories are notoriously elastic and subject to selective interpretation. Thus reliable statistical data are difficult to locate, and it is unclear what to make of those we have. Such studies as do exist tend to confirm roughly what one would expect: that different women react differently to undergoing an abortion, and that this variation may be attributed to a number of circumstantial factors.[12] If it is proper to speak of the psychological hazards of abortion at all, then once again these must be compared to the costs of being compelled to carry an unwanted pregnancy to term; the aftereffects of refused abortion seem to be at least as serious as those of abortion itself.

One factor affecting the extent to which a woman will feel guilt or remorse after abortion is her own moral attitude. Other things equal, the greater the extent to which she believes that what she is doing is evil or sinful the more likely she is to suffer pangs of conscience after the fact. Since conservatives are the ones who contend that abortion is immoral, perhaps the most effective step they could take to minimize the psychological hazards of abortion would be to cease advocating their own views.

C. BENEFIT TO THE FETUS

Liberals sometimes point to the fact that restrictive abortion policies increase the number of unwanted children, implying that the lives of these children will be particularly harsh.[13] Thus does abortion become a form of fetal euthanasia. This issue is secondary for the liberal, whose case for a permissive policy rests on the rights or interests of women and not on its benefits for fetuses or children. It is equally secondary for the conservative who is usually opposed to "active" euthanasia anyway.

It is not impossible for abortion to be beneficial for its victim.

12. Callahan (1970), chap. 3; Lane (1974), vol. 1, sections E and F; Sarvis and Rodman (1974); Greenglass (1976); Potts (1977), chap. 6.
13. Lader (1966), chap. 17, Pelrine (1971), pp. 52–53.

In order for abortion to be better for the fetus than birth two conditions must be satisfied: (1) we can predict reliably that life after birth for this person will be so miserable as to be worse than no life at all; (2) there is no means available for improving the quality of that life. There are cases in which both conditions are satisfied, as when the fetus suffers from some terrible and incurable abnormality whose only possible sequel is a life filled with suffering. Perhaps the lives of some unwanted children are so unavoidably harsh that both conditions are satisfied. But for most unwanted children (at least in developed countries) both conditions fail. Adoption, in particular, is a device for ensuring that an unwanted pregnancy produces a wanted child.

The liberal who invokes this issue flirts with some unwelcome implications. If abortion is justified at least partly by its benefits for the fetus, perhaps it is justified only when it will produce such benefits. This line of thought would lead to a moderate rather than a permissive policy. Further, if fetal benefits will justify an elective abortion, why will they not also justify a compulsory one? But then what has become of the woman's right to decide the question?

D. SPILLOVER

Conservatives contend that a permissive attitude toward abortion will diminish respect for the lives of other human beings— the aged, the mentally retarded, the unwanted. The issue is secondary for conservatives since they regard the disrespect that abortion plainly manifests for the life of the fetus as sufficient to condemn it. It is equally secondary for liberals, whose aim is to maintain the distinction between abortion and these further cases.

The contention is seldom backed with evidence. Societies in which permissive abortion policies are well entrenched do not seem to drift into genocide, or involuntary euthanasia, or abandonment of the aged. It is noteworthy that the Third Reich, which plunged headlong into both "euthanasia" and genocide, practiced a restrictive policy on abortion.

E. OVERPOPULATION

Liberals often point to the fact that in an overcrowded world, in which a decline in the birth rate is necessary, it makes no sense to compel women to complete unwanted pregnancies. The issue is secondary for the liberal, whose defense of a permissive policy does not rest on its population benefits. It is equally secondary for the conservative, who objects to homicide as a form of population control.

Permissive abortion policies do indeed lower birth rates, at least when all other factors are equal.[14] But they are far from being the most important influence on the birth rate, and abortion is an expensive means of population control. Liberals who are serious about the population problem would do well to transfer their energies to ensuring the more efficient use of contraceptives.

The mediocre arguments on side issues advanced by liberals and conservatives alike do little to encourage confidence in their stances on the central issue. Moderate views on the central issue might lead to moral conclusions about abortion that would be responsive to side-issue arguments. But uniform and extreme views of the fetus generate simple positions on the morality of abortion, and these positions are insensitive to side issues. Side-issue arguments are all consequentialist in form, appealing either to the costs or the benefits of abortion and abortion policies. Neither the liberal defense of a permissive policy nor the conservative defense of a restrictive policy is itself consequentialist; both sides hold their position as a matter of principle. Side-issue arguments are thus of the wrong form to shake either of the established views.

14. Callahan (1970), pp. 291-292; Potts (1977), chap. 4.

5. *Moral Standing*

If we are to focus attention on the central issue of the moral status of the fetus, we need a better understanding of that issue. So far moral status has been treated rather vaguely as a matter of how much the fetus "counts for" in evaluating abortion. We need both a richer and a finer vocabulary. Moral status is a determinable whose values can be ordered along a continuum. The established views have fastened upon the limits of that continuum. Thus, counting for nothing is one limiting form of moral status, as is counting for just as much as the paradigm of a normal adult human being. Every physical object has some moral status or other; it makes no more sense to say that a thing lacks moral status altogether than to say that it lacks shape or color. We therefore need some term to designate what it is that liberals withhold from and conservatives award to fetuses. This we shall call *moral standing*. To count for nothing is to have *no moral standing*. Thus to count for something is to have (some) moral standing, and to count for as much as possible is to have *full moral standing*.[15] On the liberal view a fetus has no moral standing; on the conservative view it has full moral standing. But we still need an analysis of what moral standing is.

A point of departure for such an analysis is supplied by the analogues of legal status and legal standing.[16] An entity's legal status is determined by the extent to which it possesses legal duties, rights, powers, or privileges. To have legal standing is to have some such items in one's own right and not in virtue of their

---

15. What I am here calling moral standing is what some others have characterized in terms of moral consideration; see, for example, Warnock (1971), pp. 148–152, and Goodpaster (1978). It also captures Kant's celebrated distinction between persons (full standing) and things (no standing).

16. For one explication of the notion of legal standing, see Stone (1975). Standard treatments of the cognate notion of legal personality may be found in Keeton (1949), chap. 13, and Williams (1957), chap. 15.

possession by others. Legal standing is an intrinsic condition that consists in being recognized by the law as a separate and distinct locus for such possessions. We may sharpen the notion further by treating a legal system as a set of norms distributing duties and rights, which norms are adopted by a specified procedure and backed by official sanctions. Particular legal systems may differ in two respects: the content of the duties and rights they contain and the classes of entities to which they distribute them. In any such system every duty will be implicitly or explicitly assigned to some class of duty-bearers; likewise, every right will have its class of right-bearers. Those who are bearers of one particular duty (right) need not be bearers of another (both duties and rights are discrete). Thus everyone within a given jurisdiction may have the duty to obey the criminal law, whereas only residents have the duty to pay taxes and only males have the duty to undergo compulsory military service. Similarly, citizens may have the right to vote, but only males over the age of thirty have the right to run for office and slaves have no rights at all.

One has no legal standing if one has no duties and no rights. It is possible to possess some duties and no rights (slaves) or some rights and no duties (infants). One has full legal standing if one has the same duties and rights as some appropriate paradigm—perhaps a competent adult citizen. Legal standing is always relative to some particular legal jurisdiction; it is possible to have (some) standing in one jurisdiction and none in another. It is a purely conventional attribute, containing no implication that such standing is merited or justly possessed. Whether one has legal standing in a particular jurisdiction is a question of fact. Theoretically, a legal system can award standing to whomever it pleases and withhold it from whomever it pleases.

The practical importance of having some legal standing derives from the enforcement of legal norms. Standing can consist of either duties or rights. Duties are typically burdens, constraints on one's freedom of action for the good of others. Rights are typically benefits, constraints on others' freedom of action for one's own good. Most duties require one to protect others, whereas most rights are protections against others. To lack duties is to lack restrictions. To lack rights is to lack protections—except for those that one may gain derivatively, for example, through being the property of another. To lack legal rights is thus to be legally underprivileged.

It is an easy matter to construct a concept of moral standing that is an exact analogue of legal standing. For a legal jurisdiction we substitute a homogeneous moral community, within which some shared set of norms is widely acknowledged. For simplicity we may again assume that all of these norms define and distribute duties and rights. These moral duties and rights differ from legal ones in that they are not (necessarily) written into any legal code and their sanctions are unofficial. Such sanctions may be either external (disapproval, ostracism) or internal (guilt, shame). It will be rare that the moral norms shared within a given community will coincide precisely with its legal norms. A moral system (a morality) is a conventional, customary, informal counterpart of a legal system. Thus, as is the case for legal systems: different moralities will define different duties and rights and will distribute them among different classes of duty-bearers and right-bearers; both duties and rights are discrete; to lack moral standing is to have no duties and no rights; to have full moral standing is to possess the duties and rights of the appropriate paradigm. Like legal standing, moral standing is an intrinsic condition: one's duties (rights) are not derivative from the duties (rights) of any other. Like legal standing, moral standing is always relative to some particular moral community; it is possible to have (some) standing in one community and not in another. Whether one has moral standing in a particular community is a question of fact; moral standing is purely conventional, containing no implication that it is merited or justly possessed.

The practical importance of moral standing parallels that of legal standing. Moral duties are constraints on one's treatment of others whereas moral rights offer protection against one's treatment by others. Though informal, the sanctions of morality may be more effective than the official apparatus of police, court, and prison. Thus an individual may be better off with moral rights but no legal rights than vice versa. To lack moral rights is to be morally underprivileged.

The central issue in the problem of abortion is whether the fetus has moral standing. We need an analysis of moral standing that enables us to formulate that issue perspicuously. Thus far, moral standing means possession of either duties or rights conventionally assigned within a given moral community. Although this concept is quite clear and would be well fitted to certain tasks, it is not as it stands adequate for an examination of views of abortion. The concept suffers from three defects, each of them resulting from the fact that it is modeled exactly upon legal standing. In the first place, one can have legal standing in virtue of possessing either legal duties or legal rights. But no one who inquires into the moral status of fetuses wishes to know whether fetuses have moral duties. Fetuses are incapable of being duty-bearers, as are rocks and trees and clams. The open question about the fetus concerns its moral rights, and so at the very least the notion of moral standing must be narrowed to mean possession of rights conventionally assigned within a given moral community. Such standing is then an unequivocal privilege.

But the analysis is still defective in rendering moral standing as a merely conventional property of an entity. No one who inquires into the moral status of fetuses wishes to know only whether fetuses have been granted rights in this or that moral community. Otherwise the question of the moral status of the fetus is (at least in principle) as easily answered as that of its legal status; one need only refer to the actual practices of actual communities or jurisdictions. Those on both sides of the abortion controversy are debating not how fetuses *are* treated in law or in custom but how they *ought to be* treated. The claim that fetuses have moral rights is a normative one; it is the claim that fetuses ought to be accorded certain conventional protections. The denial that fetuses have moral rights is likewise normative. Conventional rights are fully established by our actual practices, but what is at issue in the abortion debate is precisely what, so far as fetuses are concerned, those practices should be.

If we are to preserve the sense of such questions as whether fetuses have moral standing then we need concepts of moral standing and moral rights that are themselves normative. Let us say that attributing a moral right to a person is claiming that the person ought to be protected in some specified activity, or ought to be treated in some specified manner. Thus, to attribute a moral right to a person is to claim that (some or all) others have a moral duty to treat that person in some specified manner, and to propose constraints on their behavior on the person's behalf. To believe in moral rights is to hold that the conventional practices of moral communities ought to be ordered so as to guarantee certain specified protections to certain specified classes of persons—or to everyone in general. Normally it is also to hold that these protections should be supported by legal sanctions, though not all moral rights are properly converted into legal rights.

If we restrict the phrase "moral right" to its normative meaning, then having moral standing (in the sense pertinent to the abortion debate) means possessing some moral rights. Like conventional rights, moral rights need not always hang together: different rights may still be possessed by different classes of right-bearers. A given entity may therefore possess some moral rights but lack others. To lack all such rights is to have no moral standing. Presumably for the problem of abortion one particular right is of special importance: the right to life. To ask whether fetuses have moral standing is therefore to ask whether they have a moral right to life. They may possess this right and lack others, or lack this right and possess others. If fetuses have a right to life, then (some or all) other persons have a moral duty to extend to the fetus some specified protection of life. This moral constraint will limit the permissible ways in which fetuses may be treated. It may, therefore, either limit the grounds on which abortions may be performed or exclude abortions altogether as morally impermissible. Conventional recognition of the right to life may then require either a moderate or a restrictive abortion policy.

The concept of moral standing that was directly patterned upon its legal analogue has thus been revised in three respects: (1) all reference to duties has been eliminated; (2) a merely factual claim has been converted into a normative one; (3) rights in general have been narrowed to the right to life in particular. The result is a concept of moral standing that enables us to formulate concisely the views of the fetus that are at the heart of the established views of abortion: liberals hold that fetuses have no moral standing (no right to life), whereas conservatives hold that fetuses have full moral standing (a full right to life). Since moral standing is a normative property, there is no empirical procedure for discovering which side (if either) is correct. A position on the moral standing of the fetus is a moral claim, which must be defended in the manner appropriate to moral claims.

Such a defense will operate on two levels. On the intuitive level it will be connected with similar claims about the moral standing of other entities. The connection will take the form of some general criterion of moral standing, a set of properties whose possession is claimed in general to qualify their owners for moral standing. This criterion can then be applied to cases other than fetuses. An intuitive defense presupposes that some cases are hard and others are easy. The former might include, besides fetuses, such entities as nonhuman animals, artificial intelligences, infants, and grossly defective human beings. Competent adult human beings will constitute an easy case, assuming that any cases are easy. A resolution of a hard case may then be defended by grounding it in an easy one. One might, for instance, construct a hypothesis concerning the characteristics of

adults that earn them the right to life and then use that hypothesis to argue that fetuses therefore possess (lack) that right. The
greater the extent to which a claim about the moral standing of
the fetus employs a criterion that resolves other cases in a plausible manner the stronger its intuitive defense.

In order to be intuitively defensible a criterion for moral
standing must satisfy two conditions. The first simply stipulates
that the properties that qualify an entity for moral standing
must be empirical properties. The function of a criterion is to
distribute a certain moral right among the entities in the world
in accordance with their possession or lack of certain properties.
It cannot serve this function unless we have some independent
means of ascertaining which entities possess the properties in
question. These means will be empirical ones, since they are our
normal means of discovering the (nonmoral) properties of objects in the world. The second condition is that the criterion
must be applicable in contexts other than abortion and to entities other than fetuses. A criterion must be general—it must be
capable of resolving most (preferably all) questions of moral
standing.

Beyond these two initial conditions, a criterion will be acceptable only if it can be shown to be morally relevant. It is impossible to make this requirement very precise at this stage. What it
means is that the properties to which the criterion points must
have some plausible connection with the possession of certain
moral rights. There must, therefore, be some reason for thinking
that it is in virtue of an entity's possessing just *these* properties
that it has such rights, that *these* properties mark the crucial watershed between entities with these rights and entities without
them. Moral relevance can be partly decided by the intuitive test
of applying the criterion to other cases; bizarre criteria should
somewhere yield bizarre results. But relevance is really rooted in
the deeper theoretical level at which a view of the moral standing of the fetus must also be defended.

Criteria fail to be morally relevant by being arbitrary and shallow. It is arbitrary to seize upon certain properties of entities as the bases of their rights, properties such as membership in some favored kin group or community, nation or state, or race, gender, or species. It is arbitrary to seize upon such properties because there is no plausible deep connection between any of them and the possession of *rights*. Each of them is of the wrong kind to have a deep connection with moral rights. It might, of course, turn out that only Germans or blacks or women have rights, but if so, this must be in virtue of the fact that they alone possess some further property that does have a deep connection with moral rights. It is not (necessarily) shallow, for instance, to think that only human beings have moral standing; but it is shallow to think that they have such standing simply in virtue of being human.

The deep defense of a criterion for moral standing requires a moral theory. Such a theory will provide the needed link between the basic moral categories it contains (such as moral rights) and the natural properties of things. It is at the level of theory that a criterion is ultimately defended against the accusation of being arbitrary or irrelevant. A well-grounded theory is the best proof of relevance.

The concept of moral standing that has been developed so far will suffice for an examination of the established views. However, it still carries with it one defect it has inherited from its legal counterpart. Different moral theories employ different basic moral categories. For some theories, but not others, one such category is moral rights. Some theories see rights as basic moral facts, whereas others either treat them as derivative or ignore them altogether. A definition of moral standing in terms of rights discriminates against theories that are not (at least at the deep level) theories of rights. The definition therefore needs to be generalized. Since the established views do treat abortion as a problem of rights, and since they are grounded in moral theories that take rights seriously, this generalization can wait until the analysis of these views has been completed (Section 23).

6. *Standards*

A view of the moral status of the fetus, and thus of the morality
of abortion, must have a rational foundation. Whereas much of
the public debate over abortion consists of nonrational techniques of persuasion, assessment of the soundness of abortion
positions is concerned only with the extent to which it is reasonable to accept them. This requirement of rational justification follows from the fact that the established views are moral
views. The function of moral principles is to resolve conflicts,
especially interpersonal conflicts. To hold a moral principle is
thus to hold that not only oneself but also others ought to be-
have in some specified way. A morality is not a private matter,
not just a set of rules for guiding one's own actions. One's moral
commitments determine one's expectations concerning the behavior of others, expectations that one thinks it reasonable to
enforce upon these others in some (formal or informal) manner.
Whatever their content, moral principles impose some constraints on individual choice. No one will volunteer to conform
to such principles, or submit to their enforcement, unless he/she
is persuaded that they are reasonable. No one has been offered
any reason for accepting them unless they have a rational foundation.

The interpersonal dimension to morality, and especially the
appropriateness of enforcing moral rules, ensures that moral
commitments belong to a distinctive sector of one's practical
life. Let us assume that every individual picks out some objects,
events, or states of affairs as ends of action that are worth pursuing or realizing. A person's mode of attachment to a particular
end will fall into one of two mutually exclusive categories: the
end may be treated as a *taste* or as a *value.*[17] It is characteristic of

---

17. "Taste" and "value" are functioning here as technical terms; I do not
pretend to have captured the nuances of their ordinary language. The
taste/value distinction is similar to one drawn by utility theorists between
subjective and ethical preferences.

tastes that commitment to them is seen as merely personal. The holder of the taste is able to recognize that others may have different tastes without being either mistaken or unreasonable. In matters of mere taste there is no implicit claim that every reasonable person ought to agree; tastes are rooted in the temperamental differences among individuals rather than in a common rationality. A taste is ultimately defended, therefore, by referring it to the attitudes, feelings, or preferences of its holder. Tastes are subjective. To report one's tastes is not to make a statement about the properties of objects "out there" in the world; the truth of such reports is not questioned by someone else's expressing a contrary taste. For tastes the subjective refuge is always available: "Well, it is (tastes, looks, sounds) good *to me.*" Because contrary tastes may be equally reasonable, it is appropriate that the realm of taste be the realm of toleration. Uniformity in matters of taste can be achieved only by nonrational means. Anyone who enforces personal tastes against others claims for those tastes what cannot be true: that they ought to be shared by all rational persons.

It is characteristic of values that they are thought by their holders to be impersonal and objective. The object that is valued is thought to (really) possess the property of being good or worthwhile. Because the value is thought to be "in the object," value statements are treated as statements about the world. Epistemologically, they are on a par with empirical statements. If one is committed to the truth of such a statement, one is also committed to holding that those who disagree are mistaken. To hold a given value is to claim that all reasonable persons ought to hold it as well; values therefore transcend the temperamental differences among individuals. It is always appropriate to demand reasons for a person's values and these reasons must be impersonal—reasons for anyone to hold that value. For values, the subjective refuge will not serve, for it provides no one else with any reason for sharing the value. Since incompatible value judgments cannot all be true, it may be appropriate that the realm of value be the realm of enforcement. Diversity of value points to a failure of rationality; to enforce a value against dissenters is only to compel them to be reasonable.

Moral commitments are values and not merely tastes.[18] That is, to advance them as moral is to identify them as values. The language of morals is for the most part objective: this object (person, event, action, state of affairs) is good, right, obligatory (evil, wrong, forbidden). Moral values are advanced as claims about the way the world is. To regard a moral belief as reasonable for oneself is to judge it as equally reasonable for others. Contrary judgments are therefore false, mistaken; those who hold them are misguided or (perhaps) unreasonable. It is always in place to demand reasons for a person's moral beliefs, and these reasons must be impersonal. It is no defense of a moral judgment to retreat to the subjective refuge, for this retreat abandons all claim upon the agreement of others and converts a moral belief into a mere taste. Morality is a realm for argument, whose purpose is to discover which of a set of incompatible moral views is supported by the best reasons. The model here is one of the weighing of reasons issuing in judgment, rather than of the conflict of tastes issuing in compromise.

Whether moral judgments are *in fact* objective is a question in epistemology. The claim here is only that they are held and advanced *as though* they are objective and that, given the interpersonal function of morality, this must be the case. A person's moral commitments, therefore, are necessarily among his/her values. It is quite possible to make an assessment of some subject either as a matter of taste or as a matter of value. One's view of abortion, for example, may simply be a taste. It is not uncommon for women to find the idea of abortion distasteful but not to condemn other women who feel differently and who choose the procedure for themselves. Such a person does not assume

18. It was the mistake of emotivism to treat moral commitments as tastes rather than values.

that others will share her feelings, does not regard them as mistaken if they do not, and does not expect her sentiments to be enforced against them. One's personal reaction to abortion *for oneself* can be very strong, but as long as it remains "nonjudgmental" and is not extended to others, it is being treated as a subjective preference—a taste.

Both of the established views are moral views. Each side advances an objective claim about the moral status of abortion. Each side offers arguments in favor of its own view—arguments that are designed to persuade the uncommitted. Each side claims to have the view to which all reasonable persons ought to assent. Each side regards its opponent's position as mistaken and unreasonable. Each side expects its view to serve as the foundation of an abortion policy that will be equally applied to all.

It is difficult to see how the established views could fail to be moral ones. A liberal believes that abortion is a private matter because it lacks a victim. To believe that in one's own case is to believe it equally in the case of others. It is true that the liberal's favored policy of laisser faire makes room for diversity of taste concerning abortion by protecting freedom of choice. But laisser faire is only appropriate where an activity is (really) a private one. *This* objective claim the liberal cannot abandon, and it is a moral claim. A conservative believes that abortion is homicide, and if it is homicide in one case it is also homicide in all relevantly similar cases. Thus the conservative's favored policy is the enforcement of his own objective assessment of the status of abortion; those who disagree will still find themselves governed by it.

The fact that the established views are moral ones entails that they must be supported by impersonal reasons. The preceding section explored briefly what such support would look like for claims about the moral status of the fetus. Now we must generalize. The requirement that reasons be impersonal imposes three conditions on arguments for a view of abortion. The first is that only those methods of argument be employed that are com-

monly accepted as establishing the truth of their conclusions.
Thus arguments must be grounded in orthodox canons of in-
ductive and deductive logic. No idiosyncratic or eccentric standards of reasoning will be admissible.

The second condition is that personal feelings or sentiments
cannot themselves count as reasons in favor of a moral view of
abortion. Feelings about the fetus obviously play a prominent
role in the abortion debate; some feel a strong bond of sympathy
to the fetus whereas others do not. For most persons a view of
abortion is indissolubly connected to these primitive feelings.
But feelings are not in themselves reasons—though reasons for
the feelings may be reasons for a view of abortion. Nothing
whatever follows from the mere fact that a certain attitude to
abortion is held with passionate intensity. What *could* follow,
since opposed attitudes are held with equal intensity?

The third condition is that any facts marshaled in favor of a
particular view must be publicly accessible. Since science is our
established procedure for confirming or disconfirming beliefs
about the world, factual claims must be subject to some form of
empirical verification. This condition entails that, unless some
form of natural theology is correct, religious beliefs cannot
count as reasons in favor of a moral view of abortion. If a natural
theology *is* correct, then religion is a part of science and its
claims are empirically testable. Otherwise those claims are supernatural, beyond confirmation or disconfirmation. Such claims
cannot be impersonal reasons, since it is not irrational or unreasonable to deny them. A moral view of abortion is addressed to
us irrespective of our private commitments of faith. If reasons
are to be impersonal, then what is a reason for the believer must
also be a reason for the unbeliever. Since both of the established
views claim a rational foundation, we may safely ignore any connections between them and the supernatural beliefs of particular
religious sects. Religious commitments may serve as reasons for
tastes but not as reasons for moral values.

Beyond these minimal conditions the rational case for a moral view of abortion will be made on both the intuitive and the theoretical level. The former involves showing that one's assessment of abortion coheres with plausible and relatively settled judgments on cognate questions. Building a theoretical foundation requires outlining a moral theory, adducing considerations that make it reasonable to accept that theory, and then showing that the theory grounds one's moral conclusions about abortion. Obviously there are connections between the two levels of argument, since one way of defending a theory is by showing that it generates intuitively acceptable results in particular cases. As reasonable and conscientious persons we ought to prefer the view of abortion for which the best intuitive and theoretical cases can be made. The next two chapters will explore the cases that can be made for the two established views.

CHAPTER TWO

The Liberal View

The liberal's defense of a permissive abortion policy rests on the claim that abortion is a private activity, which rests in turn on denying moral standing to the fetus. To be denied moral standing is to be reduced to the status of a mere thing that may be manipulated as the needs of others dictate. Withholding moral standing from any being, especially a human being, is therefore a step that requires careful justification. If the liberal's position on the fetus is to be persuasive, it must not only cohere with credible treatments of connected issues; it must also be grounded in some reputable moral theory. In order to evaluate the liberal view, we need to locate the theory that serves as its deep structure.

7. Rights

The liberal view employs the rhetoric of rights in both its positive and negative claims. In the United States, where this rhetoric is applied to every political issue, the National Organization for Women has supported its demand for the repeal of abortion laws by invoking "the right of women to control their own reproductive lives."[1] The same theme is visible in the familiar slogan "the right to control our own bodies" and is given a prominent role by Lucinda Cisler:

> Repeal is based on the quaint idea of *justice*: that abortion is a woman's right and that no one can veto her decision and compel her to bear a child against her will. All the excellent supporting

1. Morgan (1970), p. 514.

reasons—improved health, lower birth and death rates, freer medical practice, the separation of church and state, happier families, sexual privacy, lower welfare expenditures—are only embroidery on the basic fabric: *woman's right to limit her own reproduction.*[2]

It is clearly intended that a woman's exercise of these rights may include seeking an abortion. Since abortion kills the fetus, an unspoken implication of attributing these rights to women is denying the right to life to the fetus.

The possession of rights by an individual imposes duties on some other individuals.[3] Rights are thus constraints on the ways in which individuals may be treated. To invoke rights is to claim that those individuals who are right-bearers are salient entities in the moral world whose autonomy or welfare is worthy of respect. Whatever this respect may require, it will insulate individuals to some extent against having their positions eroded in the name of social utility. Rights impose constraints on a utilitarian calculus; they are barriers against the mechanical subordination of individual to collective welfare.

A moral theory contains rights if any of its principles, basic or derivative, attribute some rights to some classes of entities. A theory may contain rights without treating them as basic. Rights are basic in a theory if the principles that specify and distribute them are themselves basic to the theory, that is, are not supported by yet more fundamental principles that make no mention of rights. A moral theory in which rights (and nothing else) are basic is a *rights theory.* For any such theory individual rights are the deepest features of the moral landscape. All further moral facts—truths about duty and justice, for example—are to be explained by reference to rights. However far such a theory

2. Cisler (1970), p. 276; emphasis in the original.

3. Rights are throughout this discussion assumed to be claim-rights rather than mere liberties or privileges; cf. Feinberg (1973), pp. 56–59. They are also assumed to belong to individuals.

may extend, its contents are bound always by these rights; they are both the substructure of the theory and the skeleton of its superstructure.

In the arguments of liberals there is no suggestion that rights are anything but basic. We may assume, therefore, that the liberal view is grounded in some rights theory. On any such theory some rights must be natural rights. Many rights are the products of convention or contract: I have the right to drive your car because of an agreement between you and me. Conventional rights cannot be basic. Somewhere a theory must explain why conventions ought (normally) to be adhered to. The explanation cannot without circularity invoke conventional rights. If it invokes individual or social utility, the theory is not a rights theory, since rights are then grounded in something more basic. The only alternative for a rights theory is to treat some rights as natural, that is, as belonging to individuals independently of any agreements or conventions. Such rights are possessed by their bearers simply because of the *nature* of those bearers. It is at the level of natural rights that we may raise the two basic questions of the *content* of rights (What rights do individuals possess?) and their *scope* (Who possesses these rights?). It is also at this level that we may demand a criterion for the distribution of rights.

In the arguments of liberals there is also no suggestion that the right to either autonomy or life is anything but natural. But if we wish to specify further the theory that is the deep structure of the liberal view, we encounter a difficulty: rights theories are a family whose members are divided on the content and scope of rights. If we assume that the scope of a right will be at least partly determined by its content, then we may focus on divisions of content. The deepest such division is between liberty-rights and welfare-rights.[4]

---

4. This distinction is made by various writers in various terms: negative v. positive rights, action-rights v. receiving-rights, etc. See, for example, Feinberg (1973), pp. 59–61.

Liberty-rights are rights to act as one pleases, free of the interference of others. They are therefore all special cases of the general right to be self-determining. Liberty-rights protect individual autonomy.[5] To have the right to travel, for instance, is to have the right to decide for oneself whether one will travel or not. One violates no duty by traveling and also violates no duty by staying home. Thus to have a liberty-right to do something is also to have the right not to do it—it is to have an open option with respect to that action. The duty of others is not to close this option by imposing constraints on one of the alternatives. To be free with respect to some action is to be unconstrained by others in the doing or omitting of that action. If we assume that constraints take the form of the use or threat of force, then to be unconstrained by others is to be free of the coercion of others. Liberty-rights are special cases of the right not to be coerced. They impose on others the duty not to use coercion.

A theory of liberty-rights thus protects individual autonomy with respect to some class of actions. If such a theory is not to fall into inconsistency, it must carefully delimit this class of actions. It obviously cannot protect one individual's right to coerce another, for then the agent would have the right to do something that he/she has the duty not to do. The theory requires a version of the private/public dichotomy. Liberty-rights apply only to private acts: those that do not coerce others, thus those that respect the liberty-rights of others. One has the right to do anything, therefore, that respects the like rights of others. The limits of one individual's rights are defined by the limits of the rights of all other individuals. A theory of liberty-rights thus pictures the moral landscape as consisting of boundaries around the private (protected) spheres of individuals.[6] Precisely where those boundaries are to be located will be determined by a suit-

5. Golding (1968), Feinberg (1978).
6. This picture is nicely painted in an unpublished paper by Peter Danielson entitled "Natural Rights are Property Rights" (read at the 1977 Annual Congress of the Canadian Philosophical Association).

able analysis of liberty and coercion.[7] However the boundaries are drawn, the space within them consists only of rights; there can be no duties in the private sphere. All duties are public (interpersonal)—specifications of the general duty not to cross the boundaries of others (without their consent). All duties correlated with liberty-rights are negative; each individual has the duty not to violate the liberties of others, but liberty-rights generate no further duty to promote their good. For a theory of liberty-rights, the moral world is well ordered when all interpersonal contact is by mutual consent and everyone's security is respected. The private ends individuals elect to pursue, the projects in which they choose to engage, the kinds of lives they lead—all these are matters of taste and not of morality. Individuals are sovereign with regard to these questions; there is in them no right and wrong.

Welfare-rights are rights to receive from others goods or services that are not required by bare respect for liberty-rights. They are therefore all special cases of the general right to live a decent or satisfying life. Welfare-rights protect individual well-being.[8] I respect your liberty-rights if I refrain from aggressing against you, if indeed I have nothing to do with you. In order to respect your welfare-rights I must interact with you, at least by making available to you commodities that will enhance your good. Welfare-rights thus impose positive rather than merely negative duties. The right to a fair trial entails the duty of legal officials to ensure a fair trial, the right to a decent education entails the duty of parents (and perhaps government) to supply a decent education, and so on. The rules of duty in a theory of welfare-rights will not stop at prohibiting harm to others; they will require that one benefit others, at least on some occasions and in some respects. Such a theory pictures the moral world as one of mutual dependence in which each of us bears some responsibility

7. For an attempt at such an analysis, see Nozick (1969).
8. Peffer (1978).

for ensuring that others fare well. On such a theory, but not on a theory of liberty-rights, being a Good Samaritan can be a moral duty.

Liberty-rights and welfare-rights have different content, define different kinds of duties, and generate different theories. Such theories may be sorted along the following lines. A theory is either *pure* (containing one category of rights only) or *mixed*. The rights it contains are either *absolute* (no violations justified, whatever the circumstances) or *defeasible*. A theory containing some defeasible rights is either *ordered* (with priority rules to adjudicate conflicts among rights) or *unordered*. These categories enable us to define three types of theory, each of which has its modern adherents.

A *libertarian* theory is a pure theory of absolute liberty-rights.[9] Because it admits no welfare-rights, it need not confront collisions between the two kinds of rights. Welfare-rights can conflict with one another (as when scarce resources prevent us from serving everyone's needs) and with liberty-rights (as when we must injure one person to aid another). A theory that includes welfare-rights cannot treat all such rights as absolute. Liberty-rights, however, need not conflict with one another. A theory that restricts itself to liberty-rights may treat each such right as absolute, as long as it is careful in drawing the boundaries among private spheres. Since respecting liberty-rights requires only leaving a person alone, it is in principle always possible to respect everyone's rights. Respect for the rights of some will thus never require violation of the rights of others. Holding liberty-rights as absolute entails that they may never be violated whatever the circumstances and whatever the consequences. Liberty is absolute against every other good, and even against itself: a person's liberty may not be violated in order to preserve his/her

---

9. The canonical modern version of such a theory is Nozick (1974). Donagan (1977) presents a proof that absolute negative moral rules are internally consistent.

own future liberty. Thus defined, libertarianism leads by a familiar route to a defense of the free market, civil liberty, and the minimal nonredistributive state (or anarchy).

A *lexical* theory is a partly ordered mixed theory in which liberty-rights remain absolute and therefore dominate welfare-rights.[10] Negative duties (duties not to aggress against individuals) are absolute in such a theory, as they are for libertarians. But a lexical theory contains a further category of defeasible welfare-rights, and thus defeasible positive duties (duties to aid others). Welfare-rights are not themselves strongly ordered on such a theory, though some goods may be considered more important than others. Defeasible duties therefore contain a good deal of flexibility: one need not promote everyone's good on every occasion in every way. Just what one's positive duties are in particular circumstances may be somewhat uncertain, though there are also likely to be clear cases. What is not at all uncertain is the lexical priority of liberty-rights over welfare-rights, and thus of negative over positive duties. The ordering rule states that it is always forbidden to violate any negative duty in order to perform any positive duty: one may not do evil that good may come. Welfare-rights may be promoted only when doing so violates no liberty-rights.

An *intuitionist* theory is an unordered mixed theory.[11] In it all

10. The notion of a lexical ordering is borrowed from Rawls (1971), pp. 42–43. I know of no formulation of an explicitly lexical rights theory. Donagan (1977) contains the near analogy of a lexical theory of duties. However, Donagan's strict (absolute) duties are not correlated with liberty-rights. Natural-law theories generally order duties lexically but disavow liberty-rights by imposing moral duties in the private sphere.

11. "Intuitionist" is being used here to pick out a class of moral theories that contain a set of equally basic principles with no ordering rule for deciding overlap and conflict among them; intuitionist rights theories are a subdomain of this class. Thus a theory is intuitionist in terms of its structure; no question is being raised here of how its principles are to be justified. For an explication of this sense of "intuitionist," see Rawls (1971),

rights in both categories are defeasible. For any right there are some circumstances in which it is overridden by some other right. Because this is still a rights theory, rights can be overridden only by other rights. All duties, negative and positive alike, are merely prima facie. The theory contains no priority rules for deciding conflicts; each such conflict is adjudicated as a separate instance. An intuitionism of rights is the counterpart of the more familiar intuitionism of duties. An intuitionist rights theory is readily convertible into an intuitionist theory of duties. The reverse, however, need not be the case: whereas all rights entail duties, there may be duties with no correlated rights.

Given that the liberal view of abortion is grounded in some rights theory, what sort of theory must this be? Much liberal rhetoric leads one to expect a libertarian theory. The right that liberals explicitly attribute to women—the right to control their own bodies, or more generally the right of autonomy—is a liberty-right. Liberals also make use of the private/public distinction, using the fact that abortion is (in their view) a private act as a decisive reason for rejecting regulation of it by the state. The liberal ideal is a free market in abortion in which individual women decide whether or not to seek abortions and are not denied access to them. The liberal view is "prochoice," that is, proliberty.

It would, however, be ludicrous to attribute a libertarian moral theory to most feminist groups, and indeed to most abortion liberals. At least many liberals hold other views on abortion (that abortions ought to be publicly funded, for example), and on further social issues as well, which are incompatible with libertarianism. To be committed to one particular liberty-right is not to be committed to other such rights, or to the view that liberty-rights are absolute, or to the exclusion of welfare-rights. There is even some reason for thinking that the liberal view it-

---

pp. 34–40. I take the theory presented in Feinberg (1973) to be an intuitionist theory of rights; see also Peffer (1978).

self is incompatible with libertarianism. The liberal goes to some length to deny fetuses the right to life. That very effort suggests that liberals would not deny this right to some other entities: to infants, perhaps, or children. Certainly most liberal defenses of abortion are not intended also as defenses of infanticide or the slaughter of children. It is not entirely clear yet just what is meant by the right to life. For competent adults this might mean only the right to live one's life free of threats by others— thus the right not to be murdered. In this case the right to life is a liberty-right. But for others (incompetents, children, infants, fetuses) it might mean both this and more: the right to have one's life supported, nurtured, enhanced by others. In this case the right to life would at least contain a welfare-right. And if one thinks that the idea of protecting the liberty or autonomy of fetuses and infants is absurd, then it would be nothing but a welfare-right. In any case, one of the rights that liberals acknowledge (though they may deny it to fetuses) looks very much like a welfare-right. How can such a right be compatible with a libertarian morality?

Libertarianism is a moral theory for competent and mature human beings. Incompetent and/or immature beings are an embarrassment to the theory (so are some nonhuman beings, but that is another matter). It makes little sense to award liberty-rights to those who are incapable of acting autonomously. If liberty-rights are all the rights there are, then infants and children, as well as fetuses, will lack moral standing entirely. Since this outcome seems somewhat harsh, one possible solution is to adopt a graded theory that attributes liberty-rights to competent adults, welfare-rights to children and infants, and no rights to fetuses. If this is treated as a sympathetic interpretation, rather than a revision, of libertarianism, it will still be possible to build a liberal view of abortion on a libertarian foundation.

Most liberals do not identify the moral theory they are presupposing. When they do not, we have no means of determining whether that theory is libertarian, lexical, or intuitionist.

This absence of theoretical depth is a significant defect in the liberal view. It may of course turn out that any of these theories will ground a criterion that will deny moral standing to fetuses. If this is the case, abortion liberals need not commit themselves to some specific variety of rights theory. But if it is not, they may find avoidance of such commitment costly.

8. *Abortion and Infanticide*

One of the attractive features of most rights theories is the breadth of their humanism: natural rights (of one kind or another) are extended across human beings without distinction of gender, race, nationality, or creed.[12] A (human) fetus is a stage in the life history of a human being. To deny it moral standing is to authorize modes of treatment of it that would otherwise be indefensible. Given that rights theories usually refuse to draw other distinctions among human beings, some case must be made for discriminating on grounds of age. Natural rights are held by their bearers simply in virtue of the kind of beings those bearers are. What is it about the nature of the fetus that disqualifies it from possessing a right to life?

Treatments of abortion in most feminist writings have given only the most cursory attention to this question. The pattern for such treatments was laid down by Simone de Beauvoir and consists of three steps.[13] The first is to embed discussion of abortion in the wider context of women's control, or lack of it, over their

12. Thus natural rights are often described as human rights. I am avoiding this terminology because it begs the question of the scope of rights. Whether, for instance, nonhuman animals have natural rights is a substantive question, as is the question whether all human beings have such rights.

13. Beauvoir (1953), pp. 456–464. For other treatments following the same pattern, see Lader (1966), Guttmacher (1967), Cisler (1970), Hardin (1971), Pelrine (1971), Women's Liberation Movement (1972), Watters (1976).

reproductive lives. At this stage abortion is given no special notice at all; it is treated as though it were a form of contraception.
The second step is to acknowledge the existence of moral opposition directed specifically to abortion but to classify all such opposition as religious. Those who assign rights to fetuses are assumed to do so on the ground that fetuses have souls. Because
the existence of souls is a matter of faith rather than reason, objections to abortion are therefore irrational. Finally, the third
step is to attribute restrictive abortion laws to a general pattern
of patriarchy.

There is much in these contentions that is quite valid, but
they fail utterly to confront the central question. Indeed, by
branding conservatives as both superstitious and sexist, feminists
imply that there is no rational case against abortion that they
need address. But in this they are simply mistaken: most conservative arguments invoke no articles of faith and are rooted in
principles that are free of discriminatory assumptions about the
nature and status of women. By and large, conservatives have
been more resourceful than liberals in constructing a purely rational foundation for their views on abortion. By failing to confront conservative arguments, and by choosing instead to dis-
credit their opponents, feminists have fostered the impression
that their own position lacks such a foundation. In any case, it is
liberals who must offer some reason for denying moral rights to
a particular class of human beings. Even if conservative arguments were as disreputable as feminists have claimed, this task
could not be shirked.

Many feminists fail not only to defend their view of the fetus
but even to define it. The liberal's practical goal is the removal of
legal restrictions on abortion. Even in the absence of such restrictions abortions are rarely performed beyond the conventional
point of fetal viability (sometime during the sixth month). In
order to secure their practical objective it is sufficient for liberals
to deny moral standing to fetuses up to this point; viability is

the earliest time in ontogenesis at which the liberal can concede a right to life to the developing individual.

On the other hand most liberals show no eagerness to treat infanticide as a private act for which a similarly permissive policy would be appropriate. If such a defense of infanticide is to be avoided, birth is the latest time at which the liberal can concede a right to life to the developing individual. We may therefore assume that for most liberals the right to life is acquired sometime between viability and birth.

Lucinda Cisler is one of the few feminists writing on abortion who has committed herself to one of the available options. She rejects both viability and quickening (the point at which fetal movement is first perceived by the mother) and then concludes: "We are left with the inescapable conclusion that the only event in the sequence of pregnancy that can be assigned a specific time is birth itself, at the time that it occurs. All else is mystique and conjecture."[14] She has stated what many feminists seem simply to assume: that fetuses lack moral standing throughout pregnancy, that infants have such standing, and that birth is the crucial moral watershed. Birth is of course unsatisfactory as a general criterion of moral standing because it is tied too closely to the specific context of abortion. However, it might be an indicator that is supported by some suitably general criterion. Birth is the point at which the special relation between mother and child is terminated and the child begins to rely on its own body systems for survival. The liberal is claiming that birth alters the *na-*

---

14. Cisler (1970), p. 274. For one feminist's opinion that quickening is a morally significant event, see Mannes (1971), p. 176. Other liberals have seemed disposed to draw a line before birth, thus (in effect) granting moral standing to some developed fetuses; see Hardin (1971), p. 169; Szasz (1971), p. 181; Williams (1974), pp. 230–232. It is often difficult to make out whether liberals are actually defending a permissive policy with no time limit ("the repeal of all abortion laws") or whether they are assuming that abortions will not be performed after fetal viability.

ture of the child: as fetus it lacked whatever natural properties earn one moral standing, and as infant it now possesses these properties. The transformation of the relation between mother and child has transformed one of the parties to that relation. How, then, is the fetus changed by birth?

Birth occasions at least the following changes in the child who undergoes it: (1) it ceases to inhabit another person's body; (2) it becomes more accessible to other creatures of its kind; (3) it begins to handle its own respiration, digestion, and excretion; (4) its direct physical link to another person's body is severed. In principle, any of these newly acquired characteristics could be assembled into at least a necessary condition of moral standing. Thus one might say that creatures have a right to life only when they are not lodged within other creatures, or when they are not connected to life-support systems. None of the resulting criteria, however, would be very plausible, since it is difficult to see why any of these characteristics should matter where a being's moral rights are concerned. We would hesitate to say that individuals lose moral standing when they enter the bodies of others (like scientists in *Fantastic Voyage*), or become inaccessible (like astronauts in quarantine), or are connected to life-support systems (like patients on respirators or dialysis machines). If so, we should equally hesitate to say that individuals gain moral standing only when these special conditions terminate.

There are two respects in which birth might be an event of moral significance. On the one hand it does alter the relation between mother and child. The relations among individuals certainly affect what it is permissible for them to do to one another; I may be justified in killing you when you are attacking me but not when you are merely passing me on the street. Pregnancy is a relation between host and parasite. It might be permissible for hosts to act on parasites in ways in which it would be impermissible for them to act on other creatures. This may be so, even if parasites have precisely the same natural rights as other creatures (perhaps *no one* has the right to continued life support by another person). In general, morally significant relations among right-bearers do not affect the sets of rights they possess (which is part of what is meant by calling rights natural) but only what those rights require or permit *in those circumstances.*[15] Birth might also have a conventional significance: there might be pragmatic (consequentialist) reasons for locating the threshold of moral standing just there rather than somewhere else. But in this case moral standing is no longer tied directly to the natural properties of entities, and the right to life is not being treated as a natural right. This avenue is closed to the holder of a rights theory.

Birth is a shallow and arbitrary criterion of moral standing, and there appears to be no way of connecting it to a deeper account. In most respects, an infant shortly after birth has the same natural characteristics (is the same kind of creature) as a fetus shortly before birth: the same size, shape, internal constitution, species membership, capacities, level of consciousness, and so forth. Biologically a full-term fetus resembles a newborn infant much more than it resembles a zygote or an embryo. Treating birth as the threshold of moral standing commits one to saying that morally a full-term fetus resembles a zygote or an embryo much more than it does a new-born infant, that *being unborn* is more significant than all of the other natural characteristics of fetuses combined.

Many of the same problems afflict the choice of viability as the crucial threshold. Viability is the capacity to survive birth. If birth is itself an arbitrary criterion, viability must be arbitrary as well. Beyond this there is the problem that impressed Lucinda Cisler: we can at least identify when in an individual's life-history birth occurs, but viability is not a datable event at all. This vagueness, however, may not be entirely a liability, since at least part of the implausibility of birth as a moral watershed is the suddenness with which it occurs. There is a further respect as well in which viability might seem a more promising candidate

15. This issue is pursued further in Section 9.

than birth as an indicator of moral standing. Becoming viable does require biologically significant changes in the nature of the fetus, rather than just in its circumstances. A fetus becomes viable in virtue of acquiring previously absent capacities. It is possible to imagine supporting the choice of viability as the crucial threshold by pointing to these underlying changes. But then viability would very likely become an epiphenomenon in a deeper account that attributed moral significance to these changes themselves.

Selecting any precisely datable point as the threshold of moral standing seems at odds with the pattern of human prenatal development. It is characteristic of mammals that their young mature both slowly and gradually. In the human species the cumulative results of the forty weeks of gestational development are enormous, but during that period there are few abrupt transitions. This pattern of continuous and gradual acquisition of natural capacities is not easily fitted to a view on which moral standing is acquired suddenly. This view might be appropriate if human beings sprang forth fully developed like armed men from dragon's teeth, or could be assembled in an afternoon like robots, or underwent metamorphosis like insects. But human beings are not such creatures and we need an account of the acquisition of moral standing that fits the kind of creatures they are. It may not be arbitrary to deny standing to a zygote and to confer it upon a full-term fetus, for in doing so we may be attending to the enormous cumulative results of prenatal development. But it will be arbitrary to pick any *point* during (or at the end of) gestation as the one at which standing is acquired.

In the rather naive view we have thus far attributed to liberals, the moral transition, when it occurs, is not only abrupt but total. The fetus coasts along through its prenatal existence with no moral standing whatever, and then suddenly it has full standing. The liberal does possess some resources for rendering this picture a little more plausible. Moral standing is defined, for the abortion context, in terms of the right to life. If rights are dis-

crete, then it is open to the liberal to say that fetuses acquire
other rights before they acquire this one. Fetuses might, for instance, have the right to be spared unnecessary suffering before
they have the right not to be killed, and so they might not lack
all possible forms of moral standing. (We would, however, want
an explanation of why some rights antedate others.) But the liberal view would be still more plausible if the right to life could
be acquired gradually, by degrees, just as most of the fetus' natural characteristics are acquired gradually. This sort of account
could produce a better fit between the curve of biological development and that of the development of moral standing.

The distinction between welfare-rights and liberty-rights
might be regarded as a step in this direction, for a liberal could
reasonably hold that the former are acquired earlier in an individual's life history than the latter. But a distinction among categories of rights is not quite what is required, for the transition
from being a bearer of welfare-rights to being a bearer of liberty-
rights might still, for all that has been said, be quite abrupt. Liberals need an account of how rights (of whatever kind) can be
acquired by degrees. Further, the categories threaten to work in
just the wrong way for the liberal. Whatever the precise definitions of a welfare-right to life and a liberty-right to life, it is
usually assumed that the former imposes *more* duties on others
than does the latter. Thus we are commonly supposed to owe
children both protection of life against violent attack and also
provision of the necessaries of life. If welfare-rights are acquired
before liberty-rights, the curve of moral standing seems to peak
early and decline thereafter.

What the liberal requires is an account of how the welfare-
right to life can itself be acquired gradually. Although such an
account will be a complication for a rights-theory, there seems to
be no barrier against rights admitting of degrees.[16] Rights corre-

16. Something like this notion of degree or strength would seem to be
required by any intuitionist rights theory.

late with duties; the degree or strength of a right might be determined by the kinds of duties it imposes on others. If a being has no right to life, others have no duties with regard to that being's life; they need attach no weight whatever in their practical deliberations to consequences for that life. If a being has a weak right to life, then others have some duties with regard to that being's life, but duties that can be easily negated or overridden by other considerations. Thus they might have the duty not to kill the being just for pleasure but no duty to refrain if doing so is inconvenient. A stronger right to life will further shrink the class of considerations that defeat the duty to protect or support life. In general, as a right to life approaches a full right, the justifications available for either killing or allowing to die diminish. A complete ordering of such rights from minimal to maximal would certainly be complex but need not be incoherent. A theory of graded rights might be just what is needed in contexts other than abortion—to explain, for example, the moral status of nonhuman animals. In any case, such a theory looks more plausible than a simple on/off account. With it the liberal could maintain that a fetus (or an infant) acquires moral standing gradually, beginning at some stage with a weak right to life (one easily overridden by most grounds for abortion) and progressing to a full right. Whatever the details of such a view, it would at least avoid the artificiality of maintaining that full standing is acquired all at once.

No rights theory exists that can provide liberals with the resources they need. Rights theories have generally been formulated for the paradigm right-bearer—a competent adult human being. The existence of nonparadigm beings (children, infants, fetuses, the severely abnormal, nonhuman animals, perhaps also artificial intelligences) is awkward for such a theory. Indeed, the fact that human beings grow slowly into maturity instead of just popping into existence as adults is awkward for the theory. Too often rights theories seem to be devised for a world populated entirely by competent adults, in which no one is mad or retarded or young. It should be no surprise, then, that rights theories do not apply easily to the problem of abortion, or to the cognate problems of the rights of children, the incompetent, and animals. No internal defect impedes the further elaboration of such theories; they are simply themselves in a state of arrested development.

In feminist treatments of abortion few meaningful steps have been taken toward clarifying the status of the fetus, locating the threshold of moral standing, developing a general criterion, or deploying a theory that can support such a criterion. By and large the fetus has simply been ignored or forgotten. More philosophical liberals have done somewhat better. Michael Tooley (1973) has produced the most interesting attempt to date to ground a liberal view.[17] Tooley recognizes that moral rights may be discrete and defines a (moral) person as any being with "a (serious) moral right to life."[18] He then enumerates those natu-

---

17. See also Tooley (1972), Purdy and Tooley (1974). There is a structurally similar account in Warren (1978); Warren and Tooley, however, differ in some significant respects.

18. Tooley (1973), p. 55. Tooley thus defines *being a (moral) person* in the way in which I have defined *having moral standing*. It is a common practice in philosophical discussions of abortion to cast the issue of moral standing in terms of whether a fetus is a person; see, for example, English (1975) and Newton (1975). This terminology has the virtue of distinguishing the moral question of the status of the fetus from the biological question of whether it is human. The otherwise fruitful discussions in Thomson (1974a) and Brody (1974, 1975) are marred by formulating the moral question as one of the humanity of the fetus. I have avoided the terminology of personhood (or personality) because it invites confusion between the conditions for being a moral person and the conditions for being a natural person.

Warren (1978) also employs the concept of a person. However, unlike Tooley, she assumes that rights form a package; to be a person is to have full moral rights (pp. 222, 224-225). She is forced by this device to deny all rights to the fetus—thus, for instance, the right not to be tortured as well as the right not to be killed. Her position is therefore more extreme than Tooley's.

ral properties that are both necessary and sufficient for possessing a right to life. In order to have moral standing a being must

(1) possess the capacity to envisage a future for itself and to have desires concerning its own future states;

(2) possess the capacity to have a concept of a self (as a continuing subject of experiences and other mental states);

(3) be such a self;

(4) be self-conscious (i.e., believe that it is such a self);

(5) possess the capacity for self-consciousness.[19]

These criteria are clearly not logically independent. We may focus on the first two, which Tooley thinks entail all the rest. These are the requirements he attempts to ground in the very concept of a right to life, indeed in the very concept of a right.

(1) In order to have a right to something, an individual must be capable (at some time) of desiring that thing.

(2) The right to life is the right to future existence as a subject of experiences or other mental states.

(3) Therefore, in order to have a right to life an individual must be capable (at some time) of desiring its own future existence as a subject.

(4) To desire something is to desire that the appropriate proposition be true.

(5) In order to desire that a proposition be true an individual must possess the concepts the proposition contains.

(6) Therefore, in order to have a right to life an individual must be capable (at some time) of possessing the concept of a self (as a continuing subject of experiences and other mental states).[20]

A fetus is clearly not (yet) capable of possessing the concept of a self. If it is killed it will never have this capacity. Thus abortion kills a being that is at no time capable of desiring its own future existence. But then the fetus cannot have a right to life and abortion cannot violate such a right.

19. Adapted from Tooley (1973), pp. 59–60.
20. Ibid., pp. 60–72.

Tooley's argument attempts to remedy all of the defects of the more naive liberal treatments. He provides a criterion for moral standing that is applicable in contexts other than abortion. In principle at least, this criterion enables us to locate the threshold at which moral standing is acquired in the life history of a normal human individual. Since concepts and desires will not appear suddenly, this threshold will be a stage rather than a precise point in that life history. Such datable events as birth will not have the slightest relevance for the development of moral standing, since they are not closely linked to the development of concepts and desires. Though Tooley's right to life does not admit of degrees, nonetheless on his view moral standing is not acquired suddenly.[21] When *is* it acquired? To this question Tooley gives no definite answer. He resists connecting the possession of concepts with linguistic abilities, so moral standing may antedate language use. But if nonlinguistic evidence for possession of concepts is admissible, it is not clear how we are to determine when an individual has mastered the difficult concept of a self. Tooley is quite definite on one point: this stage occurs sometime after birth, and so his defense of abortion is also a defense of infanticide. Tooley is not troubled by any further indeterminacy in locating the threshold:

> ... there is no serious need to know the exact point at which a human infant acquires a right to life. For in the vast majority of cases in which infanticide is desirable, its desirability will be apparent within a short time after birth.... The practical moral problem can thus be satisfactorily handled by choosing some short

21. The conditions that constitute Warren's criterion likewise are generally applicable, deny special significance to birth, and allow moral standing to be acquired gradually. In addition, Warren hints at a graded right to life: "It does seem reasonable to suggest that the more like a person, in the relevant respects, a being is, the stronger is the case for regarding it as having a right to life, and indeed the stronger its right to life is." (Warren 1978, p. 225).

period of time, such as a week after birth, as the interval during which infanticide will be permitted. This interval could then be modified once psychologists have established the point at which a human organism comes to satisfy the appropriate requirements.[22]

It seems safe to count among most people's considered moral judgments the view that, although infanticide may in some circumstances be justifiable, it is a morally serious act. Those offended by the idea of infanticide are unlikely to be consoled by Tooley's pragmatic treatment of the problem. Certainly the circumstances of infanticide are different from those of abortion. Because the infant is not connected to anyone in the direct way in which the fetus is connected to its mother, there is seldom an irresolvable conflict between the infant's interest and that of any other person. Nonetheless, Tooley's criterion implies that, prior to the threshold, infanticide is not the killing of a being with any right to life—it is not, whatever the circumstances, a wrong *to the infant*. Whatever is wrong about infanticide, when it is wrong, must be located in its side effects, never in the wrong done to its victim. Just as a woman has, on Tooley's view, the right to abort without offering any justification, so the parents of an infant have the right to kill it. Since denying the right to life to an infant frees others from duties owed to that infant, there is a serious need to know when that right is acquired. When, for instance, should we treat infanticide as homicide?

The concept of a self is a sophisticated one, requiring a distinction between oneself and other objects in the world, a further distinction between oneself and one's own mental states, and the capacity to understand persistence through time. Given the slow pace of postnatal development that distinguishes our species from all other mammals, it is inconceivable that a child

22. Tooley (1973), p. 91. Warren's criterion likewise entails that infants have no right to life and therefore that infanticide is not a violation of (the infant's) rights. She too attempts to deflect the practical importance of this conclusion. (Warren 1978, pp. 227–228).

should possess this concept before the age of two, and unlikely that he should have it by three or four. If we take Tooley's criterion seriously, children will lack a right to life for the first few years of their lives.[23] We are therefore not considering a week, or a month, or even a year after birth "during which infanticide will be permitted." The implications of Tooley's view are more extreme than he appears to realize.

Appeals to our moral convictions, even those to which we are most strongly committed, are never decisive. The challenge of Tooley's argument is to rethink whether our objections to infanticide are not themselves unfounded. But a view that generates highly counterintuitive results must have a compelling rationale. Tooley's argument contains two crucial steps: from rights to corresponding desires and from desires to corresponding concepts. The first step is the more controversial, and it rests on a general claim about moral rights:

> The basic intuition is that a right is something that can be violated and that, in general, violation of an individual's right to something involves frustrating the corresponding desire. Suppose, for example, that you own a car. Then I am under a prime facie obligation not to take it from you. However, the obligation is not unconditional: it depends in part upon the existence of a corresponding desire in you. If you do not care whether I take your car, then I generally do not violate your right by doing so.[24]

Evaluating this "intuition" is rendered difficult by the fact that little is said in its defense. Tooley offers no analysis of the concept of a right and no account of the kinds of rights individuals possess. We do not know whether rights are natural or conventional, whether they are welfare-rights or liberty-rights, whether

---

23. Warren's criterion, which in addition to self-awareness includes the ability to reason and communicate, seems likely to produce the same result. One wonders whether autistics, schizophrenics, and the severely retarded have a right to life on either Tooley's or Warren's view.

24. Tooley (1973), p. 60.

they are ordered or unordered. We are given no theory of rights.

There seems no good reason to accept the intuition for either welfare-rights or liberty-rights. Welfare-rights certainly connect with individual welfare, since they generate duties to promote that welfare. But welfare is not easily connected in turn to desire. A person can be both harmed by the satisfaction of his/her desires and benefited by their frustration. More importantly, it makes perfect sense to say that a person has been benefited (the person's welfare or interest has been promoted) by receiving a good when he/she is at no time even capable of desiring that good. Imagine a man who is sufficiently retarded or autistic as to have no sense of self but who is quite capable of enjoying life as he is living it. On Tooley's view he cannot desire to continue to live. Nonetheless, if we make it possible for him to live a happy life, within his limited capacities, then it seems clear that we have benefited him. Further, if one believes in welfare-rights, then it is not absurd to say that he has the right to such a life. It might be a necessary condition of having the welfare-right to something that the thing be a *good* for one, but this will generate no claim about desire.

The tie between liberty-rights and desires is even more tenuous. It is odd that Tooley has chosen one of the least plausible cases to illustrate his thesis. On most theories of property-rights, whether one has a right to a particular object depends on the procedure by which that object was acquired.[25] As long as that procedure violated no one else's rights, the object is justly owned and others have the duty not to appropriate it. It is not necessary that the owner continue to want the thing, or even remember that he/she owns it. If I cease to want my car, that is not the same as authorizing you to take it. It continues to be mine until I somehow dispose of it, and your taking it from me continues to be theft.

As in the case of welfare-rights, for property-rights it is not

25. See, for example, Nozick (1974), chap. 7.

necessary that an owner of a commodity ever be capable of desiring possession of that commodity in order to have the right to it. Infants or even fetuses can acquire ownership of property (by inheritance, for example) long before they have the concept of property. Nor need they ever acquire the concept. If an infant dies before the age of two or is severely retarded, this fact does not affect its property-rights; when it dies its heirs inherit the property.[26] If infants or fetuses can have property-rights though incapable of desiring property, it is not clear why they cannot have the right to life though incapable of desiring to live.

Tooley has taken an important step in attempting to link rights and desires, and thus attempting to ground his criterion of moral standing in the very concept of a right. However, his argument still suffers from the absence of a theory of rights.[27] Fa-

26. Louisell and Noonan (1970), p. 223. In Tooley (1972) we encounter the following pertinent footnote: "There are, however, situations . . . which might seem to count against the claim that a person cannot have a right unless he is conceptually capable of having the corresponding desire. Can't a young child, for example, have a right to an estate, even though he may not be conceptually capable of wanting the estate? It is clear that such situations have to be carefully considered if one is to arrive at a satisfactory account of the concept of a right. My inclination is to say that the correct description is not that the child now has a right to the estate, but that he will come to have such a right when he is mature, and that in the meantime no one else has a right to the estate. My reason for saying that the child does not now have a right to the estate is that he cannot now do things with the estate, such as selling it or giving it away, that he will be able to do later on." (p. 49n) This note does not address itself to the case of the child who never becomes mature, and the last sentence suggests a confusion between having a right and being able to claim or exercise it (see Feinberg 1974, pp. 46–49). Tooley was criticized on this point by Howell (1973), and the note does not appear in Tooley (1973).

27. Tooley's argument linking rights and desires, although it is not located within a theory of rights, at least addresses itself to the task of grounding a criterion of moral standing. There is no comparable rationale in Warren (1978), whose argument proceeds entirely on the intuitive level. Tooley's reticence to deploy a rights theory may stem from the fact that, despite his definition of a person in terms of the right to life, he does not

miliar theories of both welfare-rights and liberty-rights will not support the link between rights and desires that is crucial for Tooley's position. Perhaps other theories will be more tractable, but it is now clear that the liberal does not enjoy the luxury of avoiding specific theoretical commitment. The conceptual connections between moral rights and the natural properties of beings will depend on the kinds of rights a theory acknowledges. If an argument like Tooley's is to succeed, it must be built on some specified rights theory. Until such a theory is provided we have no reason to accept Tooley's view of the moral status of the fetus, especially when it violates some of our basic moral intuitions.

This examination of both the naive and the philosophical versions of the liberal view has uncovered a disagreeable quandary for liberals. If they wish to deny moral standing to (at least pre-viable) fetuses but not to infants, then it seems that they must defend a threshold that is arbitrary and abrupt. If, on the other hand, they devise a deeper and more general criterion, then it threatens to deny standing to infants as well and so to justify infanticide. Avoiding both of these unpleasant outcomes will place heavy demands upon a criterion of moral standing: it must pick out a threshold beyond viability but not beyond birth; it must avoid investing events like birth with a significance they do not merit; it must allow moral standing to be gained gradually; and it must be grounded in some plausible theory of rights. Given the smooth continuity of ontogenesis after viability, and indeed after birth, it is difficult to see how any criterion can satisfy all of these demands. It would be foolhardy to conclude that the liberal view cannot be given a credible defense—but the task is a daunting one.

---

espouse any such theory; see Purdy and Tooley (1974), p. 137. The point remains that if he is to provide a rationale for his criterion he will need to supply the moral theory of his choice.

9. The Right to Life

The best case for the liberal is that no fetus has moral standing. The minimal case that will still generate a permissive abortion policy is that no previable fetus has moral standing. Liberals cannot support their best case without also justifying infanticide, and it is quite possible that they cannot even support their minimal case. In this section we shall assume, without argument, the worst for the liberal—that *all* fetuses, from conception onward, have moral standing. What are the implications of conceding the right to life to fetuses? What sort of abortion policy is it then reasonable to espouse? Answering these questions will enable us to test the extent to which the liberal's advocacy of a permissive policy is dependent on denying moral standing to the fetus. It will also provide some insight into the content of the right to life—a right that has thus far remained largely unanalyzed. Finally, it will shift attention away from the special nature of the fetus to the other ingredient that complicates the abortion problem: the special relation between the fetus and the mother.

Fortunately the territory we need to cover has been well mapped by Judith Jarvis Thomson (1974a, 1974b). Although Thomson does not accept the conservative's contention that all fetuses have the right to life, she assumes it as a working hypothesis for her argument. Her question is what follows from this hypothesis for the morality both of abortion itself and of abortion policies. The argument begins by constructing an analogue of the mother/fetus relation that has the following features:

(1) The relation is parasitic: one person (the parasite) is dependent for life support on being physically connected to the body of another (the host). The parasite makes no reciprocal contribution to the well-being of the host.

(2) Both parties to the relation are adults with full rights. Specifically, the parasite has (among others) the right to life and the

host has (among others) the right to decide the use of her body.

(3) The relation is burdensome to the host: it is inconvenient, unpleasant, even dangerous while it endures and there is no benefit for the host (apart from relief from the burden) realized by its termination.

(4) The relation is involuntary, that is, it was not consented to by the host.

Thomson's contention is that in a relationship that displays these features the host has no moral duty to continue providing life support for the parasite, despite the fact that the parasite has a right to life. Thus *under analogous circumstances* a woman has no duty to continue her pregnancy, despite the fact that the fetus has a right to life. Abortion in these circumstances is justified and ought to be legally available.

The argument to this conclusion consists of an analysis of the right to life. The content of this right is defined by the duties it imposes on others—in this case on the host. It is therefore limited by the rights of these others—in this case the host's right of autonomy. Thomson tries out two interpretations of the right to life: that it is the right to be given the necessaries of life, and that it is the right not to be killed. In the former case it is clearly a welfare-right; in the latter it appears to be a liberty-right. In either case there are limits to the duties one person's possession of the right imposes on others. To have the welfare-right to life is not to have the unqualified right to whatever goods or services are necessary for continuance of one's life, for others may sometimes have no duty to provide such goods or services. In particular, "having a right to life does not guarantee having either a right to be given the use of or a right to be allowed continued use of another person's body—even if one needs it for life itself."[28] The parasite needs use of the host's body, but her prior ownership of that body and her right to control the use to be made of it imply that she has no duty to meet that need, even

28. Thomson (1974a), p. 12.

though the parasite will otherwise die. It would be nice or generous of the host to make her body available, but it is not obligatory. And if she has no duty to make her body available, the
parasite has no right to use of it.

The same result is easily reached by supposing that the right
to life is the liberty-right not to be killed. A man's possession of
this right does not entail that others have an unqualified duty
not to kill him, regardless of the circumstances. It does not entail, for example, that he may not be killed if he is threatening
the life or bodily integrity of others. The right not to be killed is
circumscribed by the rights of others. One such right, again, is
that of autonomy. The parasite has invaded the body of the host;
the host's property-right over her body includes the right to defend herself against such an invasion. As our technology now
stands, disconnecting the parasite will kill it. If the host has the
right of autonomy, she has the right to disconnect the parasite,
thereby killing it.[29] But then she has no duty not to kill the
parasite and, in this circumstance, the parasite has no right not
to be killed. Killing it would not violate its rights.

Thomson's analysis of the right to life is not a full inventory
of its content, but it does identify some items that are not part of
that content. In her analogue the right to life does not include
the right to life support provided by someone else's body. It
therefore does not include the right not to be disconnected. And
so in structurally similar cases of abortion, the fetus' right to life,
whatever its proper content, does not include the right not to be
aborted.

The strength of Thomson's analysis is the recognition that the
right to life is not a simple matter and therefore that it "will not
serve the opponents of abortion in the very simple and clear way

---

29. It is important that she has the right to disconnect the parasite, not to
kill it. If disconnecting the parasite does not cause its death she has no right
further to threaten its life (Thomson 1974a, p. 22). Abortion necessarily
involves disconnecting the fetus; it does not necessarily involve killing it.

in which they seem to have thought it would".[30] Arguments
that begin by invoking the fetus' right to life and end by con-
demning abortion will be persuasive only if that right is very
carefully unpacked somewhere along the way. Unpacking it will
require enumerating the various duties one person's possession
of the right to life imposes upon other persons—and *that* will be
a very complicated story indeed, touching (among other matters) on the right of self-defense against threats to life or well-
being, the special case in which such a threat is posed by an "innocent" person, the role of property-rights, and the difference (if
any) between killing someone and refraining from supporting
that person's life. If the liberal is right about the moral standing
of the fetus, the liberal view of abortion, including the case for a
permissive policy, follows easily. But if the conservative is right
about the moral standing of the fetus, it is not at all clear just
what follows. The conservative view must ponder the moral relevance of the mother/fetus relation and so will be more complicated than the liberal view. It is Thomson's merit to have clari-
fied just how complicated it will be.

There are two ways of responding to Thomson's argument.
One is to challenge the argument itself.[31] Because this challenge
is usually made by conservatives, and because the issues it raises
are crucial for the conservative view, it will be examined in the
next chapter. Meanwhile, we will simply assume that Thomson's
argument is sound, and thus that in the analogue she constructs
the host does no wrong by disconnecting the parasite. The second response is to explore just when this argument will justify
abortion, and thus what sort of abortion policy it will support.[32]
Can the argument support a permissive abortion policy, thus en-

30. Ibid., p. 12.
31. The main challenges have been made by Brody (1972, 1975) and
Finnis (1974).
32. See, for example, Warren (1978).

abling liberals to achieve their practical objective without denying moral standing to the fetus?

So far we know only that an abortion is justified in cases structurally similar to the analogue, namely, where pregnancy is both burdensome and involuntary. These conditions are satisfied by Thomson's case of "a sick and desperately frightened fourteen-year-old schoolgirl, pregnant due to rape."[33] Presumably an abortion law ought *at least* to permit abortions when pregnancy is due to rape (and is unwanted). What other grounds for abortion ought it to recognize? The factors that, on Thomson's argument, should affect our assessment of a particular case are the following:

(a) How the pregnancy came about, and especially the extent to which it was agreed to or invited.

(b) The burden pregnancy imposes on the woman, and especially the certainty and extent of the threat to her life, health, liberty or well-being.

(c) The benefit that continuation of pregnancy would confer upon the fetus, and especially the extent to which it will be capable of a worthwhile life.

(d) The elapsed duration of pregnancy, and especially the extent to which permitting a pregnancy to endure for some time constitutes tacit acceptance of responsibility for the fetus.

Each of these factors admits of degrees, and they may combine in an enormous number of ways. At the extremes we may locate clear cases. Pregnancy due to rape is one such clear case—the more so if we add in such further ingredients as a substantial threat to the woman's life, a severely deformed fetus, and a firm decision to abort early in pregnancy. At the opposite extreme we might find a case in which the pregnancy was clearly planned and is proceeding smoothly with a normal fetus, but the woman suddenly decides in the sixth month that she simply no longer

---

33. Thomson (1974a), p. 21.

wants the child. This case departs so radically from the analogue that Thomson's argument cannot be used to justify abortion.

What of the cases between the extremes—that is to say, almost all cases of abortion? To what extent must the pregnancy have been intended? Must a woman ensure that some reliable method of contraception is employed? What of the failure rates associated with even relatively reliable methods? To what extent does ignorance of the mechanics of conception (or contraception) constitute lack of intent? How can we be certain whether a woman wished to become pregnant? How can *she* be certain about her own aims? What if she changes her mind after intercourse? What sort of burden must pregnancy impose on a woman? How probable must a threat to her life be? Is it sufficient that childbirth has a known mortality rate, and that abortion is less risky? What counts as a threat to health? To what extent should we include anxiety, distress, or depression as such a threat? What if the burden is mild discomfort or some restriction on acitivites? What if it is economic, as it might be if a model had to forego income until she regained her formerly svelte figure? How low must the quality of life available to the fetus be in order to justify abortion? Which congenital defects are severe enough? What role is played by socioeconomic conditions affecting the child's future? How long must a pregnancy have endured before the woman will be deemed to have accepted a commitment to continue it? What considerations will override that commitment? What if the woman did not realize she was pregnant? What if she avoided finding out? And so on and on.

Clearly Thomson's argument provides no simple way of deciding particular cases. Indeed, given the *kind* of argument it is, there can be no simple way of deciding such cases. Thomson regards this as a virtue in her position: "I am inclined to think it a merit of my account precisely that it does *not* give a general yes or a general no."[34] Nonetheless she does offer some guidelines.

34. Ibid.

One is that we should think of abortion cases in terms of their analogues and come to similar decisions for similar cases. Another is that the conflict between the fetus and the mother always takes place on her territory, in a body to which she has prior claim. There is therefore always a presumption in favor of her right to be rid of the invader. This presumption may be overridden by further considerations (such as the fact that she invited the "invader" in), but it nonetheless always carries some weight. A third is that we have some minimal duty to aid others even when they have no right to that aid. It is sometimes indecent to refuse aid though one has every right to do so. There may therefore be cases in which the fetus has no right to continued life support but, because the burden to the mother is trivial and the benefit to the fetus enormous, it would be indecent to withhold it. In saying this, Thomson departs from a strict theory of rights, all of whose duties correlate with (someone's) rights. But regardless of its source, this consideration will provide some counterweight against abortion.

If one begins by granting the right to life to the fetus and then accepts Thomson's position concerning the content of that right and the duties it imposes on others, it will follow that the morality of abortion must be decided on a case-by-case basis. At best we might construct some few crude categories (pregnancy due to rape, pregnancy that threatens the woman's life, etc.) and say that abortions that fit these categories are usually permissible (or impermissible). But there could always be exceptions, and if we wanted to be sure of a particular case, we would have no choice but to weigh the various factors present in it. No formula could be devised for this weighing, since the relevant factors admit of too many variations and combine in too many novel and unexpected ways. On Thomson's view the morality of abortion will be as complicated as, say, the common law on homicide in self-defense. An abortion statute cannot afford the luxury of such unrestrained particularity. The policy supported by Thomson's argument would be a moderate one, which admitted as grounds for abortion at least pregnancy due to rape, risk to maternal life or health, and fetal deformity, and which stipulated some screening mechanism for adjudicating particular cases.[35] In addition, a policy might impose a time limit, on the basis that permitting a pregnancy to continue beyond a certain stage constitutes consent to the pregnancy.

Such a policy would clearly be cumbersome to administer—the issue of whether a pregnancy had been agreed to would be particularly difficult but also unavoidable. However it is clear that Thomson's argument cannot be used to support a simpler policy, whether permissive or restrictive. The policies of the established views, with their straightforward endorsement or condemnation of abortion, are both quite beyond its reach. If Thomson is right, then liberals who concede a right to life to the fetus must abandon their view of abortion. The liberal view is thus utterly and unalterably dependent on denying moral standing to the fetus; it cannot be supported on any other basis. The main pressure on Thomson's argument is exerted, not by liberals, but by conservatives who believe that it is too permissive toward abortion. Thomson clearly intends her analysis as an alternative to both of the established views, which she regards as simple-minded treatments of the problem. At the same time, she is aware that her analysis is incomplete and does not yet constitute a view of abortion. The working hypothesis she has granted for the sake of argument—that all fetuses have the right to life—is one that she rejects. She also rejects the liberal view that no fetuses have such a right. In order to round out her view of abortion she must somehow support her opinion that young and immature fetuses have no moral standing, whereas older and more developed fetuses have such standing, and she must do this

35. These are precisely the grounds for abortion for which there exists strong public support; see Badgley (1977), pp. 459–460. Thomson's case-by-case approach and moderate policy have an undeniable common-sense appeal, a fact she uses to her advantage.

by developing a criterion of moral standing and grounding it in the theory of rights she is presupposing.

The result of these further endeavors will be an even more complex view and an even more complex policy. (This is not meant as a criticism; perhaps only complex views do justice to abortion.) She might, for instance, support a permissive policy to some time limit, beyond which the provisions of her moderate policy would become operative. Rounding out her view will require addressing the problem of the fetus with which liberals have had so little success. She might enjoy better luck, since she is free of one of the constraints binding upon liberals: she can locate the threshold of moral standing before viability if it seems reasonable to do so. But the other constraints still apply, especially the demand that a criterion be grounded in an adequate theory of rights. It is at this level that Thomson's argument is lacking. Although she spends considerable time analyzing the right to life, and although she also offers valuable observations about rights in general, she is unspecific about the theory of rights she is presupposing.[36] We do not know what sort of theory it is or what sort of rights it contains. Different theories are likely to generate both different criteria of moral standing and different content for the right to life. Thomson's argument is promising but far from being either complete or secure.

10. The Strategy of Detachment

Liberals wish above all to make a case for a permissive abortion policy. Their preferred method is to show that abortion is a private activity and to invoke a liberal social theory in defense of

36. "... I think there does not exist any even remotely plausible theory of the logic of rights. And yet ... I think there does not exist any issue of importance in ethics in which we can avoid or side-step them." (Thomson 1974b, p. 117) Although rights are always relevant for Thomson, her discussion of Minimally Decent Samaritanism suggests that she thinks other factors are relevant as well.

toleration. But this route requires denying moral standing to the fetus, a step that is difficult to justify. Thomson's argument has shown that liberals cannot afford to concede their opponents' view of the fetus, for on that view a permissive policy becomes quite untenable. Unless some further strategy is available, the conclusion must be that a permissive policy admits of no persuasive justification.

Some liberals have attempted a further strategy. Thus far we have assumed that views of abortion are packages consisting of (1) a position on the moral standing of the fetus, (2) an assessment of the morality of abortion, and (3) a defense of an abortion policy. We have further assumed that later items in the package are built on earlier ones, so that the first step in assembling a view of abortion is to take a stand on the fetus. Some liberal arguments challenge these assumptions by detaching the political problem of choosing an abortion policy from the personal problem of the morality of abortion. If any such arguments succeed, liberals might still manage to support their preferred policy, even if their view of the fetus is exposed as utterly groundless.

One such argument is found in Daniel Callahan (1970), probably the most influential discussion of abortion to date by a philosopher. Callahan does not shrink from confronting the question of the fetus. After considerable discussion he adopts the position that moral standing is acquired gradually as the fetus develops; whereas a zygote or embryo lacks such standing, a more mature and developed fetus possesses it.[37] Moreover, Callahan recognizes that a view of the morality of abortion must be based at least in part on a view of the moral status of the fetus. One expects the story to be completed in the familiar fashion: early abortions are private matters and ought to be legally per-

---

37. Callahan (1970), chap. 11. Callahan tends to speak of when a fetus becomes a human being or a person, but the issue he is addressing is that of moral standing.

mitted, whereas later abortions are properly subject to legal regu-
lations. The appropriate policy would seem to be permissive up
to some time limit, to be located wherever Callahan thinks the
threshold of moral standing is passed.

The policy Callahan eventually supports is indeed permissive
for early abortions, with a time limit set roughly at the end of
the first trimester of pregnancy.[38] But his rationale for this time
limit is surprising in making no reference to the moral standing
of the fetus. Instead, it is based on the fact that abortions in the
first trimester are safer for women who undergo them. Neither
Callahan's time limit nor its rationale will please liberals, the former because it is so early and the latter because it is paternalistic.
But liberals might find his method of argument appealing, since
Callahan's view of the moral status of the fetus appears to have
played no role in settling on an abortion policy. He has entirely
detached the personal from the political problem: "A sharp distinction needs to be drawn between abortion on request as a
moral position and abortion on request as a *legal* position. The
weight of my criticism of abortion on request is directed at it in-
sofar as it is put forth as a moral position. As for abortion on
request as a legal position . . . I will argue that it represents good
public and legal policy."[39]

Callahan holds that the moral status of the fetus is one factor
to take into account in choosing an abortion policy. But it is not
the only one; we must attend also to pragmatic considerations
such as the enforceability of a policy, the illegal abortion rate it
will generate, and so on. Earlier in his book Callahan has argued
persuasively that on these pragmatic grounds permissive policies
are superior to all others. His eventual defense of a permissive
policy (for early abortions) appears to rest on weighting these

38. Ibid., chap. 13.
39. Ibid., p. 448. Oddly, some conservatives have drawn a similar
distinction; see Drinan (1967–68), p. 381, and compare Drinan (1967), pp.
122–123. Drinan's view is criticized in Grisez (1970), pp. 451–458.

pragmatic grounds more heavily than his own view of the moral status of the fetus. But this is somewhat odd, since it is the moral status of the fetus that determines whether or not abortion ought to be classified as a form of homicide. If Callahan thinks that first-trimester fetuses have no moral standing, he ought to rely principally on that conviction in defending a permissive policy. The further pragmatic considerations would merely reinforce a case that had already been given strong moral support. If Callahan thinks that at least some first-trimester fetuses have moral standing, he ought not to defend a policy whose time limit is set at the end of this trimester, whatever its further pragmatic justification. The moral status of the fetus cannot fail to be the central issue in settling on an abortion policy, for one's stand on that issue will determine whether one regards a permissive policy as a license for mass homicide. The pragmatic considerations are all side issues, dominated by the central question of the fetus. The gap between Callahan's view of the fetus and his favored abortion policy appears to result from allowing the side issues to dominate the central issue.

In fact, Callahan's argument effectively discounts the central issue entirely. The crucial step is the claim that even if abortion is (in at least some cases) homicide, a permissive policy may still be justified if this form of homicide poses no "threat to the common good."[40] Callahan glosses a threat to the common good as "a threat to the peace, security and safety of the whole society," and his conclusion is that abortion even when it is homicide poses no such threat: "Despite all the possible moral objections to abortion, the social harm of permissive abortion laws has not been shown; there exist, then, no grounds for society to forbid abortions to those women who want them."[41] No grounds, that is, except the safety of those very women. The obvious question is whether or not the good of fetuses has been

40. Ibid., p. 474.
41. Ibid., pp. 474, 478.

included in this reckoning of the common good. Callahan's own position commits him to including at least those fetuses to whom he ascribes moral standing. But it is quite evident that fetal welfare has by this stage of the argument entirely dropped from sight; Callahan bends his efforts to showing that abortion is no threat to "the life of those already living."[42] Since abortion is palpably a threat to the lives of fetuses, they are obviously not being reckoned among "those already living." This despite Callahan's contention that at least some fetuses have moral standing (surely they are *all* living!). In his defense of a permissive policy, Callahan's own view of the fetus has not merely been outweighed by other considerations—it has come to count for nothing whatever.

It is inconsistent (indeed schizoid) to establish a view of the moral status of the fetus and then to ignore it in arguing for an abortion policy. The wiser tactic for the liberal is to urge that the issue of the fetus is inherently undecidable. Perhaps there is no way of showing either that fetuses have moral standing or that they lack it.[43] It may be that all moral issues are undecidable, in the sense that equally strong (or weak) cases can always be made for opposed positions on such issues. Or it may be that the distribution of moral standing is a particularly vexed issue, one on which rational and impartial persons might reasonably disagree. Or perhaps the moral status of fetuses is peculiarly difficult to establish with confidence. Fetuses may constitute a borderline case that it is equally reasonable (or arbitrary) to resolve

---

42. Ibid., p. 475.

43. As is argued by Wertheimer (1974): ". . . we seem to be stuck with the indeterminateness of the fetus' humanity. This does not mean that, whatever you believe, it is true or true for you if you believe it. Quite the contrary, it means that, whatever you believe, it's not true—but neither is it false. You believe it, and that's the end of the matter." (pp. 44–45) Much feminist rhetoric concerning abortion also implies that the question of the fetus is subjective and undecidable—so much moral hairsplitting—and that abortion laws should therefore be repealed.

in both directions. Sceptical doubts may be broad or narrow, but if any of them are justified, the liberal may be able to make a case for a permissive policy after all. If no view of the fetus can be given a firm rational foundation, all such views are mere matters of taste. In a pluralistic society we should tolerate diversity of individual taste on this question. The rules of a liberal social theory forbid any group from enforcing its own standards of taste against other groups. The only social policy compatible with such a theory would be one that left each woman free to follow her own private convictions. But that would be a permissive policy.

The argument from scepticism detaches the personal from the political problem by treating the former as subjective and irrational. The first thing to note about this argument is that it means a significant retreat for liberals, who typically advance a view of the morality of abortion that they regard as objective and rational. Liberals treat the personal problem as decidable, for they promote a view that decides it. The retreat to scepticism is a last resort for liberals who are unable to supply a rational foundation for that view; it amounts to the claim that none of their opponents will succeed where they have failed. Certainly the case in favor of scepticism will not itself be easy to establish. The broader the scepticism the more likely it is to dissolve some of the liberal's own cherished values. If it extends across moral questions generally, liberals may be committed to a permissive policy on all human activities, that is, to anarchism. If it is narrowed to questions of moral standing (but why should they be different?), liberals may still need to exercise an embarrassing quantity of toleration. What would be done, for example, with rapists who argued that women did not possess liberty-rights? Liberals are committed to a private/public distinction on which most cases are clear cases, and therefore to a legal framework whose rationale is for the most part settled and beyond dispute. They would do well to treat the moral standing of the fetus, and thus the problem of abortion, as a special case for which scepticism has some special justification.

But what would that justification be? Why should the moral status of the fetus be less decidable than other moral questions? The sceptic's claim is not just that it is a difficult question but rather that it is not a question on which reason is competent. Nothing can here be established by rational means, not even that some views are mistaken; where truth and knowledge are not to be found, neither are falsehood and error. But we already have some reason for thinking that this pessimism is ungrounded. The liberal's own favored view of the fetus appears to be false; the arguments in its favor are bad arguments. This may be a negative result, but it is a rational one—the sort of result that is unavailable in genuine matters of taste. It is as yet unclear whether positive results will be forthcoming, whether eliminating bad theories will lead us to better ones. At this stage in the argument, where we cannot know just how much can be achieved by purely rational means, scepticism about the moral status of the fetus is mere dogmatism. If liberals are to give us any reason to share their scepticism, they must show that no other view of the fetus will fare any better than their own. Making a persuasive case for this negative thesis promises to be at least as difficult as making a persuasive case for the liberal view itself. In any case, whether the thesis is correct or not will emerge only at the end of our investigation.

What follows if it is correct? Liberals argue from scepticism to toleration and a permissive policy. Ironically, conservatives sometimes employ a similar device to support regulation and a restrictive policy.[44] We cannot tell, the argument goes, whether

44. See, for example, Kremer (1974). Kremer makes the question at issue appear objective by casting it in terms of the humanity of the fetus (a matter of fact). He does not think that no answer to this question can be defended but is trying to undermine liberal arguments from pluralism by showing that the fact of disagreement ought to incline us toward the safer policy.

or not fetuses have a right to life. But either they do or they do not. If they do, then a permissive policy allows mass homicide, whereas a restrictive policy (if it is effective) prevents it. If they do not, then a permissive policy expands the autonomy of women, whereas a restrictive policy confines it. If we cannot determine which is the case, we ought to choose the policy that avoids the worst possible outcome. Allowing creatures with a right to life to be slaughtered is worse than making inroads on the autonomy of women. Thus the safer course of action, the rational choice under uncertainty, is a restrictive policy.

The liberal and conservative arguments, although similar in some respects, make incompatible assumptions about the question of the status of the fetus. For the liberal there can in principle be no rational answer to the question; thus it is a matter for personal decision. For the conservative there is a correct answer "out there" that we could in principle discover, but so far it is hidden from our view. The conservative treats the choice of abortion policies as analogous to deciding whether or not to fire into the bushes when it is unclear whether a child is hiding in them. The conservative argument is not genuinely sceptical. It involves conceding that no extant view of the status of the fetus (including the conservative view) is persuasive, while contending that if we work at the problem long enough we will finally discover the truth. Given what they are conceding, conservatives will need to justify their confidence that there is an objective truth to be discovered. If all of our best efforts to date have been unsuccessful, perhaps we have been asking questions to which there are no answers. Conservatives who employ this argument thus flirt dangerously with the very scepticism that liberals are trying to exploit to their own advantage.

If liberals could justify their scepticism, they would indeed have a case for a permissive policy. A liberal social theory relies on a determinate distinction between private and public acts, requiring toleration of the former and permitting regulation of (some of) the latter. What is at stake in the abortion controversy is precisely whether fetuses have moral standing, thus whether abortion is a private act. If that issue is rationally unde-cidable, we have no better reason for assigning abortion to the one category than to the other; neither assignment would be mistaken. It might seem, then, that we have no better reason for choosing a permissive policy than a restrictive one; neither choice would be mistaken. And this would in fact be correct *so far as the central issue of the fetus is concerned.* If *that* issue is unde-cidable it cannot enable us to choose between abortion policies. But in that case the central issue simply drops out of the account and we are left to choose a policy on the basis of the side issues. These issues, as Callahan argues, favor toleration, since permis-sive policies enhance the liberties and opportunities of women, reduce the death rate from illegal abortions, lower the birth rate, and so on. On a liberal social theory it is always state coercion that requires justification, not individual liberty. If abortion can-not be shown to be homicide, there is no case for a restrictive policy.[45] Thus if liberals are right in claiming that the question of the fetus is ultimately one of subjective preference, they can use that fact to support a permissive policy. But first they must show that they are right.

The liberal view of the fetus lacks a persuasive defense. If liber-als compensate for this defect by simply ignoring the question of the fetus, their case for a permissive abortion policy loses by de-fault. If they concede moral standing to at least some (previable) fetuses, that case is incoherent. The liberals' only chance is that all other views of the fetus will turn out to be as ill grounded as their own.

---

45. Wertheimer (1974) uses a similar argument (p. 50).

CHAPTER THREE

The Conservative View

The conservative's defense of a restrictive abortion policy rests on the claim that abortion is (or involves) one sort of homicide, which rests in turn on ascribing full moral standing to the fetus. To attribute full moral standing to a creature is to award that creature the same right to life as is possessed by the paradigm of a mature and normal human being. It is therefore to impose the strictest constraints on the circumstances in which the creature can be killed or its life left unprotected. If the conservative view of abortion is to be persuasive, there must be a good case for attributing a strong right to life to all fetuses from conception onward.

Part of that case will consist in grounding this view of the fetus in a moral theory. Liberals have tended to ignore this level of theory in defending their view of abortion. Those who have not failed entirely in this regard have attempted to connect their view of the fetus with a rights theory, but have been unspecific about the sort of rights theory they are presupposing. Conservatives have by and large been both more forthcoming and more consistent. The conservative view has its roots in the moral tradition of natural law. It therefore has a deep structure whose counterpart liberals are now only beginning to assemble for their own position. Evaluating the conservative view of the fetus, and of abortion, requires familiarity with this natural-law tradition.

11. *Natural Law*

All natural-law theories share two features. The first is a content and structure defined by a set of moral rules and by priorities ordering these rules. There is room here for some variation—

"natural law" is also the name of a family of theories—but there are also limits to such variation. There are some rules and some priorities that are elements common to all natural-law theories. The second feature is a claim about the justification of such theories, namely, that moral principles are somehow grounded in the nature of things and thus are not merely conventional. The truth of moral principles can be established by rational procedures at least analogous to those appropriate to laws of nature. Moral theories are thus ultimately grounded in either science or metaphysics; moral philosophy is not autonomous and the choice of ultimate moral principles is not unconstrained by reason.

We shall here be concerned only with the content and structure of natural-law theories, and not with their further epistemological claims. In Section 7 three types of rights theories were distinguished: libertarian, lexical, and intuitionist. This distinction is one of content (the sorts of rights a theory contains) and structure (the ordering relations among those rights). If a natural-law theory is a rights theory, it is a lexical theory. Natural-law theories are usually formulated as theories of duty. Donagan (1977) employs the traditional terminology of perfect and imperfect duties.[1] Perfect duties are expressed by rules that prohibit the performance of specified kinds of acts (killing, assault, enslavement, etc.). These rules are absolute, admitting of no exceptions whatever the circumstances. Agents must fulfil their perfect duties on every possible occasion. Imperfect duties are expressed by rules that enjoin the pursuit of specified ends (giving aid, etc.). These rules are not absolute, leaving agents some

1. Donagan (1977), pp. 153-155. Donagan does not call his theory a natural-law theory, probably because he attempts to give it a Kantian foundation rather than the sort of grounding in the natural order more typical of the natural-law tradition. However, its content and structure satisfy the conditions for a natural-law morality—as do the duties in Kant's *Metaphysics of Morals*. Donagan does recognize Aquinas as well as Kant as a source for his theory.

latitude in deciding what to do in specific circumstances. Agents need not fulfil their imperfect duties on every possible occasion. This perfect/imperfect dichotomy has been drawn by various authors in various terms: as the distinction between strict and loose duties, duties of justice and duties of charity or beneficence, or (as in Section 7) negative and positive duties. Whatever one's favored vocabulary, the essential difference is between the duty not to do a certain kind of act and the duty to promote a certain general end.

If one assumes that all duties are correlated with reciprocal rights (and vice versa), this distinction of kinds of duty is congruent with the distinction between liberty-rights and welfare-rights. If one has the duty to promote the good, happiness, or well-being of others, or to rescue them from misfortune or evil, these others have a right to these forms of treatment. Such rights, however, will all be defeasible, and the rules of duty they entail will all be prima facie. Strict negative duties will likewise correlate with inviolable liberty-rights, and the rules formulating such duties will be absolute. A system of moral principles that invokes both inviolable liberty-rights and defeasible welfare-rights, and that thus imposes both absolute and prima facie duties, implicitly contains its own priority rule. In Donagan's theory, that ordering rule is the Pauline principle that *evil is not to be done that good may come of it.*[2] What this principle requires is that perfect duties never be violated in the course of carrying out imperfect duties. Perfect duties thus have lexical priority over imperfect: the latter may be done only when none of the former are omitted. Thus, if a natural-law theory is a rights theory, it is a lexical theory.

A natural-law theory is partly defined by this division of negative and positive duties and by the lexical Pauline ordering rule. But another essential element has thus far been omitted, and when it is included it becomes clear that a natural-law theory

2. Ibid., p. 155.

cannot be a rights theory. Moral theories may be divided into those that are *ideal* and those that are *discretionary*. The difference between the two sorts of theory emerges in their treatment of the private realm, where the interpersonal dimension of action is absent. A discretionary theory contains no duties for the private realm—no duties to oneself. It treats the private sphere as one of taste rather than morality; here individuals are free to decide their ends and pursuits for themselves, free of moral constraints. On a discretionary theory all duties are duties to others, and no private act can be morally right or wrong.[3] An ideal theory lays down some conception of the good life, some end or ideal that it is good for human agents to pursue in their own lives, and it enjoins pursuit of this ideal as a duty. An ideal theory thus includes the private realm within the scope of morality; here there are moral duties and an objective distinction of right and wrong. An ideal theory thus contains duties to oneself—duties to pursue one's development or perfection—as well as duties to others.[4]

Natural-law theories are ideal theories: this is the third element that, together with the division of negative and positive duties and the Pauline principle, defines their characteristic content and structure. Such theories cannot recognize a general right to liberty in the private sphere. A liberty-right protects the freedom of its possessors to decide for themselves what they will do or the ends they will pursue. A general right to liberty in the private sphere converts that sphere into the realm of taste. Such a right is therefore incompatible with private duties: one cannot have the right either to do or to omit a certain act if one has either the duty to do it or the duty to omit it. The inclusion in natural-law theories of a class of duties to oneself entails that some duties are not correlated with any reciprocal rights. But then the duties in such theories extend beyond the rights recog-

3. See, for instance, Nozick (1974). A rights theory that contains absolute liberty-rights is necessarily a discretionary theory.
4. See, for instance, Donagan (1977), chap. 3.

nized by the theories, and this cannot be true in a rights theory. In natural-law theories the basic deontic concept is not that of a right but that of a duty .

If the conservative view of abortion is grounded in a natural-law theory, then it is not grounded in a rights theory. Nonetheless, the rhetoric of the conservative view is that of rights: the right to life, the right to be born, and so forth. Further, many (not all) natural-law defenses of the conservative view invoke fetal rights.[5] But this fact should not be surprising, even though natural-law theories are not rights theories. The concept of a rights theory is an exclusive one, requiring that nothing but rights are basic in the theory. A theory may contain rights without making such rights basic, and thus without being a rights theory. Duties to oneself cannot be correlated with rights, but the same does not hold for duties to others. Positive duties to others (duties to give aid) may entail rights on the part of these others. Negative duties to others (duties not to injure) likewise may entail rights on the part of these others. These rights will lack the element of personal autonomy essential to liberty-rights but they are still rights *against others* and we can still distinguish the former (defeasible) from the latter (inviolable).[6] The abortion context is one of interpersonal conflict (at least it is if conservatives are correct). Duties to oneself do not therefore play a

5. See Bourke (1951), chap. 11; Kenny (1962), chap. 5; Drinan (1967, 1967–68); Granfield (1969). Those who prefer the language of duty include Kelly (1958), chaps. 9–11; McFadden (1967), chaps. 6–8; Noonan (1970). Finnis (1974) argues, to little effect, against treating the morality of abortion in terms of rights.

6. I shall assume that welfare-rights also include the option to accept and use the good in question or not, as one pleases. Where rights do not include this option, then so far as the private sphere is concerned they seem identical with duties (to oneself). (See Feinberg 1978, p. 105). In discussing the natural-law treatment of morality I shall therefore speak of negative v. positive rights, or absolute v. defeasible rights, but not of liberty-rights v. welfare-rights.

central role in this context. If duties to others imply rights owned by those others, the morality of abortion can be analyzed indifferently by natural-law conservatives either in terms of duties toward the fetus or in terms of rights of the fetus. As Germain Grisez has contended, in the interpersonal realm the two currencies are entirely convertible: "Rights and duties are correlative. If I have an unalienable right to life, then it is always wrong for others to kill me. If it is sometimes justified for them to kill me, then my right to life is not unalienable."[7]

A natural-law theory supplies conservatives with two different sorts of duty that may be applicable to abortion: the absolute duty not to kill and the prima facie duty to provide life support. It therefore also supplies two different sorts of rights: the inviolable right not to be killed and the defeasible right to life support. In what follows it will be assumed that these duties translate into these rights, and vice versa. Thus, despite the fact that natural-law theories are not rights theories, the natural-law defense of the conservative view can be treated as one that attributes certain kinds of rights to fetuses. Our analysis of moral standing thus requires no modification.

Since abortion nearly always involves killing the fetus, it seems natural to focus on the absolute prohibition on killing. Whenever rules are treated as absolutes they must be formulated very carefully. For reasons that will emerge more fully in what follows, we will assume that a natural-law theory contains the following rule concerning killing: it is always wrong (impermissible) directly to kill an innocent creature who possesses moral standing. In order for it to be wrong to kill some particular creature three conditions must therefore be satisfied: (1) the creature must have moral standing, (2) the creature must be innocent, and (3) the killing must be direct. If we apply these conditions to the case of abortion, the first fastens on the moral status of the fetus and the other two on the relation between the

7. Grisez (1970a), p. 204.

fetus and the mother. In order for conservatives to justify their view of abortion, they must show both that fetuses have moral standing and that the special circumstances of abortion are those in which killing a creature with moral standing is impermissible.

12. *Abortion and Contraception*

The liberal and conservative views of the fetus are in many respects mirror images of one another. So as to deny fetuses the right to life, the liberal wishes to defend a moral threshold at, or shortly before, birth. So as to award fetuses the right to life, the conservative wishes to defend a threshold at, or shortly after, conception. Each view, at least in its naive version, invests one of the temporal boundaries of pregnancy with enormous moral significance. The liberal's problem is to show that birth can carry that moral weight, and thus to distinguish abortion from infanticide. The conservative's problem is to show that conception can carry that moral weight, and thus to distinguish abortion from contraception.

If all fetuses have moral standing, what are the natural properties that earn them this standing? In what morally relevant respects do they resemble the paradigm of a normal human adult? One answer we can dismiss straight off is that they possess souls. In much Catholic moral theology the moral status of a fetus is assumed to depend upon the point during gestation at which it gains a soul. Possession of a soul is not a natural property whose presence or absence is verifiable by any empirical test. But then no claim about fetal ensoulment can serve as an impersonal reason in favor of a view of abortion. The Catholic Church itself has no official position on when ensoulment occurs, and the issue is warmly debated by theologians.[8] Different views on this matter can intelligibly lead to different views of the morality of abortion, but they will in all cases be *personal* views. They will

8. See, for instance, Donceel (1970).

have no claim upon the assent of the unbeliever, and certainly no claim to be enshrined in public policy.[9]

Conservative rhetoric might lead one to think that the crucial property possessed by all fetuses is that they are alive. Conservatives often invoke the "sanctity of life" against abortion and advance their cause through "prolife" organizations. Since conservatives do not scruple at destroying some forms of life (cells, organs, etc.), perhaps what is decisive is that a fetus is an organism, a living individual distinct from all others. If this obvious fact is combined with some appropriate reverence-for-life ethic, the moral standing of the fetus (and of all other organisms) might easily follow. But this interpretation cannot be correct, and the label "prolife" cannot be meant seriously. A natural-law morality does not treat the killing of all organisms, whatever their species, as morally serious. Neither do most conservatives who are not exercised by the extermination of cockroaches or mosquitoes and who do not typically object even to the practice of slaughtering animals for food or clothing. What the conservative wishes to protect is not the sanctity of life in general but the sanctity of human life.

On this narrower view the morally relevant property that a (human) fetus shares with a normal (human) adult is simply that they are both human beings. A human being in the purely biological sense is an organism belonging to the species homo sapiens.[10] The abortion debate concerns fetuses who are human,

---

9. Most conservatives have recognized this limitation on theological arguments. Thus Häring (1973): "It cannot be the task of a pluralistic state to protect the religious teaching of a church where this does not coincide with the generally acknowledged common good of that society . If we argue on the basis of natural law, this can be effective only to the extent that we give, in addition to the official teaching of ecclesiastical authority, reasons and motives that could be convincing to sincere and intelligent people who are not under the authority of the Church." (p. 117)

10. There is room for caviling over even the biological definition of humanity. Having caviled in Sumner (1974) I feel entitled not to do so

not bovine or canine. Human fetuses, at whatever stage of development, are plainly members of our species. If moral standing is distributed on the basis of humanity, then fetuses plainly have such standing. Equally plainly, they have such standing from the beginning. Species membership is not a characteristic acquired during development; a human fetus has been human for as long as it has existed (it has never belonged to any other species, nor to none at all). If conception is the beginning of fetal existence, (human) fetuses have moral standing from conception.[11]

This assumption that being human is the natural property that serves as the criterion of moral standing has permeated the entire abortion debate. Its intuitive force derives from the obvious fact that we do select the model member of our own species as the exemplar of moral standing, and that force can be measured by the common, almost reflex, identification of moral rights and human rights. The assumption has led both liberals and conservatives to engage in a rather odd debate over whether, or when, a fetus becomes human.[12] As long as "human" is held to its purely biological sense, this seems an empirical question that admits of a ready answer—an answer that could be agreed to without risk by both sides. But if the question is up for consideration against the shared background assumption that being human is the criterion of moral standing, an answer to it is no longer morally innocuous. In this context "human" itself begins to take on a normative meaning, so that conceding that a fetus is human is conceding that it has rights. This dual aspect of the term has immeasurably aided the conservative cause, for liberals

---

here. As I argued in that paper, the issues are the same whatever one's preferred categories.

11. For simplicity I will assume that the life history of an individual begins at conception. There are reasons for doubting this, having to do with the possibility of both fission and fusion between conception and implantation, but I do not wish to make anything of them.

12. See, for instance, Noonan (1968, 1970).

foolish enough to grant the background assumption have been forced to defend the implausible claim that a new individual member of our species only becomes human at or near its birth.[13] Wiser liberals have refused to play by these rules and have insisted on separating the factual question of whether fetuses are human from the moral question of whether they have rights.[14]

That separation is necessary if abortion arguments are not to equivocate or beg the question. Being human is not identical with having moral standing; rather, it is advanced by (some) conservatives as a criterion of moral standing. The implication of accepting it as a criterion is that full standing is distributed to all members of our own species and withheld from all other entities, including all members of all other species. It is possessed by all human beings regardless of their departure from the paradigm in other respects, and in particular regardless of how immature or abnormal they may be. It is not possessed by any nonhuman beings regardless of their resemblance to the paradigm in other respects, and in particular regardless of how mature, normal, developed, or intellligent they may be. On this view we need look to no characteristics of living beings save their species membership, and so the human/nonhuman boundary marks a sharp division between moral persons and mere things. Given the implications for protection of life both of including all members of our own species and of excluding all members of other species, drawing this moral circle around our own kind requires some rationale, lest it seem mere self-serving chauvinism.

Many conservatives who have employed humanity as a criterion of moral standing have supplied no such rationale. In their arguments this step functions as an unexamined axiom, so natu-

---

13. This defect of strategy afflicts the otherwise useful accounts by Brody (1974, 1975) and Engelhardt (1974).

14. See, for instance, Tooley (1973) and Newton (1975).

ral as to need no defense.[15] Their position is as shallow and naive
as that of liberals who simply assume without argument that
birth or viability is a moral watershed. There is a good deal of
attention in conservative writings to the question of when abortion is permissible if all fetuses have a right to life. Justifications
for the contention that they have this right *simply because they are
human* tend to be much more perfunctory. This scanty support
for a claim that is central for conservatives is all the more puzzling when it is noticed that species membership is an arbitrary
and superficial criterion of moral standing.

A biological species is a natural kind, as is a gender or race. No
one would entertain seriously the proposition that men have
moral standing *just because they are male* or that whites have such
standing *just because they are white*. Denying women and non-
whites the right to life simply on the ground of their sex or race
would (obviously) be sexist or racist. It is just as obvious that
denying all nonhuman creatures the right to life simply on the
ground of their species would be speciesist.[16] The defect in all
three cases is the same: there is no plausible deep connection between the natural property selected and possession of moral
rights; an individual's gender, race, or species does not *in itself*
have any implications for his/her moral status, and so fastening
upon any of these divisions as significant in itself is mere bigotry.
Attending exclusively to any of these properties means ignoring
all further characteristics of individuals; their sentience, intelligence, rationality, linguistic ability, moral agency, and so forth.
But these are the very properties that may have a deep connection with moral standing; we can imagine successfully constructing such a connection. Predicating possession of rights on

15. Häring (1973) is typical; the assumption that "our concern is not just
for biological life but for *human* life" (p. 111, emphasis in original) is
nowhere defended. See also Kelly (1958), McFadden (1967), Granfield
(1969).

16. See Singer (1975), chap. 1.

mere membership in some natural kind promises no such success.

If being human fails as a criterion, this does not imply that it is irrelevant to the distribution of moral standing. It is simply not intrinsically relevant, as a criterion must be. But it could still turn out as a matter of fact that all and only human beings have moral standing, because all and only human beings have some further property that is a plausible criterion of moral standing. If this does turn out to be the case, then species membership can function as an indicator of moral standing (we will be able to pick out the class of creatures with a right to life by attending to their species), though not as a criterion. It is inconceivable that gender or race will turn out even to be an indicator. It is not inconceivable that species membership will turn out to be an indicator, though it is unlikely. But in order to test out this possibility we still need a criterion.

Some conservatives have sought such a criterion in the level of intelligence or rationality, or the capacity for a rich life or for moral agency, typical of normal adult members of our species. Here two quite distinct questions arise. The basic one is how to connect any of these characteristics to the possession of moral rights. This issue will be explored in the next chapter, where a criterion of moral standing will be defended. At this stage it will simplify the discussion if we just assume that there is a reasonable case to be made for employing at least one of these properties as a criterion. For present purposes it will be convenient to fasten upon rationality as the relevant characteristic, since it has the greatest frequency of occurrence in conservative arguments, and to leave the notion of rationality pretty well unanalyzed. Thus we shall suppose that creatures have moral standing in virtue of being rational. The further question concerns the implications of this assumption for the case of the fetus.

This much is clear: if rationality is the criterion of moral standing, membership in homo sapiens is at best a highly imperfect indicator. There are two separate problems: creatures who are rational but not human, and creatures who are human but not rational. Depending on one's favored analysis of rationality, the former category might include other animal species (apes, dolphins, whales, etc.), machines (computers and robots), and (for all we know) intelligent extraterrestrials. It may of course be possible to define rationality so that of all the creatures known to us, natural and artificial alike, only human beings are rational. But then one would need to show that building this conception of rationality into a criterion of moral standing was not merely a device for indirectly limiting such standing to our own species. In any case it would still be impossible to rule out future encounters with other life forms who were rational in the relevant respect. Being human is not a necessary condition for being rational, and therefore is not a necessary condition for having moral standing.

The second problem is more troublesome for the conservative. However rationality is construed, it is a set of abilities: to use language, adapt means to ends, form realistic beliefs about the world, reflect on one's own mental states, or whatever. These abilities are dispositions; a creature has them if it displays them in the appropriate circumstances. They are gradually achieved by human beings in the normal course of development. A creature is rational while it possesses these abilities; it is not rational before the abilities are achieved or after they have been permanently lost. At any given time, not all members of the species have achieved rationality. Some (the severely retarded) will never achieve it. Others (fetuses and infants) have not yet achieved it. Still others (the irreversibly comatose or deranged) have both achieved and lost it. If being rational is the criterion for moral standing, then it seems to follow that many members of the species have no such standing—and among these members will be fetuses.

It is somewhat of an oddity that conservatives should employ the same sort of high standard for moral rights that we have already encountered in such liberals as Tooley. The liberal uses the standard to screen out fetuses (and infants). The conservative uses it to screen out other animal species, thus preserving a special status for human beings. But it threatens also to exclude many human beings, including fetuses. There is thus a tension between the conservative's resort to rationality as a criterion of moral standing and the ascription of such standing to fetuses. The same tension will afflict the choice of any other similarly exacting standard (richness of life, capacity for moral agency, etc.). As long as conservatives fasten on abilities that are typically achieved only at a relatively advanced stage of development, they will have difficulty extending moral standing backward to conception.

One technique for resolving this tension is pragmatic—the claim that we will better protect the lives of those members of our species who are rational if we accord the same protection to those who will never be rational, or are not yet rational, or are no longer rational.[17] On this view only persons who have achieved (and not lost) rationality merit moral standing in their own right, but all other members of the species should be treated as though they merited it also. This spillover argument is a last resort for the conservative, who clearly would like to show that fetuses deserve standing in virtue of their very nature. It will succeed only if it can be shown that protection of the nonrational is necessary for the security of the rational. So far as fetuses are concerned there is little evidence that the practice of abortion, even on a large scale, raises the general homicide rate or otherwise makes us more careless of the lives of normal adults than we are already. Consequentialist arguments are two-edged swords, and the evidence on this question does not favor the conservative's case. In Secton 26 pragmatic arguments for a

---

17. Thus Granfield (1969): "To give moral justification to abortion is to condemn all men to the level of expendable things. Morally, the fight against abortion is not primarily to protect the human dignity of the unborn, but is above all to safeguard that dignity in all mankind." (p. 144)

moral threshold will be examined in more detail; it will there be argued that there is no good reason for locating that threshold at conception.

What the conservative requires is some means of extending moral standing to fetuses in virtue of their very nature. Two such arguments are available, one that relies on the concept of a natural kind, and one that introduces the notorious notion of potentiality. The natural-kind argument is favored by Donagan (1977), who grounds his moral rules in the respect that is due rational creatures and treats rationality as a state a creature is in at a given stage of its life—that is, as an achievement. The question then is: why extend respect to creatures who have not yet reached that state?

> Let it . . . be provisionally conceded that, in the first instance, respect is recognized as owed to beings by virtue of a state they are in: say, that of rational agency. If there are beings who reach that state by a process of development natural to normal members of their species, given normal nurture, must not respect logically be accorded to them, whether they have yet reached that state or not? The principle underlying this reasoning is: if respect is owed to beings because they are in a certain state, it is owed to whatever, by its very nature, develops into that state.[18]

This principle is in turn a special case of a more general one:

> The duties of human beings to others are duties to them as human beings, that is, as rational creatures of a certain kind. The forms which may be taken by the fundamental moral duty of respect for a rational creature as such will vary with the degree to which that creature is actually in possession of the reason a mature creature of that kind would normally possess; but such variations in no way annul the duty.[19]

---

18. Donagan (1977), p. 171. For a similar, but rather less perspicuous, account see Melden (1977), pp. 220–223.

19. Ibid., p. 82.

The natural-kind argument converts deciding the moral status of an individual creature into a two-stage process. At the first stage we determine whether mature creatures of that kind normally are rational.[20] If they are, then the individual has moral standing regardless of whether he/she is rational. If they are not, then the individual lacks moral standing, again regardless of whether he/she is rational. Moral standing thus extends to the edges of a natural kind whose mature members are normally rational. The human species is such a kind; in virtue of the (achieved) rationality of normal adults, moral standing is also enjoyed by fetuses, infants, the profoundly retarded, the severely disordered, and the irreversibly comatose. All of these latter creatures ride the moral coattails of the paradigm rational being. Though a fetus has considerably less rationality than a mature dog, it has moral standing in virtue of being a creature "of a rational nature."[21] Thus, though being human is not a criterion of moral standing, and may also not be necessary for such standing, it is sufficient.

Let us assume that we understand both what a natural kind is and when rationality is normal for a mature member of such a kind.[22] The two-level structure of this view is reminiscent of rule-utilitarianism. Rule-utilitarians value the production of utility but do not determine the moral value of an individual act by

20. This two-stage process is similar to that entailed by the "species principle" in Devine (1978), pp. 53–54. Both the natural-kind argument and the species principle ascribe moral standing to some nonhuman beings. They differ, however, in one important respect. Devine considers a species rational (or intelligent) if any member of that species displays the requisite abilities, however freakish this phenomenon. Thus he must worry that the appearance of some superintelligent cat would require us to extend moral standing to all its backward feline kin. On Donagan's principle a species is rational only if it is normal for mature members of the species to be rational. This is the work done by the notion of a natural kind.

21. Kremer (1974), p. 103.

22. For one explication of the concept of a natural kind, see Brody (1975), chap. 6.

reference to its own utility; instead they look to the utility of the kind of act it is. Donagan values rationality but does not determine the moral standing of an individual creature by reference to its own rationality; instead he looks to the rationality of the kind of creature it is. In both cases the crucial test is applied only to kinds and not to individual members of those kinds. Donagan regards any other procedure as inconsistent: "To reject this principle would be arbitrary, if indeed it would be intelligible. What could be made of somebody who professed to rate the state of rational agency as of supreme value, but who regarded as expendable any rational creature whose powers were as yet undeveloped?"[23] One is tempted to retort: what could be made of somebody who professed to rate the state of rational agency as of supreme value, but who extended moral rights to creatures who will never at any time achieve that state (the profoundly retarded) or will never again achieve it (the irreversibly deranged or comatose)? Ex hypothesi moral standing belongs "in the first instance" to beings "in virtue of a state they are in." It is then awarded to beings who are not in that state because they stand in a certain relation (belonging to the same natural kind) to beings who are in that state. A philosopher who has managed this step shows a certain hubris in accusing his opponents of inconsistency.

The basic fault in the two-stage argument from natural kinds is an analogue of the traditional complaint against rule-utilitarianism.[24] If we appeal to utility in comparing kinds of acts, why should we not also appeal to utility in comparing individual acts? *Why should we not if utility is what we value?* Likewise, if we appeal to rationality in comparing kinds of creatures, why should we not also appeal to rationality in comparing individual creatures? *Why should we not, if rationality is what we value?* Rule-utilitarianism can lead us to choose the act of lesser utility,

23. Donagan (1977), p. 171.
24. See Smart (1956).

if it belongs to a kind that is generally of greater utility. The natural-kind argument can lead us to favor the creature of lesser rationality, if it belongs to a kind that is generally of greater rationality.[25] The inconsistency in both cases lies in admitting the relevance of a criterion (utility, rationality) at the level of a rough sort (kinds of acts, kinds of creatures) but then denying its relevance at the level of a fine sort (individual acts, individual creatures). That makes as much sense as valuing juiciness in fruit and then choosing this peach over this pear because normally mature peaches are juicier than mature pears. This peach is "a fruit of a juicy kind" though unluckily it is also rock-hard.

The natural-kind argument looks much like a devious attempt to reinstate humanity as a criterion of moral standing. Fetuses, although obviously not rational, resemble the paradigm right-bearer in being human. The appeal to natural kinds selects that resemblance as morally relevant while denying the relevance of all differences—including differences of rationality. Plainly there is another alternative available to those who wish to predicate moral standing on (achieved) rationality: they may award such standing to fetuses (or infants or children) when, but only when, they have achieved this rationality. That is the straight route to follow, but unfortunately it leads directly to the liberal view.

The potentiality argument closely resembles the argument from natural kinds but manages to avoid some of the latter's deficiencies. Devine (1978) gives it the following form:

> According to this principle, there is a property, self-consciousness or the use of speech for instance, such that (i) it is possessed by

25. In the case of Devine's supercat (note 20, above) the natural-kind argument would withhold standing from the freakish feline since, however rational it may be, rationality is not normal for its species. Neither the natural-kind argument nor Devine's species principle handles this case felicitously. It is also unclear what each would pick out as the natural kind or species of a superintelligent machine, should we learn how to construct one. Can rationality be normal for some specified model of computer?

adult humans, (ii) it endows any organism possessing it with a serious right to life, and (iii) it is such that any organism potentially possessing it has a serious right to life even now—where an organism possesses a property potentially if it will come to have that property under normal conditions for development.[26]

He provides it with the following rationale:

> The basis of the potentiality principle is quite simple: what makes the difference between human beings and other life is the capacity human beings enjoy for a specially rich kind of life. The life already enjoyed by a human being cannot be taken away from him, only the prospect of such life in the future. But this prospect is possessed as much by an infant or fetus as by a full-grown adult.[27]

The potentiality argument coincides with the natural-kind argument to the extent that they both award moral standing to healthy (nondefective) fetuses: those who "under normal conditions for development" will come to display the crucial ability that we will assume still to be rationality. They part company on the status of persons suffering from severe congenital retardation (who will not under normal conditions achieve rationality) and the irreversibly comatose (who have irretrievably lost their rational capacities). The argument from potentiality thus stops short of extending moral standing to the boundaries of the species; being human is no longer sufficient for having a right to life.

This line of thought certainly appears more promising for the conservative than the natural-kind argument, and reliance on fetal potential is a common theme in conservative treatments of abortion.[28] The principal defect in the earlier argument is that

26. Devine (1978), p. 94. One could interpret the passage quoted above from Donagan (1977), p. 171, as a statement of the potentiality argument instead of the natural-kind argument. Perhaps that is how Donagan there intends it. But his treatment of the case of the insane (p. 82) commits him to the natural-kind argument.

27. Devine (1978), p. 95.

28. See, for instance, Wade (1975).

nonrational human beings are awarded moral standing simply in virtue of a resemblance (conspecificity) that holds between them and rational beings, and it is difficult to see why that resemblance should be thought more significant than either the resemblances between human beings and many nonhuman beings or the differences among human beings. On the potentiality argument one can point to a property of an individual fetus that seems relevant to its moral status: the fact that this very fetus, if allowed to develop in the normal manner, will someday be rational. It is not astonishing that someone who values rationality should care for creatures who will be rational in the future as well as those who are rational at present. Protecting the lives of the potentially and the actually rational are merely two different means of promoting rationality.

There is a straightforward consequentialist defense available for the argument from potentiality. Suppose that one regards the existence of rationality as an intrinsic good, so that the more of it there is the better, and the best state of affairs is that in which there is as much as possible. One will then be inclined both to protect rationality where it already exists and to foster its development where it does not yet exist, since both tactics promise to prevent needless rationality losses. On such a view the existence of a potentially rational creature will clearly not be a matter of indifference, for ensuring the development of that creature will be one way of increasing the pool of rationality. On the other hand neither the severely retarded nor the irreversibly comatose have any rationality in their future; from the point of view of a "utilitarianism of rationality" they are therefore not worth an investment of effort.[29]

A principle enjoining us to maximize rationality will support

---

29. As is recognized by Devine (1978): "But this prospect [of future rational life] is not possessed by the irreversibly comatose, and thus they are morally speaking dead from the standpoint of the potentiality principle." (p. 95)

something like the argument from potentiality; moreover, it is just such a principle that is suggested by Devine's rationale (quoted above). However, adopting this principle would be exceedingly dangerous for a conservative, indeed for any natural-law theorist. A utilitarianism of rationality threatens to permit the sacrifice of either actually or potentially rational beings when such a course of action will maximize rationality. Thus it might permit killing one rational being to save the lives of ten, or ten to save the lives of a hundred, where doing so results in the largest obtainable net sum of rationality. If it is the quantity of rationality that matters (assuming this is a meaningful notion), then in principle the life of any individual rational being is dispensable. But this maximizing approach is inconsistent with the natural-law ordering of negative and positive duties (the Pauline principle), the absoluteness of the duty not to kill, and the conservative view of abortion.[30] Historically, natural-law theorists in general and abortion conservatives in particular have been vehement in their denunciation of any form of utilitarianism. Though they may value rationality, the structure of their moral theory is not adequately expressed by a maximizing principle.

But then what support remains for the potentiality argument? We must remember that there is an obvious alternative account available to one who wishes to connect rationality and the right to life: a graded account on which those who are actually rational (have achieved rationality) have a full right to life, those who are merely potentially rational (have not begun to achieve rationality) have no right to life, and those who are in process of becoming rational (have begun to achieve rationality) have a partial right to life. This account seems to cohere much more easily with a moral theory that trades in rights and duties. Rights are normally owned by (and duties owed to) creatures in

30. See the treatment of homicide in Donagan (1977), chap. 3. Donagan clearly regards rationality as an end to be promoted, both in one's own case and in that of others, but not at the cost of violating perfect duties.

virtue of the properties or abilities those creatures actually possess, not in virtue of those they will come to possess in the future. Thus the right to vote is owned by those who have actually
achieved a stipulated age, and not by those who will reach that
age in the normal course of development. Lest it be thought that
this feature is peculiar to conventional rights, it holds as well for
natural liberty-rights. Such rights are owned by those capable of
autonomous action (competent adult human beings), and not
by those who will someday possess this capacity. Rights are
dated—individuals possess a particular right when they satisfy
the relevant criterion. When they no longer satisfy the criterion
they no longer possess the right; this much the potentiality argument concedes. When individuals do not yet satisfy the criterion, they do not yet possess the right; they will achieve both
rationality and the rights appropriate to rational beings in the
same developmental process. There will then be a time to talk of
rights. Thus fetuses who are not yet rational do not yet have a
right to life, *if the criterion of moral standing is rationality.* Again
setting a high standard leads inevitably to the liberal view of the
fetus.

A graded account is certainly not simple in its structure and is
not easy to work out in practice. How, for instance, should we
correlate the various levels of human ontogenesis (and the rights
appropriate to each) with the various levels of animal phylogenesis (and the rights appropriate to each)? Should a human infant
count for more or less than a mature chimpanzee? It should not
be assumed, however, that no such account can be satisfactorily
worked out. The next chapter will confront the task of assembling a graded view, though not one that employs rationality as
a criterion for the right to life.

The potentiality argument is also likely to prove much more
than the conservative wishes. It assigns moral standing to that
which in the normal course of development will come to display
rationality. Devine is careful to deny that normality is statistical;

thus it is normal for zygotes to develop into fetuses and infants even if most are spontaneously aborted.[31] In that sense it is also normal for ova to be fertilized (though it is unlikely than any given ovum will be fertilized) and for spermatozoa to fertilize (though it is overwhelmingly unlikely that any particular spermatozoon will do so). Since both are gametes (sex cells) fertilization is what they are *for*. But then if protection of life is to be extended back to fetuses, embryos, or zygotes in virtue of their potential, it must by parity of reasoning be extended back also to ova and spermatozoa in virtue of theirs. Of course a zygote, say, is a genetically complete member of the species (a human being), whereas gametes are not. But that entails only that killing gametes is not homicide, not that it is not wrong (and just as wrong as homicide). Some forms of abortion (the IUD, the "morning-after" pill) work by interfering with implantation (the natural sequel to fertilization). Most forms of contraception work by interfering with fertilization (the natural sequel to intercourse). This latter fact, indeed, is the basis of the natural-law prohibition of the use of "artificial" contraceptive methods.[32] Such techniques run afoul of the potentiality argument as surely as do methods of abortion. But, if so, then as far as the potentiality argument is concerned, abortion and contraception are both wrong, both equally wrong, and both wrong for precisely the same reason.[33]

It follows that conception cannot serve as a threshold of moral standing; such standing (and the duties it entails) must be extended back beyond conception to the processes and materials

31. "Pregnancy for instance is a normal result of coitus, even though it results from coitus with relative infrequency. Hence also statistics on infant mortality and fetal loss are of little relevance to the question of what the normal development of a human infant or fetus is." (Devine 1978, p. 99)

32. See, for instance, Paul VI (1968) and Noonan (1965).

33. This suggests that the Catholic Church behaves consistently only when it agitates for the legal enforcement of its views on both contraception and abortion.

that normally result in conception. From the point of view of potentiality, conception is an event of no more significance than viability or birth; it is simply another step in the actualization of the potential for creating a rational being that is contained in male and female gametes. From the point of view of potentiality, the fact that conception for the first time assembles the complete genetic material for a new individual is also of no significance; it is entirely arbitrary to protect a creature who is potentially rational and to not protect the potential for a rational creature. Thus, if conservatives embrace the potentiality argument, and especially if they value rationality as an end-state that it is intrinsically good to bring about, they will be unable to maintain a moral distinction between abortion and contraception.

Liberals have difficulty in establishing birth as a moral threshold, and thus in distinguishing abortion from infanticide. Preserving the significance of birth requires resort to a shallow criterion of moral standing (spatial location, physical connection to another, etc.). A deeper criterion, if it denies moral standing to fetuses, will deny it also to infants; the liberal's defense of abortion thus also exonerates infanticide. Conservatives have difficulty in establishing conception as a moral threshold, and thus in distinguishing abortion from contraception. Preserving the significance of conception requires resort to a shallow criterion of moral standing (membership in the human species). A deeper criterion, if it awards moral standing to fetuses, will award it also to gametes; the conservative's attack on abortion thus also condemns contraception. Neither view can prevent seepage of its treatment of abortion across the boundaries separating abortion from contraception and infanticide. Yet one of the intuitions shared by almost everyone who reflects on these matters is that abortion is morally more serious than contraception, and infanticide more serious than abortion. Neither of the established views can make sense of these judgments.

The implausibility of the liberal and conservative views of the fetus stems from a common source: their mutual insistence that all fetuses, regardless of the differences among them, have precisely the same moral status. Gestation is a sequence of events that begins with a single-celled zygote and ends with a full-term fetus. The process that links these termini is one of enormous quantitative and qualitative change; the dissimilarities between the initial product and the end product are much more obvious and striking than the similarities. Both of the established views require us to overlook these changes entirely in assigning moral status to fetuses. Neither assigns any weight at all to the primary feature of gestation—the *development* of the fetus. Neither allows us to treat a zygote as a different sort of thing from a full-term fetus: the former more akin to the gametes whose union produced it, the latter more akin to a newborn infant. If the common-sense judgment of the contraception/abortion/infanticide triad as one of increasing moral seriousness is to be honored, uniform views of the status of the fetus must be abandoned.

13. *Self-Defense*

If the conservative view of the fetus cannot be established, the conservative view of abortion is groundless. Since we wish to analyze the conservative view further we must assume, contrary to fact, that it is possible to justify attributing a full right to life to all fetuses, from conception onward. The focus of attention then shifts away from the nature of the fetus to the relation between fetus and mother. If we assume that all fetuses have moral standing, when (if ever) is abortion justified? In the previous chapter we explored Thomson's treatment of this question and set out her argument for a case-by-case analysis of the morality of abortion and for a moderate abortion policy. Since conservatives advocate a restrictive policy, the question is whether or not it is possible for them to avoid Thomson's conclusions.

We have been assuming that the conservative accepts the natural-law rule that it is always wrong directly to kill an innocent being who possesses a right to life. If all fetuses have a right to life, and if abortion always involves killing the fetus, then abortion can be justified only when *either* (1) the fetus is not innocent, *or* (2) the killing is not direct. Each of these possibilities might define a class of permissible abortions. The former invokes the right of self-defense, whereas the latter rests on the principle of double effect. Virtually all conservatives agree that there are some circumstances in which abortion is morally permissible. They differ both over precisely what these circumstances are and over whether appeal should be made to the double effect.[34] Since there is no reason at the outset for thinking that these two kinds of appeal will generate the same classes of permissible abortions, they will be examined separately. This section will explore the implications for abortion of the right of self-defense.

The natural-law tradition has long recognized an individual's right to use force or violence in order to repel an attack against his/her life, even when doing so will result in the death of the attacker.[35] In the paradigm case of justified self-defense, all of the following conditions are satisfied:

The Attacker
(1) The attacker is a responsible agent (a competent adult human being).

34. All conservatives limit the justification of abortion to cases in which the mother's life is at stake. They differ over whether it is justified in all such cases. The narrowest view is that of the Catholic Church, which employs the principle of double effect; see Kelly (1958), Kenny (1962), and McFadden (1967) for standard accounts and Noonan (1970) for a useful history. Generally speaking, conservatives who argue from the right of self-defense hold a somewhat broader view in which abortion is permissible whenever it is the indispensable means of saving the mother's life; see Donagan (1977), pp. 162–163, and Devine (1978), pp. 152–156. Grisez (1970b) defends a broader view on the basis of a reinterpretation of the double effect.

35. In Aquinas the right of self-defense is supported by an appeal to the double effect; see Grisez (1970b). For a contemporary treatment that eschews this derivation, see Donagan (1977), pp. 84–88.

The Defender

(2) The defender is a paradigm bearer of a right to life (a competent adult human being).

The Attack

(3) The attacker is about to commit, or is in process of committing, some act.

(4) If that act is committed, it will certainly result in the death of the defender.

(5) In committing the act, the attacker intends to kill the defender.

(6) The attack is gratuitous; it has not been provoked, invited, or consented to by the defender.

(7) The attack is unjust; it is not warranted by any circumstances involving the attacker and defender.

The Defense

(8) Only the defender can successfully repel the attack.

(9) The defender cannot repel the attack without causing the death of the attacker; thus, if the attack is repelled, the defender will live and the attacker will die.

(10) If the attack is not repelled, the defender will die and the attacker will live.

Departures from the paradigm will weaken or violate one or more of these conditions. As we move away from the paradigm it will become less clear that killing in self-defense is justified, although on any reasonable view it will be permissible in some nonparadigm cases. A casuistry of homicide in self-defense will need to proceed on a case-by-case basis.

Abortion is never a paradigm case of justified self-defense. The closest approximation to the paradigm is found in those cases in which the continuation of pregnancy will kill the mother. Even these cases depart from the paradigm because a fetus is not a responsible agent, indeed not an agent at all. The fetus is therefore incapable of committing an act that threatens the mother's life and, a fortiori, incapable of doing so intentionally or unjustly. It is the life-support relation between mother and fetus that places the former's life in jeopardy. It is therefore inappropriate to think of the fetus as an attacker, though its presence in the woman's body is a threat to her life. Abortions to save the mother's life will also tend to be nonparadigm in other respects: the woman may have consented to the pregnancy that now threatens her life, the defense against that threat will probably be carried out by a third party (the physician), and the fetus will seldom survive the death of the mother since it is dependent on her for life support. For the moment we will hold these additional complications to one side and focus on the importance of the fact that a fetus is incapable of launching an unjust attack.

The issue here is whether or not the fetus is innocent, and therefore protected by the natural-law rule governing homicide. The innocence condition in that rule can be construed in two different ways. The first way contrasts innocence with guilt and thus fastens upon such elements of *mens rea* as voluntariness, intention, negligence, and recklessness. On this construal an agent is guilty when he/she is culpable for some act or omission. Moral guilt thus requires a capacity for moral agency; a being incapable of acting as a moral agent must be morally innocent. Nonhuman animals are innocent in this way, as are infants and fetuses. Thus if the homicide rule protects the morally innocent, it is always wrong to kill the fetus, even if the continuation of pregnancy threatens one's life.[36]

The other construal treats innocence as a purely technical matter: a being is innocent if it is not now threatening the life (or some other basic good) of another being.[37] Being technically

36. Leaving aside exceptions justified by appeal to the double effect, this is the view of Pius XI (1939), pp. 94-96; Paul VI (1968), p. 5; Kelly (1958); Kenny (1962); McFadden (1967).

37. I have borrowed the notion of technical innocence from Thomson (1974b), p. 122. Devine (1978) makes much the same distinction between moral (and juridical) innocence and causal innocence (p. 152). See also Nozick (1974), pp. 34-35. Donagan (1977) employs a moral conception of innocence: the innocent are "those who are neither attacking other human beings nor have been condemned to death for a crime" (p. 87). This device enables him to claim that neither killing an attacker in self-defense nor

innocent thus contrasts not with being guilty but with being a threat. Beings incapable of moral agency may still be threats; this is often true of nonhuman animals, rarely true of infants, and sometimes (as in the cases under consideration) true of fetuses. Thus, if the homicide rule protects the technically innocent, it is not always wrong to kill the fetus; it may be permissible to kill it when the continuation of pregnancy threatens one's life.

The natural-law recognition of the right to kill in self-defense suggests that innocence in the homicide rule must be taken in the technical rather than the moral sense. Certainly the fact that a being is morally guilty is not sufficient to justify taking its life (otherwise who would be safe?). Capital punishment is sometimes defended by natural-law theorists on the ground that at least one variety of moral guilt (culpable homicide) deprives the guilty party of the normal protection of the person; to commit murder is to forfeit one's right to life.[38] But it is difficult to reconcile this approach with a theory of *natural* rights and duties. If rights are grounded in our rational nature, how can they be lost or forfeited except by our ceasing to share in that nature? But that would suggest that we ought to execute only murderers who are incurably insane. And if the murderer's right to life has been forfeited, why is it only the state that has the right to kill him? Is he not then defenseless against everyone? But then won't private vengeance or vigilante justice also be permissible?

---

capital punishment is killing of the innocent (which is absolutely impermissible). Later, however, he takes the line that although the fetus who threatens the mother's life is clearly innocent, nonetheless abortion to save the mother's life is justified: "what matters is not the innocence of the assailant but what is due to the victim" (p. 163). It is difficult to reconcile this passage with the absolute prohibition against killing the innocent.

38. Donagan (1977), p. 163. It is not clear whether Donagan requires that the death penalty be necessary as a protection for the members of a society (as a deterrent, or to prevent recidivism among murderers), in which case capital punishment becomes a special case of killing in self-defense. Grisez (1970b) objects, quite rightly, to this line of argument (pp. 66–73).

Forfeiture of rights by the assailant, it should be noted, is not required to explain the defender's right to use violence in resisting the attack. The attacker does not have (never had) the right to cross the boundary protecting the defender's private sphere.

But the fact that a being is morally guilty is also not necessary to justify taking its life. If my life is being threatened by a gun-wielding agent incapable of *mens rea* (a madman or a child or a sleepwalker or an automaton), my right of self-defense permits me to kill the attacker if that is the only means of protecting myself.[39] Nor is it necessary that the threat to life take the form of an act, or that it be posed by a creature capable of agency.[40] In Thomson's example where you are trapped in a tiny house with a rapidly growing child, you need not passively wait to be crushed to death. The right to defend one's life encompasses the right to repel threats to life that involve no malice, no intention, no awareness, and even no act on the part of their source. On the other hand it must be true that the source is actually posing a threat. The homicide rule must therefore be read as protecting the lives of all those (with a right to life) who are not themselves threatening others. This interpretation will allow (in appropriate circumstances) for killing in self-defense, and thus it will allow, in principle at least, for abortion in self-defense.[41]

39. As is recognized by Donagan (1977), pp. 162–163, and Devine (1978), p. 152.

40. The criticisms of Thomson's argument by Brody (1972, 1975) are vitiated by his contention that the threat to life must be posed by some action on the part of another, rather than by the mere continued existence of that other. It is not the continued existence of the fetus that threatens the mother; in principle the fetus could continue to exist (somewhere else) without posing the slightest danger to her (which is why Brody's medicine case is not pertinent). It is the physical connection between the fetus and her body that threatens her life; that connection will *cause her death*. Although the threat does not take the form of an action by the fetus, she is clearly justified in repelling it.

41. It will not allow for capital punishment, except perhaps for killers so dangerous that no other means will prevent them from further murders.

A clear case of an abortion justified by the right of self-defense would be one in which continuation of pregnancy will certainly kill the mother, the fetus will in that case die anyway, and the pregnancy is due to rape. The fact that the abortion will be carried out by a third party does not alter the case; if a woman has the right to defend herself against the fetus, then she has the right to invoke third-party assistance.[42] We move one step away from the clear case by supposing that the fetus will survive the death of the mother. This situation is sometimes presented as though, from an onlooker's point of view, it is an equal choice between two lives in conflict. Some even claim that, just as the fetus is a threat to the woman's life, so the woman is a threat to the fetus' life.[43] There are such situations, as when two people are trapped in a room with only enough food (owned by neither) for one to survive; here it is not clear that either has the right pre-emptively to kill the other. But this cannot be the right model for the mother/fetus relation. Pregnancy is not a problem of distributive justice in which it is uncertain who ought to be awarded the scarce resources. Here all of the resources for both parties are being provided by the woman. (Imagine that you have just enough food for your survival and I invade your house, demanding that you give it to me). The conflict between mother and fetus is being played out entirely on territory (her body) to which she has a prior claim. The fetus is the invader of that territory; she is its defender.

The right of self-defense includes the right to employ as much violence (and no more) as can reasonably be predicted to succeed in repelling the threat. In pregnancy the threat is the life-support connection between the fetus and the mother. It is

---

42. The positive duties in a natural-law morality can entail a duty to render assistance to others whose lives are being threatened. This is explicitly recognized by Donagan (1977), pp. 86-87. A physician might, therefore, have a duty to perform an abortion to save a woman's life.

43. Devine (1978), p. 153.

therefore permissible to employ some means to terminate that connection. Most abortion techniques in current use kill the fetus in utero. If the fetus were capable of extrauterine survival, the right of self-defense might require use of some nonlethal technique that terminates pregnancy while preserving the life of the fetus. However, almost all abortions are carried out on pre-viable fetuses who cannot be saved by current technology once the placental connection is severed. All available means of de-fending the mother's life before viability require killing the fetus. In these circumstances, any abortion technique appears to be permissible.[44] On the other hand, if the fetus is viable and a hysterotomy is performed, there will be a clear duty to save the life of the fetus if possible. The right to kill where necessary is not the right to kill where unnecessary.

As we move further away from the clear case, it is easy to see the direction that the analysis will take. The factors relevant to assessing a particular case of abortion will be precisely those that were isolated in our earlier discussion of Thomson. Other things equal, the right to abort in self-defense will be weakened as the woman becomes more responsible for her pregnancy, the threat to life becomes more remote, the value threatened alters from life to some lesser good (health, liberty, well-being), the benefits to the fetus of continued life increase, and the woman comes voluntarily to accept responsibility for completing the preg-nancy.[45] However, none of these conditions will invariably over-ride the right of self-defense. In contexts other than abortion

---

44. As is argued by Nicholson (1978), pp. 57 –58.

45. Leaving aside questions of when pregnancy is voluntary, it should be noted that having consented to a pregnancy that now threatens life is not the same as having consented to that threat to life. Perhaps in voluntarily becoming pregnant a woman consents to the normal risks of pregnancy, but certainly not to abnormal ones. On a natural-law morality agents may have the duty not to be reckless with their lives. Devine (1978) discusses self-defense against nonlethal threats (pp. 153-154), but his fixation on threats to life is given no justification.

that right extends to at least some situations in which the defender has placed herself at risk, in which the threat to her life is
merely probable, or in which it is not life but liberty or bodily
integrity that is at stake. Obviously the further we move from
the paradigm case of justified self-defense the harder it will become to exonerate killing in self-defense, even if no other means
is available. But the right of self-defense will cover a good many
cases beyond the strict confines of the paradigm, and also beyond
the clear case of abortion where pregnancy due to rape threatens
the mother's life.

Tracing out the implications of the woman's right of self-defense against an invasion of her body would require a case-by-
case analysis of the morality of abortion and a moderate abortion
policy. Examination of the right of self-defense has thus led us to
the same conclusion that Thomson extracted from the fetus'
right to life. This is hardly surprising, since the rights of different parties in conflict are mutually limiting. The fetus' right to
life is bounded by the mother's right of self-defense and vice
versa.[46] To map the former is therefore also to map the latter.
We now have support for Thomson's argument, which was left
largely unexamined in the previous chapter. The rights that bear
upon the mother/fetus relation yield a moderate view of the morality of abortion and a moderate abortion policy. Thus, even if
all fetuses have a right to life, abortion will be justified in many
circumstances. At most, conservatives can allow that it is justified whenever the mother's life is at stake. But then the conservative view of abortion cannot be derived from the conservative
view of the fetus. Or rather—it cannot be so derived if conservatives rely on a moral rule prohibiting homicide where the victim
is innocent. It remains yet to be seen whether appeal to the double effect will better serve their cause.

46. The right of self-defense is a special case of the right to autonomy.
Thus the conflict of rights mirrors the conflict between the fetus' life and
the woman's autonomy.

14. *The Double Effect*

Since a being who is threatening the life (or some other basic good) of another is not (technically) innocent, invoking the right of self-defense is consistent with an absolute rule against killing the innocent. Appeal to the double effect, on the other hand, entails that killing an innocent being is sometimes permissible, as long as the killing is indirect. For the discussion to follow we will assume that innocence is to be construed in a moral sense, so that fetuses are innocent even when pregnancy places the mother's life at risk. The principle of double effect is intended to distinguish in such cases between direct and indirect homicide.

The principle had its origin in Aquinas' justification of killing in self-defense.[47] It has been refined by subsequent Catholic moralists into the following form:

> When an act will produce two effects, one good and one evil, the act is permissible when all of the following conditions are satisfied:
>
> (1) *Intrinsic quality of the act.* The act, considered in itself and independently of its effects, is not impermissible.
>
> (2) *Causality.* The evil effect is not the means of producing the good effect.
>
> (3) *Intention.* Only the good effect is intended; the evil effect is merely tolerated.
>
> (4) *Proportionality.* The good effect and the evil effect are more or less equally balanced in importance.[48]

When these conditions are satisfied, and when the evil effect is the death of a being with moral standing, we have a case of indirect killing. When one or more of the conditions is violated, the killing is direct. The intrinsic-quality condition presupposes

47. See Grisez (1970b), for an excellent account.
48. This formulation has been adapted from Kelly (1958). For similar renderings, see Bourke (1951), Kenny (1962), McFadden (1967), and Grisez (1970b).

that certain acts are absolutely impermissible simply in virtue of the kinds of acts they are. This is a standard feature of a natural-law theory, whose absolute rules forbid acts of these kinds. The causality and intention conditions are closely related and follow from the Pauline principle plus the postulate that an agent who intends an end must also intend the causally necessary means to that end. The proportionality condition, although somewhat vague, requires weighing the good and evil effects and is intended to screen out cases (satisfying the other conditions) in which bringing about a trivial good will entail also producing a substantial evil.

Not all natural-law theorists subscribe to the principle of double effect, but it is a tempting way of moderating what might otherwise be a harsh and inflexible morality. Although agents are strictly forbidden to *do evil,* the principle defines those conditions under which they may *bring about evil.* Where the mother's life is at stake, the good effect of an abortion is the preservation of that life, whereas the evil effect is the death of the fetus. In its orthodox employment in Catholic morality the principle is not used to justify all abortions to save the mother's life. Instead, the following division of cases is made:

A. *Direct Abortions*

CASE A1: Early in her pregnancy a woman is diagnosed as suffering from chronic hypertensive heart disease. If her pregnancy is continued to the stage at which the fetus is viable, she will very likely die from the overload on her cardiovascular system.

CASE A2: While a woman is in labor it is discovered that the fetus is hydrocephalic. The fetus' abnormally large cranium makes normal vaginal delivery impossible; both the woman and the fetus will die if it is attempted. She will also not survive a Caesarean section, nor will the fetus. The only way to save her life is to crush the skull of the fetus (craniotomy), thus rendering a vaginal (stillborn) delivery possible.

B. *Indirect Abortions*

CASE B1: Early in her pregnancy a woman is diagnosed as suffering from cancer of the cervix. If a hysterectomy is performed then her survival chances are good; otherwise she will very likely die.

CASE B2: Early in pregnancy the fetus is discovered to be developing in the fallopian tubes instead of the uterus. Unless the fetus is aborted or the tube excised (salpingectomy) the woman is in danger of dying from tubal rupture.[49]

All of these cases have two features in common: (a) if the appropriate operation is not performed, the woman will certainly or probably die; (b) the fetus will certainly die if the operation is performed and will certainly or probably die if it is not. Neither feature, therefore, distinguishes direct from indirect abortions. Further, the first pair of cases cannot be distinguished from the second by either the intrinsic-quality or the proportionality conditions. In each case what is envisaged is a surgical procedure that is not intrinsically evil, since there are circumstances in which the procedure is permissible. And life surely balances life, especially when we remember that the fetus' life cannot in all likelihood be saved in any case. In terms of consequences, operating cannot be worse than not operating; if the operation is successful, one life is saved, whereas if it is unsuccessful, both lives are lost.

Thus if $A1/A2$ are to be distinguished from $B1/B2$ it must be on the basis of the causality and intention conditions. The standard account is that in the former cases killing the fetus is the means of saving the mother's life, whereas in the latter cases it is not. Thus in the former cases the physician must intend to kill the fetus if she intends to save the mother, whereas in the latter cases she need not (and must not) so intend. The physician may foresee with certainty that, if she performs the hysterectomy or salpingectomy, the fetus will die, but the death of the fetus is not itself causally necessary in order to save the woman's life. It

49. I have slightly modified the four cases presented by Nicholson (1978), p. 21. Nicholson's critique of the principle of double effect is the best yet available. For a history of the controversy among Catholic moralists, see Noonan (1970).

is the surgical procedure that is causally necessary since if it is not performed, the woman will die. If there were some means available of saving the fetus' life (by transferring it to an artificial placenta), the survival of the fetus would in itself be no threat to the woman's life.

On the standard account, appeal to the double effect will therefore justify fewer abortions than even the strictest rendering of the right of self-defense. It is doubtful, however, that the principle of double effect enables us to draw any moral distinction between A1/A2 and B1/B2, since the former cases also appear to satisfy the causality and intention conditions.[50] In the former cases (as in the latter) the medical procedure involved produces two effects: the death of the fetus, and preservation of the mother's life. The physician may foresee with certainty that if she performs the procedure the fetus will die, but the death of the fetus is not itself causally necessary in order to save the woman's life. The termination of pregnancy, and thus the surgical procedure, are causally necessary, since otherwise the woman will die. But if there were some means available of saving the fetus' life, the survival of the fetus would in itself be no threat to the woman's life. It is disconnecting the fetus that is causally indispensable, not killing it.

The principle of double effect thus threatens to justify any abortion to save the mother's life. The elasticity of act-descriptions will always permit us to describe the medical procedure in question in such a way that (a) it is not impermissible in itself, (b) it will both kill the fetus and save the woman's life, and (c) the death of the fetus will not itself be a means of ensuring the woman's survival. This result is guaranteed by the fact that it is only the termination of pregnancy, and not the securing of the death of the fetus, that is essential to abortion. This unwelcome inflation of the class of indirect abortions might be resisted by either of two countermeasures. One is to claim that in the in-

50. As is also argued by Nicholson (1978), pp. 23ff.

direct cases it is not the fetus that is the source of the threat to the woman's life.[51] Thus, in B1 the woman would be in danger even were she not pregnant, whereas in both A1 and A2 it is the pregnancy itself (the physical connection between mother and fetus) that is the threat. The problem with this line of thought is that in B2 also it is the pregnancy (the presence of the fetus in the tube) that is the threat; if the woman were not pregnant, or if the fetus were located normally, she would be in no danger. The distinction between A1/A2 and B1/B2 thus cannot depend on whether the fetus threatens to be the cause of the woman's death.

A more promising approach is to argue that the causal connection between the medical procedures used in A1/A2 and the death of the fetus is too intimate for these cases to count as indirect killings.[52] Although the notion of an intimate causal connection is far from transparent, it might be urged that it is physically impossible for a fetus to survive craniotomy or such standard abortion techniques as vacuum aspiration, dilatation and curettage, and saline induction. No conceivable medical technology could preserve the life of a fetus subjected to these destructive procedures. It is not, however, physically impossible for the fetus to survive hysterectomy or salpingectomy, for in both these cases it is at least removed intact from the mother. If we were to develop a technology of fetal transfer, such fetuses could conceivably be saved. Indirect abortion might then be distinguished as those in which fetal survival is compatible with known laws of nature.

This line of thought focusses attention on abortion techniques, ruling out those that destroy the fetus in the uterus. It will still fail, however, to draw the direct/indirect line where the

---

51. See, for example, McFadden (1967), p. 194, for the claim that in B2 it is not "the fetus as such" that constitutes the danger to the mother.

52. See, for example, Foot (1967). This gambit is criticized in Bennett (1966) and in Nicholson (1978).

conservative wants it. Some abortion techniques (the IUD and hysterotomy) deliver an intact fetus; the use of such techniques will therefore be exonerated on this account, at least where necessary to save the mother's life. Thus A1 could qualify as an indirect abortion. Further, the same distinction does not seem to be applied to cases other than abortion. If I am attacked, the principle of double effect allows me to defend myself by means whose use it is physically impossible for the assailant to survive, as long as my aim is to repel the attack and not to kill. If the only means available of repelling the attack is to blow the assailant to pieces, and if doing so is therefore justified, it is not clear why one may not also cut a fetus to pieces. We do not now possess a technology that enables us to save previable fetuses; thus it is in present circumstances impossible to save the fetus' life whatever abortion technique we use. If we develop a method of abortion compatible with fetal survival, then doubtless the principle of double effect will obligate us to use it wherever possible. But while such a technology is unavailable, we have no morally relevant distinction between direct and indirect life-saving abortions.

If the principle of double effect will justify all abortions to save the mother's life, it also will not stop there. Where another good such as health or bodily integrity or autonomy is at stake, nothing will prevent the double effect from permitting abortion save the proportionality condition. This result is explicit in Grisez (1970b) who, for excellent reasons, revises the principle of double effect so that it will justify all abortions to save the mother's life. Grisez is then faced with the prospect of likewise exonerating all abortions that are genuinely therapeutic: those in which the aim is to benefit the mother (by terminating the pregnancy), and not to kill the fetus. His defense against this unwelcome outcome is to point to the fact that in these further cases the fetus will generally survive if the abortion is not performed, and to contend that therefore the greater good (the fetus' life) is being sacrificed to the lesser (the woman's health, or liberty, or whatever). This is to invoke the proportionality condition.[53]

It is unclear just which goods the proportionality condition will count as offsetting the evil of fetal death. In principle one could take the strict line that only life balances life, but it seems more reasonable to grant that other injuries to the woman (disablement, permanent impairment of health, insanity) will justify abortion. Perhaps the balance need not be precisely equal, the aim being to exclude abortions for trivial reasons. The range of abortions that will be admitted by the principle of double effect will depend on just how strictly or loosely the proportionality condition is interpreted. However this goes in detail, the double effect promises to be more permissive concerning abortion than the conservative view allows. Obviously cases will need to be assessed on an individual basis, and the key factor will be the nature and probability of the harm threatened to the woman by the continuation of pregnancy. The natural end of appeal to the double effect is thus a case-by-case analysis of abortion and a moderate abortion policy.

Since the argument from self-defense also led us to a moderate view, it is tempting to conclude that invoking self-defense and the double effect come in the end to the same thing, perhaps even that they are disguised versions of one another. This hypothesis is strengthened by observing that the double effect is the traditional natural-law grounding of the right of self-defense. However, the temptation should be resisted. The appeal to self-defense stresses an asymmetry in the mother/fetus relation; since the fetus is the intruder and the parasite, it is the mother who is defending herself against a threat. On the principle of double ef-

---

53. Grisez needlessly imperils his own position by denying (pp. 78–79) that good and evil effects can be weighed against one another. However, he later (p. 95) argues that it is irrational to sacrifice life for such further goods as health.

fect the situation is symmetrical: the mother's life (or other good) is causally incompatible with the fetus' life, and vice versa. Since both parties are innocent, neither occupies a morally privileged position. Thus, if abortion can be justified so that the mother lives and the fetus dies, so can an alternative course of action on which the fetus lives and the mother dies. It is in virtue of this symmetry that in the end the deciding factor is the balance of benefits and burdens for both parties. Neither the fact that the drama is being played out within the body of one of the parties nor the question of whether this party is responsible for her condition plays any role. The outcome of the argument from the double effect, although it is more permissive than the conservative view, does not coincide with the outcome of Thomson's argument. Where they diverge, the appeal to self-defense offers the intuitively more satisfying result. The fact that on the double effect one would in A2 "be equally justified in cutting away the mother to rescue the baby"[54] casts the gravest doubt on its adequacy as a moral principle. It can be brought to yield less grotesque results only if it comes to treat the fetus as an invader. To do so it must recognize that the fetus is not (technically) innocent; but then it will simply reduce to the argument from self-defense.

Whether appeal is made to the right of self-defense or to the principle of double effect, a natural-law morality will justify abortions beyond the narrow confines of saving maternal life. The conservative view of abortion is thus doubly unfounded. Conservatives cannot make a convincing case for their position on the moral status of the fetus; but even if they could, that position would support neither their own view of the morality of abortion nor their favored abortion policy. By contrast, the lib-

54. Grisez (1970b), p. 94. Grisez thus treats the mother/fetus case as an analogue of the case in which Siamese twins cannot both survive, but separating them would kill one while saving the other. Here neither twin has prior ownership of the body parts they share and so neither has a privileged moral claim to survival.

eral view fails in only one of these crucial respects. Liberals cannot establish their position on the moral status of the fetus, but were they able to do so, their view of abortion and their defense of a permissive policy would both follow readily enough. Thus, however badly the liberal view has fared, conservatives are in an even less enviable position.

So far as the moral status of the fetus is concerned, we have a merely negative result: neither of the established views is persuasive on this question. But Thomson's argument has also furnished us with a positive (if hypothetical) result: for those cases in which the fetus has full moral standing, only a case-by-case approach to evaluating abortion, and only a moderate policy, will be acceptable. We thus have some support for a middle way with the abortion question.

CHAPTER FOUR

A Third Way

The established views have failed on both the intuitive and theoretical levels. Their conceptions of the moral status of the fetus, if they are not shallow and arbitrary, violate widely shared moral convictions concerning contraception and infanticide. The conservative's defense of a restrictive policy violates equally widely shared convictions concerning the individual's right of self-defense against threats to life, liberty, or personal integrity. Moreover, both views are underdetermined by their own moral theories. Liberals have been unable to ground their view of the fetus in a theory of rights, whereas conservatives have been served even less well by a natural-law morality that not only fails to support their view of the fetus but would lead from that view to a moderate abortion policy.

The demise of the established views deprives us of our familiar reference points in the abortion landscape. It is the simplicity of these views that has rendered them easy to grasp and thus easy to market in the public forum. Unfortunately, it is also that simplicity—especially their uniform views of the fetus—which has proved to be their fatal weakness. When confronted with a problem as complex as that of abortion, we have some initial reason to suspect simple solutions. Our critique of the established views has amply justified this suspicion. We need a view of abortion responsive to all of the elements whose conjunction renders the problem of abortion so perplexing and so divisive. Such a view cannot be a simple one.

If an alternative to the established views is to be developed, three tasks must be successfully completed. The first is to construct this third way and to show how it is essentially different from both of the positions it supersedes. The indispensable ingredient at this stage is a criterion of moral standing that will generate a view of the fetus and thus a view of abortion (including an abortion policy). The second task is to defend this view on the intuitive level by showing that it coheres better than either of its predecessors with our considered moral judgments both on abortion itself and on cognate issues. Then, finally, the view must be given a deep structure by grounding it in a moral theory. This chapter will undertake the first two tasks by outlining a position on the abortion problem and justifying it by appeal to moral intuitions. The more daunting theoretical challenge will be confronted in the two succeeding chapters.

15. *Specifications*

Although our critique has produced negative results, it will also point the way to a more constructive outcome. The established views have failed in certain specific respects. Collating their points of weakness will provide us with guidelines for building a more satisfactory alternative. It will be convenient to divide these guidelines into two categories corresponding to the two ingredients that complicate the problem of abortion: the nature of the fetus and the implications of the mother/fetus relationship.

The conservative view, and also the more naive versions of the liberal view, select a precise point (conception, birth, etc.) as the threshold of moral standing, implying that the transition from no standing to full standing occurs abruptly. In doing so they rest more weight on these sudden events than they are capable of bearing. A view that avoids this defect will allow full moral standing to be acquired gradually. It will therefore attempt to locate not a threshold point, but a threshold period or stage.

Both of the established views attribute a uniform moral status to all fetuses, regardless of their dissimilarities. Each, for example, counts a newly conceived zygote for precisely as much (or as little) as a full-term fetus, despite the enormous differences between them. A view that avoids this defect will assign moral status differentially, so that the threshold stage occurs sometime during pregnancy.

A consequence of the uniform approach adopted by both of the established views is that neither can attach any significance to the development of the fetus during gestation.[1] Yet this development is the most obvious feature of gestation. A view that avoids this defect will base the (differential) moral standing of the fetus at least in part on its level of development. It will thus assign undeveloped fetuses a moral status akin to that of ova and spermatozoa, whereas it will assign developed fetuses a moral status akin to that of infants.

So far, then, an adequate view of the fetus must be gradual, differential, and developmental. It must also be derived from a satisfactory criterion of moral standing. The conditions of adequacy for such a criterion were set out in Section 5: it must be general (applicable to beings other than fetuses), it must connect moral standing with the empirical properties of such beings, and it must be morally relevant. Its moral relevance is partly testable by appeal to intuition, for arbitrary or shallow criteria will be vulnerable to counterexamples. But the final test of moral relevance is grounding in a moral theory.

An adequate view of the fetus promises a morally significant division between early abortions (before the threshold stage) and late abortions (after the threshold stage). It also promises borderline cases (during the threshold stage). Wherever that stage is located, abortions that precede it will be private matters, since the fetus will at that stage lack moral standing. Thus the provisions of the liberal view will apply to early abortions: they

1. Both Tooley (1973) and Warren (1978) allow moral standing to be acquired gradually in the normal course of human development. But since both believe that such standing is only acquired after birth, neither attributes any importance to prenatal development—except as the groundwork of postnatal development.

will be morally innocent (as long as the usual conditions of maternal consent, etc., are satisfied) and ought to be legally unregulated (except for rules equally applicable to all other medical procedures). Early abortion will have the same moral status as contraception.

Abortions that follow the threshold stage will be interpersonal matters, since the fetus will at that stage possess moral standing. The provisions of Thomson's argument will apply to late abortions: they must be assessed on a case-by-case basis and they ought to be legally permitted only on appropriate grounds. Late abortions will have the same moral status as infanticide, except for the difference made by the physical connection between fetus and mother.

A third way with abortion is thus a moderate and differential view, combining elements of the liberal view for early abortions with elements of (a weakened version of) the conservative view for late abortions. The policy that a moderate view will support is a moderate policy, permissive in the early stages of pregnancy and more restrictive (though not as restrictive as conservatives think appropriate) in the later stages. So far as the personal question of the moral evaluation of particular abortions is concerned, there is no pressing need to resolve the borderline cases around the threshold stage. But a workable abortion policy cannot tolerate this vagueness and will need to establish a definite time limit beyond which the stipulated grounds will come into play. Although the precise location of the time limit will unavoidably be somewhat arbitrary, it will be defensible as long as it falls somewhere within the threshold stage. Abortion on request up to the time limit and only for cause thereafter: these are the elements of a satisfactory abortion policy.

A number of moderate views may be possible, each of them satisfying all of the foregoing constraints. A particular view will be defined by selecting (a) a criterion of moral standing, (b) the natural characteristics whose gradual acquisition during normal

fetal development carries with it the acquisition of moral standing, and (c) a threshold stage. Of these three steps, the first is
the crucial one, since it determines both of the others.

16. *A Criterion of Moral Standing*

We have thus far assumed that for a creature to have moral
standing is for it to have a right to life. Any such right imposes
duties on moral agents; these duties may be either negative (not
to deprive the creature of life) or positive (to support the creature's life). Possession of a right to life implies at least some im-
munity against attack by others, and possibly also some entitle-
ment to the aid of others. As the duties may vary in strength, so
may the corresponding rights. To have some moral standing is
to have some right to life, whether or not it may be overridden
by the rights of others. To have full moral standing is to have
the strongest right to life possessed by anyone, the right to life of
the paradigm person. Depending on one's moral theory, this
right may or may not be inviolable and indefeasible and thus
may or may not impose absolute duties on others.

Although this analysis of moral standing will later be broad-
ened, it will still suffice for our present purposes. To which creatures should we distribute (some degree of) moral standing? On
which criterion should we base this distribution? It may be easier to answer these questions if we begin with the clear case and
work outward to the unclear ones. If we can determine why we
ascribe full standing to the paradigm case, we may learn what to
look for in other creatures when deciding whether or not to include them in the moral sphere.

The paradigm bearer of moral standing is an adult human
being with normal capacities of intellect, emotion, perception,
sensation, decision, action, and the like. If we think of such a
person as a complex bundle of natural properties, then in principle we could employ as a criterion any of the properties common
to all normal and mature members of our species. Selecting a

particular property or set of properties will define a class of creatures with moral standing, namely, all (and only) those who share that property. The extension of that class will depend on how widely the property in question is distributed. Some putative criteria will be obviously frivolous and will immediately fail the tests of generality or moral relevance. But even after excluding the silly candidates, we are left with a number of serious ones. There are four that appear to be the most serious: we might attribute full moral standing to the paradigm person on the ground that he/she is (a) intrinsically valuable, (b) alive, (c) sentient, or (d) rational. An intuitive test of the adequacy of any of these candidates will involve first enumerating the class of beings to whom it will distribute moral standing and then determining whether that class either excludes creatures that upon careful reflection we believe ought to be included or includes creatures that we believe ought to be excluded. In the former case the criterion draws the boundary of the moral sphere too narrowly and fails as a necessary condition of moral standing. In the latter case the criterion draws the boundary too broadly and fails as a sufficient condition. (A given criterion may, of course, be defective in both respects.)

Beings may depart from the paradigm along several different dimensions, each of which presents us with unclear cases that a criterion must resolve. These cases may be divided into seven categories: (1) inanimate objects (natural and artificial); (2) nonhuman terrestrial species of living things (animals and plants); (3) nonhuman extraterrestrial species of living things (should there be any); (4) artificial "life forms" (androids, robots, computers); (5) grossly defective human beings (the severely and permanently retarded or deranged); (6) human beings at the end of life (especially the severely and permanently senile or comatose); (7) human beings at the beginning of life (fetuses, infants, children). Since the last context is the one in which we wish to apply a criterion, it will here be set aside. This will enable us to settle on a criterion without tailoring it specially for the problem of abortion. Once a criterion has established its credentials in other domains, we will be able to trace out its implications for the case of the fetus.

The first candidate for a criterion takes a direction rather different from that of the remaining three. It is a commonplace in moral philosophy to attribute to (normal adult) human beings a special worth or value or dignity in virtue of which they possess (among other rights) a full right to life. This position implies that (some degree of) moral standing extends just as far as (some degree of) this intrinsic value, a higher degree of the latter entailing a higher degree of the former.[2] We cannot know which things have moral standing without being told which things have intrinsic worth (and why)—without, that is, being offered a theory of intrinsic value. What is unique about this criterion, however, is that it is quite capable in principle of extending moral standing beyond the class of living beings, thus embracing such inanimate objects as rocks and lakes, entire landscapes (or indeed worlds), and artifacts. Of course, nonliving things cannot literally have a right to *life,* but it would be simple enough to generalize to a right to (continued) *existence,* where this might include both a right not to be destroyed and a right to such support as is necessary for that existence. A criterion that invokes intrinsic value is thus able to define a much more capacious moral sphere than is any of the other candidates.

Such a criterion is undeniably attractive in certain respects: how else are we to explain why it is wrong to destroy priceless icons or litter the moon even when doing so will never affect any living, sentient, or rational being?[3] But it is clear that it cannot serve our present purpose. A criterion must connect moral

2. Tom Regan appears to defend this position in his (unpublished) essay "Sumner on the Wrongness of Killing" (however, see note 9, below). Basing moral standing on intrinsic value also seems to be implied by the ideal utilitarianism of Moore and Rashdall.

3. On the other hand, why should we assume that all wrongs are moral wrongs?

standing with some property of things whose presence or absence can be confirmed by a settled, objective, and public method of investigtion. The property of being intrinsically valulable is not subject to such verification. A criterion based on intrinsic value cannot be applied without a theory of intrinsic value. Such a theory will supply a criterion of intrinsic value by specifying the natural properties of things in virtue of which they possess such value. But if things have moral standing in virtue of having intrinsic value, and if they have intrinsic value in virtue of having some natural property, then it is that natural property which is serving as the real criterion of moral standing, and the middle term of intrinsic value is eliminable without loss. A theory of intrinsic value may thus entail a criterion of moral standing, but intrinsic value cannot itself serve as that criterion.

There is a further problem confronting any attempt to ground moral rights in the intrinsic worth of creatures. One must first be certain that this is not merely a verbal exercise in which attributing intrinsic value to things is just another way of attributing intrinsic moral standing to them. Assuming that the relation between value and rights is synthetic, there are then two possibilities: the value in question is moral or it is nonmoral. If it is moral, the criterion plainly fails to break out of the circle of moral properties to connect them with the nonmoral properties of things. But if it is nonmoral, it is unclear what it has to do with moral rights. If there are realms of value, some case must be made for deriving moral duties toward things from the nonmoral value of these things.

The remaining three candidates for a criterion of moral standing (life, sentience, rationality) all satisfy the verification requirement since they all rest standing on empirical properties of things. They may be ordered in terms of the breadth of the moral spheres they define. Since rational beings are a proper subset of sentient beings, which are a proper subset of living beings, the first candidate is the weakest and will define the broadest sphere, whereas the third is the strongest and will define the narrowest sphere.[4] In an interesting recent discussion, Kenneth Goodpaster (1978) has urged that moral standing be accorded to all living beings, simply in virtue of the fact that they are alive.[5] Although much of his argument is negative, being directed against more restrictive criteria, he does provide a positive case for including all forms of life within the moral sphere.[6]

Let us assume that the usual signs of life—nutrition, metabolism, spontaneous growth, reproduction—enable us to draw a tolerably sharp distinction between animate and inanimate beings, so that all plant and animal species, however primitive, are collected together in the former category. All such creatures share the property of being *teleological systems:* they have functions, ends, directions, natural tendencies, and so forth. In virtue of their teleology such creatures have needs, in a nonmetaphorical sense—conditions that must be satisfied if they are to thrive or flourish. Creatures with needs can be benefited or harmed; they are benefited when their essential needs are satisfied and harmed when they are not. It also makes sense to say that such creatures have a good: the conditions that promote their life and health are good for them, whereas those that impair their normal functioning are bad for them. But it is common to construe morality as having essentially to do with benefits and harms or with the good of creatures. So doing will lead us to extend moral

---

4. Or so we shall assume, though it is certainly possible that some (natural or artificial) entity might display signs of intelligence but no signs of either sentience or life. We might, for instance, create forms of artificial intelligence before creating forms of artificial life.

5. Goodpaster employs the locution "moral considerability" where we are speaking of moral standing. The notions are identical, except for the fact that Goodpaster explicitly refrains from restricting moral considerability to possession of rights, let alone to the right to life. Nothing in the assessment of Goodpaster's view will hang on the issue of rights, and the notion of moral standing will later be generalized so as to drop essential reference to rights.

6. In the paragraph to follow I have stated that case in my own words.

standing to all creatures capable of being benefited and harmed, that is, all creatures with a good. But this condition will include all organisms (and systems of organisms), and so life is the only reasonable criterion of moral standing.

This extension of moral standing to plants and to the simpler animals is of course highly counterintuitive, since most of us accord the lives of such creatures no weight whatever in our practical deliberations. How could we conduct our affairs if we were to grant protection of life to every plant and animal species? Some of the more extreme implications of this view are, however, forestalled by Goodpaster's distinction between a criterion of inclusion and a criterion of comparison.[7] The former determines which creatures have (some) moral standing and thus locates the boundary of the moral sphere; it is Goodpaster's contention that life is the proper inclusion criterion. The latter is operative entirely within the moral sphere and enables us to assign different grades of moral standing to different creatures in virtue of some natural property that they may possess in different degrees. Since all living beings are (it seems) equally alive, life cannot serve as a comparison criterion. Goodpaster does not provide such a criterion, though he recognizes its necessity. Thus his view enables him to affirm that all living creatures have (some) moral standing but to deny that all such creatures have equal standing. Though the lives of all animate beings deserve consideration, some deserve more than others. Thus, for in-

7. These are my terms; Goodpaster distinguishes between a criterion of moral considerability and a criterion of moral significance (p. 311). It is odd that when Goodpaster addresses the practical problems created by treating life as an inclusion criterion (p. 324) he does not appeal to the inclusion/comparison distinction. Instead he invokes the quite different distinction between its being reasonable to attribute standing to a creature and its being (psychologically and causally) possible to act on that attribution. One would have thought the question is not what we *can* bring ourselves to do but what we *ought* to bring ourselves to do, and that the inclusion/comparison distinction is precisely designed to help us answer this question.

stance, higher animals might count for more than lower ones, and all animals might count for more than plants.

In the absence of a criterion of comparison, it is difficult to ascertain just what reforms Goodpaster's view would require in our moral practice. How much weight must human beings accord to the lives of lichen or grass or bacteria or insects? When are such lives more important than some benefit for a higher form of life? How should we modify our eating habits, for example? There is a problem here that extends beyond the incompleteness and indeterminacy of Goodpaster's position. Suppose that we have settled on a comparison criterion; let it be sentience (assuming that sentience admits of degrees in some relevant respect). Then a creature's ranking in the hierarchy of moral standing will be determined by the extent of its sentience: nonsentient (living) beings will have minimal standing, whereas the most sentient beings (human beings, perhaps) will have maximal standing. But then we are faced with the obvious question: if sentience is to serve as the comparison criterion, why should it not also serve as the inclusion criterion? Conversely, if life is the inclusion criterion, does it not follow that nothing else can serve as the comparison criterion, in which case all living beings have equal standing? It is difficult to imagine an argument in favor of sentience as a comparison criterion that would not also be an argument in favor of it as an inclusion criterion.[8] Since the same

8. Goodpaster does not defend separating the two criteria but merely says "we should not expect that the criterion for having 'moral standing' at all will be the same as the criterion for adjudicating competing claims to priority among beings that merit that standing" (p. 311). Certainly inclusion and comparison criteria can be different, as in Mill's celebrated evaluation of pleasures. For Mill every pleasure has some value simply in virtue of being a pleasure (inclusion), but its relative value is partly determined by its quality or kind (comparison). All of this is quite consistent (despite claims to the contrary by some critics) because every pleasure has some quality or other. Goodpaster's comparison criterion threatens to be narrower than his inclusion criterion; it certainly will be if degrees of standing are based on sentience, since many living things have no

will hold for any other comparison criterion, Goodpaster's view can avoid its extreme implications only at the price of inconsistency.

Goodpaster's view also faces consistency problems in its claim that life is necessary for moral standing. Beings need not be organisms in order to be teleological systems, and therefore to have needs, a good, and the capacity to be benefited and harmed. If these conditions are satisfied by a tree (as they surely are), then they are equally satisfied by a car. In order to function properly most machines need periodic maintenance; such maintenance is good for them, they are benefited by it, and they are harmed by its neglect. Why then is being alive a necessary condition of moral standing? Life is but an (imperfect) indicator of teleology and the capacity to be benefited and harmed. But Goodpaster's argument then commits him to treating these deeper characteristics as the criterion of moral standing, and thus to according standing to many (perhaps most) inanimate objects.[9]

This inclusion of (at least some) nonliving things should incline us to re-examine Goodpaster's argument—if the inclusion of all living things has not already done so. The connection between morality and the capacity to be benefited and harmed appears plausible, so what has gone wrong? We may form a conjecture if we again consider our pradigm bearer of moral standing. In the case of a fully normal adult human being, it does appear that moral questions are pertinent whenever the ac-

---

sentience at all. It is inconsistent to base degrees of standing on (variations) in a property and also to extend (some) standing to beings who lack that property entirely.

9. Tom Regan (1976), who argues that moral standing should be distributed on the basis of possession of a good (or the capacity to be benefited and harmed), explicitly accepts the implication that inanimate things may have standing. Regan sometimes fails to distinguish between "x has a good (can be benefited and harmed)" and "the existence of x is good (has intrinsic value)." Thus his apparent endorsement of both an intrinsic value and a benefit/harm criterion.

tions of another agent promise to benefit or threaten to harm such a being. Both duties and rights are intimately connected with benefits and harms. The kinds of acts that we have a (strict) duty not to do are those that typically cause harm, whereas positive duties are duties to confer benefits. Liberty-rights protect autonomy, which is usually thought of as one of the chief goods for human beings, and the connection between welfare-rights and benefits is obvious. But if we ask what counts as a benefit or a harm for a human being, the usual answers take one or both of the following directions:

(1) *The desire model.* Human beings are benefited to the extent that their desires (or perhaps their considered and informed desires) are satisfied; they are harmed to the extent that these desires are frustrated.

(2) *The experience model.* Human beings benefited to the extent that they are brought to have experiences that they like or find agreeable; they are harmed to the extent that they are brought to have experiences that they dislike or find disagreeable.

We need not worry at this stage whether one of these models is more satisfactory than the other. On both models benefits and harms for particular persons are interpreted in terms of the psychological states of those persons, in terms, that is, of their interests or welfare. Such states are possible only for beings who are conscious or sentient. Thus, if morality has to do with the promotion and protection of interests or welfare, morality can concern itself only with beings who are conscious or sentient.[10] No

---

10. Goodpaster (1978) does not shrink from attributing interests to nonsentient organisms, and Regan (1976) does not shrink from attributing interests to both nonsentient organisms and artifacts. Both authors assume that if a being has needs, a good, and a capacity to be benefited and harmed, then that being has interests. There is much support for this assumption in the dictionary definitions of both "interest" and "welfare," though talk of protecting the interests or welfare of plants or machines seems contrived and strained. But philosophers and economists have evolved technical definitions of "interest" and "welfare" that clearly tie these notions to the

other beings can be beneficiaries or victims *in the morally relevant way*. Goodpaster is not mistaken in suggesting that nonsentient beings can be benefited and harmed. But he is mistaken in suggesting that morality has to do with benefits and harms as such, rather than with a particular category of them. And that can be seen the more clearly when we realize that the broadest capacity to be benefited and harmed extends not only out to but beyond the frontier of life. Leaving my lawn mower out in the rain is bad for the mower, pulling weeds is bad for the weeds, and swatting mosquitoes is bad for the mosquitoes; but there are no moral dimensions to any of these acts unless the interests or welfare of some sentient creature is at stake. Morality requires the existence of sentience in order to obtain a purchase on our actions.

The failure of Goodpaster's view has thus given us some reason to look to sentience as a criterion of moral standing. Before considering this possibility directly, it will be helpful to turn to the much narrower criterion of rationality.[11] The rational/nonrational boundary is more difficult to locate with certainty than the animate/inanimate boundary, since rationality (or intelligence) embraces a number of distinct but related capacities for thought, memory, foresight, language, self-consciousness, objectivity, planning, reasoning, judgment, deliberation, and the like.[12] It is perhaps possible for a being to possess some of these

---

psychological states of sentient beings. It is the existence of beings with interests or welfare *in this sense* that is a necessary condition of the existence of moral issues.

11. Rationality is the basis of Kant's well-known distinction between persons (ends in themselves) and mere things (means). It is also advanced as a criterion by Tooley (1973), Donagan (1977), and Warren (1978).

12. Possession of a capacity at a given time does not entail that the capacity is being manifested or displayed at that time. A person does not lose the capacity to use language, for instance, in virtue of remaining silent or being asleep. The capacity remains as long as the appropriate performance could be elicited by the appropriate stimuli. It is lost only when this

capacities and entirely lack others, but for simplicity we will assume that the higher-order cognitive processes are typically owned as a bundle.[13] The bundle is possessed to one extent or another by normal adult human beings, by adolescents and older children, by persons suffering from the milder cognitive disorders, and by some other animal species (some primates and cetaceans for example). It is not possessed to any appreciable extent by fetuses and infants, by the severely retarded or disordered, by the irreversibly comatose, and by most other animal species. To base moral standing on rationality is thus to deny it alike to most nonhuman beings and to many human beings. Since the implications for fetuses and infants have already been examined, they will be ignored in the present discussion. Instead we will focus on why one might settle on rationality as a criterion in the first place.

That rationality is sufficient for moral standing is not controversial (though there are some interesting questions to be explored here about forms of artificial intelligence). As a necessary condition, however, rationality will exclude a good many sentient beings—just how many, and which ones, to be determined by the kind and the stringency of the standards employed. Many will find objectionable this constriction of the sphere of moral concern. Because moral standing has been defined in terms of the right to life, to lack moral standing is not necessarily to lack all rights. Thus one could hold that, although we have no duty to (nonrational) animals to respect their lives, we do have a duty

---

performance can no longer be evoked (as when the person has become catatonic or comatose). Basing moral standing on the possession of some capacity or set of capacities does not therefore entail silly results, such as that persons lose their rights when they fall asleep. This applies of course, not only to rationality but also to other capacities, such as sentience.

13. The practical impact of basing moral standing on rationality will, however, depend on which particular capacities are treated as central. Practical rationality (the ability to adjust means to ends, and vice versa) is, for instance, much more widely distributed through the animal kingdom than is the use of language.

to them not to cause them suffering. For the right not to suffer, one might choose a different (and broader) criterion—sentience, for example. (However, if this is the criterion appropriate for that right, why is it not also the criterion appropriate for the right to life?) But even if we focus strictly on the (painless) killing of animals, the implications of the criterion are harsh. Certainly we regularly kill nonhuman animals to satisfy our own needs or desires. But the justification usually offered for these practices is either that the satisfaction of those needs and desires outweighs the costs to the animals (livestock farming, hunting, fishing, trapping, experimentation) or that no decent life would have been available for them anyway (the killing of stray dogs and cats). Although some of these arguments doubtless are rationalizations, their common theme is that the lives of animals do have some weight (however slight) in the moral scales, which is why the practice of killing animals is one that requires moral justification (raises moral issues). If rationality is the criterion of moral standing, and if (most) nonhuman animals are nonrational, killing such creatures could be morally questionable only when it impinges on the interests of rational beings (as where animals are items of property). In no case could killing an animal be a wrong against it. However callous and chauvinistic the common run of our treatment of animals may be, still the view that killing a dog or a horse is morally no more serious (ceteris paribus) than weeding a garden can be the considered judgment of only a small minority.

The standard that we apply to other species we must in consistency apply to our own. The greater the number of animals who are excluded by that standard, the greater the number of human beings who will also be excluded. In the absence of a determinate criterion it is unclear just where the moral line will be drawn on the normal/abnormal spectrum: will a right to life be withheld from mongoloids, psychotics, the autistic, the senile, the profoundly retarded? If so, killing such persons will again be no wrong *to them*. Needless to say, most such persons (in company with many animals) are sentient and capable to some extent of enjoyable and satisfying lives. To kill them is to deprive them of lives that are of value to them. If such creatures are denied standing, this loss will be entirely discounted in our moral reasoning. Their lack of rationality may ensure that their lives are less full and rich than ours, that they consist of simpler pleasures and more basic enjoyments. But what could be the justification for treating their deaths as though they cost them nothing at all?

There is a tradition, extending back at least to Kant, that attempts just such a justification. One of its modern spokesmen is A. I. Melden (1977), who treats the capacity for moral agency as the criterion of moral standing. This capacity is manifested by participation in a moral community—a set of beings sharing allegiance to moral rules and recognition of one another's integrity. Rights can be attributed only to beings with whom we can have such moral intercourse, thus only to beings who have interests similar to ours, who show concern for the well-being of others, who are capable of uniting in cooperative endeavors, who regulate their activities by a sense of right and wrong, and who display the characteristically moral emotions of indignation, remorse, and guilt.[14] Rationality is a necessary condition (though not a sufficient one) for possessing this bundle of capacities. Melden believes that of all living creatures known to us only human beings are capable of moral agency.[15] Natural rights, including the right to life, are thus human rights.

14. Melden (1977), p. 204. Melden rejects rationality as a criterion of standing (p. 187), but only on the ground that a being's rationality does not ensure its possessing a sense of morality. Clearly rationality is a necessary condition of moral agency. Thus a criterion of moral agency will not extend standing beyond the class of rational beings.

15. Whether or not this is so will depend on how strong the conditions of moral agency are. Certainly many nonhuman species display altruism, if we mean by this a concern for the well-being of conspecifics and a willingness to accept personal sacrifices for their good. On p. 199 Melden enumerates a number of features of our lives that are to serve as the basis of our possession of rights; virtually all mammals display all of these features.

We may pass over the obvious difficulty of extending moral standing to all human beings on this basis (including the immature and abnormal) and focus on the question of why the capacity for moral agency should be thought necessary for possession of a right to life. The notion of a moral community to which Melden appeals contains a crucial ambiguity.[16] On the one hand it can be thought of as a community of moral agents—the bearers of moral duties. Clearly to be a member of such a community one must be capable of moral agency. On the other hand a moral community can be thought of as embracing all beings to whom moral agents owe duties—the bearers of moral rights. It cannot simply be assumed that the class of moral agents (duty-bearers) is coextensive with the class of moral patients (right-bearers). It is quite conceivable that some beings (infants, nonhuman animals) might have rights though they lack duties (because incapable of moral agency). The capacity for moral agency is (trivially) a condition of having moral duties. It is not obviously also a condition of having moral rights. The claim that the criterion for rights is the same as the criterion for duties is substantive and controversial. The necessity of defending this claim is merely concealed by equivocating on the notion of a moral community.

Beings who acknowledge one another as moral agents can also acknowledge that (some) creatures who are not themselves capable of moral agency nonetheless merit (some) protection of life. The more we reflect on the function of rights, the stronger becomes the inclination to extend them to such creatures. Rights are securities for beings who are sufficiently autonomous to conduct their own lives but who are also vulnerable to the aggression of others and dependent upon these others for some of the necessaries of life. Rights protect the goods of their owners and shield them from evils. We ascribe rights to one another because we all alike satisfy these minimal conditions of autonomy, vul-

---

16. The same ambiguity infects the argument in Fox (1978), who wishes to deny rights to nonhuman animals.

nerability, and dependence. In order to satisfy these conditions a creature need not itself be capable of morality: it need only possess interests that can be protected by rights. A higher standard thus seems appropriate for possession of moral duties than for possession of moral rights. Rationality appears to be the right sort of criterion for the former, but something less demanding (such as sentience) is better suited to the latter.

A criterion of life (or teleology) is too weak, admitting classes of beings (animate and inanimate) who are not suitable loci for moral rights; being alive is necessary for having standing, but it is not sufficient. A criterion of rationality (or moral agency) is too strong, excluding classes of beings (human and nonhuman) who are suitable loci for rights; being rational is sufficient for having standing, but it is not necessary. A criterion of sentience (or consciousness) is a promising middle path between these extremes.[17] Sentience is the capacity for feeling or affect. In its most primitive form it is the ability to experience sensations of pleasure and pain, and thus the ability to enjoy and suffer. Its more developed forms include wants, aims, and desires (and thus the ability to be satisfied and frustrated); attitudes, tastes, and values; and moods, emotions, sentiments, and passions. Consciousness is a necessary condition of sentience, for feelings are states of mind of which their owner is aware. But it is not sufficient; it is at least possible in principle for beings to be conscious (percipient, for instance, or even rational) while utterly lacking feelings. If rationality embraces a set of cognitive capacities, then sentience is rooted in a being's affective and conative life. It is in virtue of being sentient that creatures have interests, which are compounded either out of their desires or out of the experiences they find agreeable (or both). If morality has to do with the protection and promotion of interests, it is a plausible conjecture

17. In their several ways, Feinberg (1974), Regan (1975), and Singer (1975) have all defended the possession of interests (and thus sentience) as the criterion of moral standing.

that we owe moral duties to all those beings capable of having interests. But this will include all sentient creatures.

Most animal species, like all plant species, are (so far as we can tell) utterly nonsentient. Like consciousness, sentience emerged during the evolutionary process as a means of permitting more flexible behavior patterns and thus of aiding survival. Biologically it is marked by the emergence in the first vertebrates of the forebrain (the primitive ancestor of the human cerebral hemispheres).[18] As far as can be determined, even the simple capacity for pleasure and pain is not possessed by invertebrate animals.[19] If this is the case, then the phylogenetic threshold of moral standing is the boundary between invertebrates and vertebrates.

Like rationality, and unlike life, it makes sense to think of sentience as admitting of degrees. Within any given mode, such as the perception of pain, one creature may be more or less sensitive than another. But there is a further sense in which more developed (more rational) creatures possess a higher degree of sentience. The expansion of consciousness and of intelligence opens up new ways of experiencing the world, and therefore new ways of being affected by the world. More rational beings are capable of finding either fulfilment or frustration in activities and states of affairs to which less developed creatures are, both cognitively and affectively, blind. It is in this sense of a broader and deeper sensibility that a higher being is capable of a richer, fuller, and more varied existence. The fact that sentience admits of degrees

18. See, for example, Rose (1976), chap. 6. Psychologists and physiologists tend to use the term "consciousness" to cover perception and such higher-order cognitive processes as thought and language use, rather than sensation. In this sense conscious activities in human beings are localized in the cerebral cortex, an area of the brain that we share with most mammals. Sensation (pleasure/pain) and emotion are rooted in the limbic system, an evolutionarily more ancient part of the brain present in most vertebrates.

19. See Snyder (1977). For an outline of the physiology of pain sensation, see Melzack (1973), chap. 4. The transmission of pain requires mechanisms present only in animals with a central nervous system.

(whether of sensitivity or sensibility) enables us to employ it both as an inclusion criterion and as a comparison criterion of moral standing. The animal kingdom presents us with a hierarchy of sentience. Nonsentient beings have no moral standing; among sentient beings the more developed have greater standing than the less developed, the upper limit being occupied by the paradigm of a normal adult human being. Although sentience is the criterion of moral standing, it is also possible to explain the relevance of rationality. The evolutionary order is one of ascending intelligence. Since rationality expands a creature's interests, it is a reliable indicator of the degree of moral standing which that creature possesses. Creatures less rational than human beings do not altogether lack standing, but they do lack full standing.

An analysis of degrees of standing would require a graded right to life, in which the strength of the right varied inversely with the range of considerations capable of overriding it. The details of any such analysis will be complex and need not be worked out here. However, it seems that we are committed to extending (some) moral standing to all vertebrate animals, and also to counting higher animals for more than lower. Thus we should expect the higher vertebrates (mammals) to merit greater protection of life than the lower (fish, reptiles, amphibia, birds) and we should also expect the higher mammals (primates, cetaceans) to merit greater protection of life than the lower (canines, felines, etc.). Crude as this division may be, it seems to accord reasonably well with most people's intuitions that in our moral reasoning paramecia and horseflies count for nothing, dogs and cats count for something, chimpanzees and dolphins count for more, and human beings count for most of all.

A criterion of sentience can thus allow for the gradual emergence of moral standing in the order of nature. It can explain why no moral issues arise (directly) in our dealings with inanimate objects, plants, and the simpler forms of animal life. It can also function as a moral guideline in our encounters with novel

life forms on other planets. If the creatures we meet have interests and are capable of enjoyment and suffering, we must grant
them some moral standing. We thereby constrain ourselves not
to exploit them ruthlessly for our own advantage. The kind of
standing that they deserve may be determined by the range and
depth of their sensibility, and in ordinary circumstances this will
vary with their intelligence. We should therefore recognize as
equals beings who are as rational and sensitive as ourselves. The
criterion also implies that if we encounter creatures who are rational but nonsentient—who utterly lack affect and desire—
nothing we can do will adversely affect such creatures (in
morally relevant ways). We would be entitled, for instance, to
treat them as a species of organic computer. The same obviously
holds for forms of artificial intelligence; in deciding whether to
extend moral standing to sophisticated machines, the question
(as Bentham put it) is not whether they can reason but whether
they can suffer.

A criterion of sentience also requires gentle usage of the severely abnormal. Cognitive disabilities and disorders may impair
a person's range of sensibility, but they do not generally reduce
that person to the level of a nonsentient being. Even the grossly
retarded or deranged will still be capable of some forms of enjoyment and suffering and thus will still possess (some) moral
standing in their own right. This standing diminishes to the
vanishing point only when sentience is entirely lost (irreversible
coma) or never gained in the first place (anencephaly).[20] If all
affect and responsivity are absent, and if they cannot be engendered, then (but only then) are we no longer dealing with a
sentient creature. This verdict accords well with the contemporary trend toward defining death in terms of the permanent loss

20. The definition of irreversible coma in Harvard Medical School (1968)
includes complete unreceptivity and unresponsivity. Anencephaly is the
total absence of the cerebral hemispheres; anencephalic fetuses or neonates
never survive.

of cerebral functioning.[21] Although such patients are in one obvious sense still alive (their blood circulates and is oxygenated), in the morally relevant sense they are now beyond our reach, for we can cause them neither good nor ill. A criterion of life would require us to continue treating them as beings with (full?) moral standing, whereas a criterion of rationality would withdraw that standing when reason was lost even though sensibility should remain. Again a criterion of sentience enables us to find a middle way.

Fastening upon sentience as the criterion for possession of a right to life thus opens up the possibility of a reasonable and moderate treatment of moral problems other than abortion, problems pertaining to the treatment of nonhuman animals, extraterrestrial life, artificial intelligence, "defective" human beings, and persons at the end of life. We need now to trace out its implications for the fetus.

17. *The Morality of Abortion*

The adoption of sentience as a criterion determines the location of a threshold of moral standing. Since sentience admits of degrees, we can in principle construct a continuum ranging from fully sentient creatures at one extreme to completely nonsentient creatures at the other. The threshold of moral standing is that area of the continuum through which sentience fades into nonsentience. In phylogenesis the continuum extends from homo sapiens to the simple animals and plants, and the threshold area is the boundary between vertebrates and invertebrates. In pathology the continuum extends from the fully normal to the totally incapacitated, and the threshold area is the transition from consciousness to unconsciousness. Human ontogenesis also presents us with a continuum from adult to zygote. The threshold area

21. See Veatch (1976), especially chaps. 1 and 2.

will be the stage at which sentience first emerges, but where is that to be located?

A mental life is built upon a physical base. The capacity for sentience is present only when the necessary physiological structures are present. Physiology, and in particular neurophysiology, is our principal guide in locating a threshold in the phylogenetic continuum. Like a stereo system, the brain of our paradigm sentient being is a set of connected components.[22] These components may be roughly sorted into three groups: forebrain (cerebral hemispheres, thalamus, hypothalamus, amygdala), midbrain (cerebellum), and brainstem (upper part of the spinal cord, pineal and pituitary glands). The brainstem and midbrain play no direct role in the individual's conscious life; their various parts regulate homeostasis (temperature, respiration, heartbeat, etc.), secrete hormones, make reflex connections, route nerves, coordinate motor activities, and so on. All of these functions can be carried on in the total absence of consciousness. Cognitive, perceptual, and voluntary motor functions are all localized in the forebrain, more particularly in the cerebral cortex. Sensation (pleasure/pain), emotion, and basic drives (hunger, thirst, sex, etc.) are controlled by subcortical areas in the forebrain. Although the nerves that transmit pleasure/pain impulses are routed through the cortex, their ultimate destination is the limbic system (amygdala, hypothalamus). The most primitive forms of sentience are thus possible in the absence of cortical activity.

Possession of particular neural structures cannot serve as a criterion of moral standing, for we cannot rule out encounters with sentient beings whose structures are quite different from ours. But in all of the species with which we are familiar, the components of the forebrain (or some analogues) are the minimal conditions of sentience. Thus the evolution of the forebrain serves as

22. For an accessible account of brain structures and functions, see Rose (1976).

an indicator of the kind and degree of sentience possessed by a particular animal species. When we turn to human ontogenesis we may rely on the same indicator.

The normal gestation period for our species is 280 days from the onset of the last menstrual period to birth.[23] This duration is usually divided into three equal trimesters of approximately thirteen weeks each. A zygote has no central nervous system of any sort. The spinal cord makes its first appearance early in the embryonic period (third week), and the major divisions between forebrain, midbrain, and brainstem are evident by the end of the eighth week. At the conclusion of the first trimester virtually all of the major neural components can be clearly differentiated and EEG activity is detectable. The months to follow are marked chiefly by the growth and elaboration of the cerebral hemispheres, especially the cortex. The brain of a seven-month fetus is indistinguishable, at least in its gross anatomy, from that of a newborn infant. Furthermore, by the seventh month most of the neurons that the individual's brain will contain during its entire lifetime are already in existence. In the newborn the brain is closer than any other organ to its mature level of development.

There is no doubt that a newborn infant is sentient—that it feels hunger, thirst, physical pain, the pleasure of sucking, and other agreeable and disagreeable sensations. There is also no doubt that a zygote, and also an embryo, are presentient. It is difficult to locate with accuracy the stage during which feeling first emerges in fetal development.[24] The structure of the fetal brain, including the cortex, is well laid down by the end of the second trimester. But there is reason to expect the more primitive and ancient parts of that brain to function before the rest. The needs of the fetus dictate the order of appearance of neural

23. Standard accounts of fetal development may be found in Patten and Carlson (1974), and Torrey and Feduccia (1979). For the prenatal development of the brain, see also Rose (1976), chap. 7.

24. This is a question to which embryologists seem not to address themselves.

functions. Thus the brainstem is established and functioning first, since it is required for the regulation of heartbeat and other metabolic processes. Since the mammalian fetus develops in an enclosed and protected environment, cognition and perception are not essential for survival and their advent is delayed. It is therefore not surprising that the cortex, the most complex part of the brain and the least important to the fetus, is the last to develop to an operational level.

Simple pleasure/pain sensations would seem to occupy a medial position in this priority ranking. They are localized in a part of the brain that is more primitive than the cortex, but they could have little practical role for a being that is by and large unable either to seek pleasurable stimuli or to avoid painful ones. Behavioral evidence is by its very nature ambiguous. Before the end of the first trimester, the fetus will react to unpleasant stimuli by flinching and withdrawing. However, this reaction is probably a reflex that is entirely automatic. How are we to tell when mere reflex has crossed over into consciousness? The information we now possess does not enable us to date with accuracy the emergence of fetal sentience. Of some judgments, however, we can be reasonably confident. First-trimester fetuses are clearly not yet sentient. Third-trimester fetuses probably possess some degree of sentience, however minimal. The threshold of sentience thus appears to fall in the second trimester.[25] More ancient and primitive than cognition, the ability to discriminate simple sensations of pleasure and pain is probably the first form of consciousness to appear in the ontogenetic order. Further,

25. The view in Pluhar (1977) agrees with that defended here in basing the moral standing of the fetus on what Pluhar calls "simple consciousness" (as opposed to reflexive consciousness or self-consciousness). However, he argues that the potential for simple consciousness also qualifies its owner for moral standing; it would appear, then, that he attributes (some degree of) such standing to all fetuses. Pluhar is effectively criticized on this point by Daniels (1979). See also Carrier (1975).

when sentience emerges it does not do so suddenly. The best we can hope for is to locate a threshold stage or period in the second trimester. It is at present unclear just how far into that trimester this stage occurs.

The phylogenetic and pathological continua yield us clear cases at the extremes and unclear cases in the middle. The ontogenetic continuum does the same. Because there is no quantum leap into consciousness during fetal development, there is no clean and sharp boundary between sentient and nonsentient fetuses. There is therefore no precise point at which a fetus acquires moral standing. More and better information may enable us to locate the threshold stage ever more accurately, but it will never collapse that stage into a point. We are therefore inevitably confronted with a class of fetuses around the threshold stage whose sentience, and therefore whose moral status, is indeterminate.

A criterion based on sentience enables us to explain the status of other putative thresholds. Neither conception nor birth marks the transition from a presentient to a sentient being. A zygote has not one whit more consciousness than the gametes out of which it is formed. Likewise, although a neonate has more opportunity to employ its powers, it also has no greater capacity for sensation than a full-term fetus. Of thresholds located during gestation, quickening is the perception of fetal movement that is probably reflex and therefore preconscious. Only viability has some relevance, though at one remove. For reasons given earlier, it cannot serve as a criterion. But a fetus is viable when it is equipped to survive in the outside world. A being that is aware of, and can respond to, its own inner states is able to communicate its needs to others. This ability is of no use in utero but may aid survival in an extrauterine environment. A fetus is therefore probably sentient by the conventional stage of viability (around the end of the second trimester). Viability can therefore serve as a (rough) indicator of moral standing.

Our common moral consciousness locates contraception and

infanticide in quite different moral categories. This fact suggests implicit recognition of a basic asymmetry between choosing not to create a new life in the first place and choosing to destroy a new life once it has been created.[26] The boundary between the two kinds of act is the threshold at which that life gains moral protection. Since gametes lack moral standing, contraception (however it is carried out) merely prevents the creation of a new person. Since an infant has moral standing, infanticide (however it is carried out) destroys a new person. A second-trimester threshold of moral standing introduces this asymmetry into the moral assessment of abortion. We may define an early abortion as one performed sometime during the first trimester or early in the second, and a late abortion as one performed sometime late in the second trimester or during the third. An early abortion belongs in the same moral category as contraception: it prevents the emergence of a new being with moral standing. A late abortion belongs in the same moral category as infanticide: it terminates the life of a new being with moral standing. The threshold of sentience thus extends the morality of contraception forward to cover early abortion and extends the morality of infanticide backward to cover late abortion. One of the sentiments voiced by many people who contemplate the problem of abortion is that early abortions are importantly different from late ones. The abortion techniques of the first trimester (the IUD, menstrual extraction, vacuum aspiration) are not to be treated as cases of homicide. Those employed later in pregnancy (saline induction, hysterotomy) may, however, have a moral quality approaching that of infanticide. For most people, qualms about abortion are qualms about late abortion. It is a virtue of the sentience criterion that it explains and supports this differential approach.

---

26. The asymmetry is easily accounted for by a rights theory, since only the latter act can violate anyone's right to life.

The moral issues raised by early abortion are precisely those raised by contraception. It is for early abortions that the liberal view is appropriate. Since the fetus at this stage has no right to life, early abortion (like contraception) cannot violate its rights. But if it violates no one's rights, early abortion (like contraception) is a private act. There are of course significant differences between contraception and early abortion, since the former is generally less hazardous, less arduous, and less expensive. A woman has, therefore, good prudential reasons for relying on contracoption as her primary means of birth control. But if she elects an early abortion, then, whatever the circumstances and whatever her reasons, she does nothing immoral.[27]

The moral issues raised by late abortion are similar to those raised by infanticide. It is for late abortions that (a weakened form of) the conservative view is appropriate. Since the fetus at this stage has a right to life, late abortion (like infanticide) may violate its rights. But if it may violate the fetus' rights, then late abortion (like infanticide) is a public act. There is, however, a morally significant difference between late abortion and infanticide. A fetus is parasitic upon a unique individual in a manner in which a newborn infant is not. That parasitic relation will justify late abortion more liberally than infanticide, for they do not occur under the same circumstances.

Since we have already explored the morality of abortion for those cases in which the fetus has moral standing, the general approach to late abortions is clear enough. Unlike the simple and uniform treatment of early abortion, only a case-by-case analysis will here suffice. We should expect a serious threat to the woman's life or health (physical or mental) to justify abortion, especially if that threat becomes apparent only late in pregnancy. We should also expect a risk of serious fetal deformity to justify abortion, again especially if that risk becomes apparent (as it

27. Unless there are circumstances (such as extreme underpopulation) in which contraception would also be immoral.

usually does) only late in pregnancy. On the other hand, it should not be necessary to justify abortion on the ground that pregnancy was not consented to, since a woman will have ample opportunity to seek an abortion before the threshold stage. If a woman freely elects to continue a pregnancy past that stage, she will thereafter need a serious reason to end it.

A differential view of abortion is therefore liberal concerning early abortion and conservative (in an extended sense) concerning late abortion. The status of the borderline cases in the middle weeks of the second trimester is simply indeterminate. We cannot say of them with certainty either that the fetus has a right to life or that it does not. Therefore we also cannot say either that a liberal approach to these abortions is suitable or that a conservative treatment of them is required. What we can say is that, from the moral point of view, the earlier an abortion is performed the better. There are thus good moral reasons, as well as good prudential ones, for women not to delay their abortions.

A liberal view of early abortion in effect extends a woman's deadline for deciding whether to have a child. If all abortion is immoral, her sovereignty over that decision ends at conception. Given the vicissitudes of contraception, a deadline drawn that early is an enormous practical burden. A deadline in the second trimester allows a woman enough time to discover that she is pregnant and to decide whether to continue the pregnancy. If she chooses not to continue it, her decision violates neither her duties nor any other being's rights. From the point of view of the fetus, the upshot of this treatment of early abortion is that its life is for a period merely probationary; only when it has passed the threshold will that life be accorded protection. If an abortion is elected before the threshold, it is as though from the moral point of view that individual had never existed.

Settling on sentience as a criterion of moral standing thus leads us to a view of the moral status of the fetus, and of the morality of abortion, which satisfies the constraints set out in Section 15. It is gradual, since it locates a threshold stage rather than a point and allows moral standing to be acquired incrementally. It is differential, since it locates the threshold stage during gestation and thus distinguishes the moral status of newly conceived and full-term fetuses. It is developmental, since it grounds the acquisition of moral standing in one aspect of the normal development of the fetus. And it is moderate, since it distinguishes the moral status of early and late abortions and applies each of the established views to that range of cases for which it is appropriate.

18. *An Abortion Policy*

A differential view of the morality of abortion leads to a differential abortion policy—one that draws a legal distinction between early and late abortions. If we work within the framework of a liberal social theory, then it is understood that the state has no right to interfere in the private activities of individuals. An early abortion is a private act—or, rather, a private transaction between a woman and her physician. No regulation of this transaction will be legitimate unless it is also legitimate for other contractual arrangements between patients and physicians. It might be quite in place for the state to require that abortions be performed by qualified (perhaps licensed) personnel in properly equipped (perhaps licensed) facilities: whether or not this is so will depend on whether the state is in general competent to regulate trade in medical skills. Both the decision to abort and the decision to use contraceptives are private ones on which a woman ought to seek medical advice and medical assistance. There is no justification in either case for restricting access to that advice or that assistance.

An abortion policy must therefore be permissive for early abortions. There is at this stage no question of inquiring into a woman's reason for seeking an abortion. Her autonomy here is absolute; the simple desire not to have a child (or not to have one now) is sufficient. Grounds for abortion become pertinent only when we turn to late abortions. Since virtually all such abortions will result in the death of a being that has a right to life (though not all will violate that right), the state has a legitimate role to play in governing trade in abortion at this stage. Legal grounds for late abortion are a special case of conditions for justifiable homicide. As much as possible (allowing for the unique relation between mother and fetus) these grounds should authorize abortion when killing would also be justified in relevantly similar cases not involving fetuses. Two general conditions for justifiable homicide will be applicable to abortions: self-defense and euthanasia.

The usual legal grounds for abortion provided by moderate policies may be divided into four categories:[28] (a) therapeutic (threat to maternal life or health); (b) eugenic (risk of fetal abnormality); (c) humanitarian (pregnancy due to the commission of a crime, such as rape or incest); (d) socioeconomic (poverty, family size, etc.). If a moderate treatment of late abortion is coupled (as it should be) with a permissive treatment of early ones, only the first two categories are necessary. Therapeutic grounds for abortion follow from a woman's right of self-defense. The threat, however, must be serious in two different respects: the injury in prospect must be more than trivial and the probability of its occurrence must be greater than normal. The risks generally associated with pregnancy will not here suffice. Further, there must be good medical reason not to delay until the fetus has a better chance of survival, and every effort must be made to save the fetus' life if this is possible.[29] Thus late abortion

28. I here adapt the categories used in World Health Organization (1971), p. 6.

29. For convenience I here count as abortions procedures undertaken at or beyond the conventional point of viability (which in some jurisdictions is set as early as twenty weeks). In cases of genuine medical emergency, the desire to save the life of the fetus can be manifested by preferring hysterotomy to saline induction.

for therapeutic reasons ought to be reserved for genuine medical emergencies in which no other course of action would qualify as proper care of the mother. In many putatively moderate policies therapeutic grounds for abortion (especially mental health clauses) are interpreted so liberally as to cover large numbers of cases that are not by any stretch of the imagination medical emergencies. This is the standard device whereby a policy moderate in principle becomes permissive in practice. Since the policy here advanced is permissive in principle (for early abortions), a strict interpretation of the therapeutic grounds for late abortions will be mandatory.

The same strictures will apply to eugenic grounds. Where there is a substantial risk of some severe anomaly (rubella, spina bifida, Tay-Sachs disease, etc.), abortion may be the best course of action for the fetus. This is not obviously the case for less severe defects (Down's syndrome, dwarfism, etc.). Again there will be no justification for an interpretation of eugenic grounds so elastic that it permits abortion whenever the child is unwanted (because, say, it is the "wrong" sex). A rough rule of thumb is that late abortion for reasons of fetal abnormality is permissible only in those cases in which euthanasia for defective newborns would also be permissible. Probability will play a different role in the two kinds of case, since prenatal diagnosis of these conditions is often less certain than postnatal. But against this reason for delay we must balance the anguish of a woman carrying a fetus who may turn out at birth to be grossly deformed. Since diagnostic techniques such as ultrasound and amniocentesis cannot be employed until the second trimester, a permissive treatment of early abortions will not eliminate the need for late abortions on eugenic grounds.

Both therapeutic and eugenic grounds can be alleged for a wide range of abortions. Some of these cases will be clearly justified, others will be just as clearly unjustified, and the remainder will just be hard cases. There is no formula that can be applied mechanically to decide the hard cases. We should look to a statute for only the most perfunctory statement of justifying grounds for abortion. Particular decisions (the analogue of case law) are best undertaken by persons with the relevant medical expertise. This might be a hospital or clinic committee established especially to monitor late abortions or an "ethics committee" with broader responsibilities. In either case, establishing the right sort of screening mechanism is the best means of ensuring that the justifying grounds are given a reasonable application.

There is no need for any special notice of humanitarian grounds. It is doubtful indeed whether incest ought to be a crime, except in those cases in which someone is being exploited. In any case, any woman who has become pregnant due to incestuous intercourse will have ready access to an early abortion. If she declines this opportunity and if there is no evidence of genetic abnormality, she may not simply change her mind later. The same obviously applies to pregnancy due to rape, including statutory rape. The practical problems should be approached by providing suitable counseling.

A permissive policy for early abortions will also render socioeconomic grounds redundant. Since social constraints do not normally create an emergency for which abortion is the only solution, and since women will be able to terminate pregnancies at will in the early stages, there is no need for separate recognition of social or economic justifications for abortion.

An adequate abortion policy is thus a conjunction of a permissive policy for early abortions and a moderate policy for late abortions. The obvious remaining question is where to draw the boundary between the two classes of cases. When we are dealing with the morality of abortion, borderline fuzziness is both inevitable and tolerable. Many moral problems turn on factors that are matters of degree. Where such factors are present, we cannot avoid borderline cases whose status is unclear or indeterminate. It is a defect in a moral theory to draw sharp lines where there are none, or to treat hard cases as though they were easy. But what makes for good morals may also make for bad law. An abortion policy must be enforceable and so must divide cases as clearly as possible. A threshold stage separating early from late abortions must here give way to a cutoff point.

Since there is no threshold point in fetal development, any precise upper limit on the application of a permissive policy will be to some extent arbitrary. Clearly it must be located within the threshold period, thus sometime in the second trimester. Beyond this constraint the choice of a time limit may be made on prag- matic grounds. If a permissive policy for early abortions is to promote their autonomy, women must have time to discover that they are pregnant and to decide on a course of action. This factor will tend to push the cutoff point toward the end of the second trimester. On the other hand, earlier abortions are sub- stantially safer and more economical of scarce medical resources than later ones. This factor will tend to pull the cutoff point to- ward the beginning of the second trimester. Balancing these con- siderations would incline one toward a time limit located some- time around the midpoint of pregnancy. But it should not be pretended that there is a unique solution to this policy problem. Differential policies may legitimately vary (within constraints) in their choice of a boundary between permissiveness and moder- ation.

Since abortion is a controversial matter, a society's abortion policy ought to include a "conscience clause" that allows medi- cal personnel with conscientious objections to avoid involve- ment in abortions.[30] It is in general preferable not to require doctors and nurses to perform tasks that deeply offend their moral principles, at least as long as others are willing to meet pa- tients' needs. But it should be stated plainly that dissenting scruples are here being honored, not because they are correct (for they are not), but because a pluralistic society thrives when it promotes as much mutual respect of values as is compatible with

30. There is a good account of the debate on a conscience clause for the 1967 British Abortion Act in St. John-Stevas (1967–1968).

the common good. The position of hospitals may be quite different. Any institution that is publicly funded is obliged to provide a suitably wide range of public services. Individual persons may opt out of performing abortions without thereby rendering abortions unavailable, but if entire hospitals do so, substantial numbers of women may have no meaningful access to this service. Whether abortions ought to be subsidized by government medical insurance plans is a question of social justice that cannot be answered without investigating the moral basis of compulsory social welfare programs in general. However, once a society has installed such a plan, there is no justification for omitting abortions from the list of services covered by it.[31]

The abortion policy here proposed is not novel: a differential policy with a time limit in the second trimester is already in operation in a number of countries.[32] But these policies seem usually to have been settled on as compromises between the opposed demands of liberals and conservatives rather than as matters of principle. Such compromises are attractive to politicians, who do not seek any deeper justification for the policies they devise. But there is a deeper justification for this policy. Although it does define a middle ground between the established views, it

31. If abortion should be omitted on the ground that most pregnancies can be easily avoided, then treatment for lung cancer must also be omitted since most cases of lung cancer can be even more easily avoided. There is no justification for restricting a woman's access to abortion by requiring the consent of the father. Until men learn to become pregnant, if a man wishes to father a child he must find a woman willing to carry and bear it. Parental consent is a slightly more complicated issue, since it raises questions about the competence of minors. In most cases a girl who is mature enough to be sexually active is also mature enough to decide on an abortion; in any case no parental consent regulation is justified for abortion that is not also justified for all comparable forms of minor surgery.

32. Notably the United States, Great Britain, France, Italy, Sweden, the Soviet Union, China, India, Japan, and most of the countries of Eastern Europe. The cutoff points in these jurisdictions vary from the beginning to the end of the second trimester.

has not been defended here as the outcome of a bargaining procedure. Instead it has been advanced as the only policy congruent with an adequate criterion of moral standing and proper recognition of both a woman's right to autonomy and a fetus' right to life. A differential policy does not mediate between alternatives both of which are rationally defensible; instead it supersedes alternatives both of which have been discredited.

CHAPTER FIVE

Morality and Utility

A credible third option in the abortion debate must be a moderate, differential view of abortion. No other view can be made to cohere with considered and reasonable judgments on connected moral issues. A view of abortion requires, however, more than merely intuitive support. The counterintuitive implications of the established views are a surface manifestation of their lack of a deep structure. Both views presuppose moral theories that treat rights and/or duties as basic, but neither can be supported by appeal to such theories. The remaining task is to show that a moderate view has an adequate deep structure.

The direct route to showing this would be to continue presupposing a theory of rights and/or duties. Moral standing has thus far been defined in terms of the right to life, and a case has been made for connecting possession of this right with sentience. Moreover, justifying grounds for abortion (in the cases in which these are operative) have been largely derived from appeal to the right of self-defense, or autonomy. There is, therefore, every prospect of constructing a moderate, differential view of abortion on the foundation of some theory in which rights and/or duties function as basic notions. There are also, however, compelling reasons for rejecting any such theory. It has been convenient to cast the discussion to this point in terms of such theories, since they are the common currency of the established views. And it is not insignificant that a moderate view can defeat the established views on their own grounds. But the inadequacy of moral theories of rights and duties ensures that the process of grounding a moderate view will consist of two stages. In the first we must construct a better moral theory; then we must show that this theory can serve as the deep structure of a moderate view of abortion.

19. *Moral Theories*

A moral decision is a choice among courses of action based on
some conception of what it is morally good or right to do. A
moral rule or principle is a general formula capable of serving,
directly or indirectly, as a guide in making moral decisions. A
moral theory is a set of (one or more) basic moral principles that
can be used to generate more specific moral rules, standards, or
guidelines. A moral theory is addressed to us in our capacity as
moral agents, beings capable of regulating our practical lives by
means of beliefs about the good and the right. It is a plan for
living the moral life.

Varieties of moral theories may be distinguished along a number of dimensions. Here we will focus on two such dimensions
that, because they are independent of one another, combine to
define four types of theory. The first concerns the treatment of
the private sphere. Actions are private in so far as they do not
affect the interest or autonomy of any individual except their
agent. A moral theory will either contain (or imply) norms for
the private sphere or it will not. If it does, it is an *ideal* theory; if
it does not, it is a *discretionary* theory.[1] Discretionary theories
treat the private sphere as the realm of taste rather than value
(and therefore rather than morality). Within the private sphere
actions may be rational or irrational, prudent or imprudent—but
not moral or immoral. A discretionary theory thus limits the
scope of morality to the evaluation of interpersonal activities;
the purpose of moral principles is to resolve conflicts of interest
or autonomy among agents each of which is the center of

---

1. Brian Barry draws a similar distinction (between ideal-regarding and
want-regarding theories) in Barry (1965), pp. 38–41. Barry, however,
stresses the impact of these theories on the public rather than the private
realm. I have not taken over his terminology because I do not wish to
restrict discretionary theories to the satisfaction of wants. See also the
distinction between broad and narrow conceptions of morality in Mackie
(1977).

his/her own private sphere. When individuals impinge upon the spheres of others, they must regulate their affairs by reference to moral rules or standards; but within their own spheres they are sovereign. On a discretionary theory there may be moral duties to others, but there can be no such duties to oneself. There is no end around whose pursuit individuals must organize their private lives. Because the choice of ultimate goods or goals is left to the individual's discretion, we should expect a society that shares a discretionary theory to feature a variety of styles of life, none of them open to condemnation on moral grounds unless they prejudice the opportunities of others to pursue their own favored life styles. The private sphere would then be the realm of pluralism and mutual toleration.

An ideal theory mandates some moral norms for the private sphere. The ends that agents, when left to their own devices, may elect to pursue are sorted into the intrinsically good (noble, virtuous, exalted) and the intrinsically evil (base, vicious, degraded). This division may be grounded in a conception of a shared human nature and of ways of life appropriate (and inappropriate) to beings of that nature. In any case, an ordering of the intrinsic worth of personal goals generates moral norms governing the choice of a life style, norms that enjoin pursuit of good ends and forbid pursuit of evil ones. These norms will limit the variety of life styles in a society whose members are dedicated to the pursuit of the good life. They will not annihilate individual discretion, since the mandatory ends are necessarily vague and leave room for different means of pursuing them. But an individual must choose some style of life that can be plausibly connected to some intrinsically valuable ends. In addition to duties to others, individuals thus have moral duties to themselves. These duties constrain their sovereignty over their own personal lives and reduce the extent of the realm of taste.

The opposition between discretionary and ideal theories turns on the objectivity of a conception of the good life. Moral beliefs, because they are values and not tastes, make an implicit claim to objectivity. All moral theories agree on an objective treatment of the public, interpersonal realm. What is at issue is whether some objective conception of the good life is to be applied to the private sphere, or whether this sphere is to be treated as one of taste and therefore of subjectivity. Is there some one authoritative conception of the good life or do we here expect a plurality of individual conceptions? The opposition expresses itself in part in divergent construals of interest, well-being, or welfare. A subjective analysis sees an individual's welfare ultimately from his/her own point of view. It thus takes as basic either the individual's desires and aversions or the experiences he/she finds agreeable and disagreeable. For something to promote a person's interest, it must directly or indirectly either satisfy that person's wants or bring about experiences he/she welcomes and enjoys. A subjective account of welfare thus preserves a measure of individual sovereignty. There is of course room for errors of judgment, for believing that something will be good for one when it will not. But individuals are always the final judges of whether their welfare has been enhanced or not; in one way or another they must acknowledge that they have been made better off. Their interest is not served by providing them with goods that rank high on someone else's conception of well-being if those goods are not highly regarded by them as well. It is still possible to make some sense of the notion of basic or primary goods, since there will be certain conditions (the necessaries of life) that are likely to be indispensable on any conception of the good, however eccentric it may be.[2] But even at this basic level, it will be necessary to make allowance for idiosyncrasies of taste.

Discretionary moral theories employ a subjective analysis of interest or welfare. Because ideal theories advance an objective conception of the good life, they allow for something's benefiting an individual even though it may override his/her most

2. The concept of a primary good is borrowed from Rawls (1971), pp. 90–95.

basic desires and tastes. On this view we are unreliable authorities on what is good for us, as well as on how it may best be
attained. Since this account of welfare adopts a point of view external to the individual, it is best captured, not by the subjective
notions of desire or experience, but by the more objective notion
of need. Certain goods are necessary for the living of a good or
well-developed or at least minimally human life. Individuals are
better off for the possession of such goods, whether or not they
themselves acknowledge the benefits. Just as individuals are not
sovereign over what is best for others, they are also not sovereign
over what is best for themselves.

The second dimension along which moral theories may be divided concerns the kind of protection that they accord to individuals. Since every moral theory generates norms governing interpersonal behavior, every theory places some constraints on
how agents may treat one another. These constraints may be
either loose or strict. They are loose when any specific mode of
treatment is permitted in principle, as long as it is consonant
with the overall end promoted by the theory. They are strict
when certain specific kinds of acts are forbidden regardless of the
circumstances and regardless of the further ends that may be
served by doing them. Degrees of strength are obviously possible
as constraints against specific modes of treatment are overridden
by more or fewer considerations. A moral theory will either impose strict constraints on how individuals may be treated or it
will not. If it does, it is an *absolute* theory; if it does not, it is a
qualified theory.[3] An absolute theory contains some specific absolute moral rules, though it may contain qualified rules as well.
Violating such rules will be forbidden by the theory with no al-

---

3. Robert Nozick draws a similar distinction (between side-constraint
and end-state theories) in Nozick (1974), pp. 28–30. Nozick, however,
hedges on whether his side-constraints are absolute (p. 30n). I have not
taken over his terminology because I do not wish to restrict qualified
theories to the maximization (or minimization) of any end-state.

lowable exceptions. A qualified theory contains no absolute rules. Beyond this negative condition its content is unspecified: it may feature basic prima facie rules of duty or it may avoid the language of duty altogether. The constraints it places on specific modes of treatment of others may vary from strong (overridable only in extreme cases) to weak (subject to some social calculus). Absolute theories define one extremity on the spectrum of individualist moral constraints; qualified theories occupy all of the rest of it.

The two dichotomies enable us to define four types of moral theory. The discretionary/ideal boundary divides rights theories from natural-law theories. The function of a right, whether a liberty-right or a welfare-right, is to protect individuals' autonomy over their own lives. A theory that treats such rights as basic is therefore committed to a subjective analysis of welfare and to the denial that individuals have moral duties to themselves.[4] Natural-law theories, on the other hand, contain an objective account of the mode of life appropriate to a human being. Because this conception is applicable to any human agent, every agent has a duty to live by it.[5] The conception of welfare on a natural-law theory cannot therefore be entirely subjective. The same boundry cuts through both utilitarian and intuitionist theories. The classical utilitarians (Bentham, Mill, Sidgwick) advanced a subjective analysis of welfare in terms of desire or pleasure. They thus allowed individuals discretion in determining their objects of desire and their sources of pleasure; in order to be benefited, individuals had to receive either what they wanted or what they found agreeable.[6] No way of life was morally obligatory, not

4. Nozick (1974), esp. chap. 10.
5. Donagan (1977), chap. 3.
6. For an excellent account of how, despite appearances, the classical utilitarians were noncommittal on questions of intrinsic value, see Narveson (1967a), chap. 3. Narveson himself offers a subjective analysis of utility. Mill's notorious views on the quality of pleasures inject an ideal element into his theory. The crucial step is not the introduction of quality (or kind)

even the pursuit of personal welfare itself. It was assumed to be imprudent, perhaps even irrational, to lack concern for one's own well-being, but it was not treated as immoral. By contrast, the ideal utilitarians (Moore, Rashdall) advocated a theory of intrinsic value on which certain objects or states of affairs were worth pursuing in their own right.[7] The theory enjoined individuals to aim at producing what was in fact good, rather than what they themselves considered to be good. Since some of these intrinsic goods were private to an individual's own life, morality flowed across the private/public frontier. What was good for a person was determined by what was good in itself. The classical forms of intuitionism have also been ideal theories.[8] But there is nothing in the nature of intuitionism that guarantees that this must be so. In principle at least one could devise a discretionary intuitionism that consisted of a number of equally basic principles none of which intruded on individuals' sovereignty over their private affairs. An "intuitionism of rights" would be one case of such a theory.

The absolute/qualified boundary divides all utilitarian and intuitionist theories from natural-law theories. The latter contain some (negative) moral rules that are absolute.[9] Utilitarians, whether classical or ideal, cannot accept that there is any specific kind of action whose performance is absolutely forbidden under

---

of pleasures to supplement the Benthamite reliance on quantity, since agents may with perfect consistency prefer pleasures of one kind over pleasures of another regardless of their relative magnitudes, and anyway each could act on his/her own quality-preferences. The ideal element is the use of "the only competent judges" as an objective and authoritative measure of the value of pleasures. There is an informative discussion of Mill's ideal treatment of utility in Donner (1978).

7. Moore (1903), chap. 6, and (1912), chap. 7; Rashdall (1924), vol. 1, chap. 7.

8. Price (1974), Ross (1930, 1939).

9. Anscombe (1968), Donagan (1977), chaps. 3, 6. See also Nagel (1974).

all circumstances. For any act, however horrendous, there will be some imaginable circumstances in which it will be permissible. In general what may or may not be done to others will be determined, in one way or another, by a calculus of social utility. If utilitarian theories contain rights and duties at all, the rights must be defeasible and the duties loose. The same holds for any form of intuitionism. Because such theories lack priorities for ordering their several rules, no duty is immune to being overridden by some other.[10] But then no rules are absolute and no rights inviolable. The same boundary cuts through rights theories. A libertarian or lexical theory contains inviolable rights and absolute rules. An intuitionism of rights, being unordered, does not.

The two dichotomies thus generate the following classification of moral theories:[11]

	QUALIFIED	ABSOLUTE
DISCRETIONARY	Classical utilitarianism Intuitionism of rights	Libertarian and lexical rights theories
IDEAL	Ideal utilitarianism Classical intuitionism	Natural law

10. Ross (1930), chap. 2.

11. These categories avoid the traditional distinction between consequentialist and nonconsequentialist theories. Because of the elasticity of the act/consequence boundary, any moral theory may (trivially) be formulated in terms of the production of consequences; the interesting differences among theories concern the individualist constraints they impose on the counting of consequences. But this is the dimension reflected in the qualified/absolute distinction.

The theories that underlay the established views of abortion were both absolute. But any absolute theory is defective in principle, and so the moral basis of the established views must be abandoned.

20. *Individuality*

Before exposing the defects of absolute moral theories, it will be helpful to compare the merits of ideal and discretionary theories. At stake between them is one form of individuality. Ideal theories postulate a common good for all human beings, without regard for those respects in which individuals' tastes and styles may differ.[12] This uniformity is most evident in natural-law theories that treat human beings as a natural kind for which one conception of the good life is sufficient. The assumption of a homogeneous human nature flourished within a natural teleology in which every species was thought to have its own proper end or function. Once the nature and function of human beings are understood, we are on the way to discovering wherein lies their peculiar good. In its secular form this view of course appears in Aristotle, but its more secure refuge is a providential religion. If God is the designer of the universe and all its contents, he is the authority to whom we turn in order to discover our purpose and our good. A uniform conception of human good survives as long as some particular world view, natural or supernatural, continues to hold sway. When that framework fragments, when a set of shared assumptions is supplanted by a marketplace of diverse hypotheses, it becomes harder to maintain the distinction between truth and error. At that point the choice of a life style becomes a matter of subjective preference.

For a modern audience it is impossible to ground an ideal the-

---

12. In order to be complete, and also in order to escape the charge of arbitrarily limiting the ideal to human good, an ideal theory will also need an objective account of the good for nonhuman animals.

ory in religion, both because conceptions of God are now as diverse as conceptions of the good and also because objective values require more than a supernatural foundation. Meanwhile, belief in a natural teleology has been shaken by the rise of a mechanistic physics and biology. As science matures it relies less and less on design and purpose. Teleological explanations are still properly applied to those individual organisms to whom it is appropriate to attribute goal-seeking behavior. They are still, therefore, properly applied to individual human beings. But it is precisely for these beings that the hypothesis of a common purpose, and therefore a common good, is least plausible. The direction of evolution is toward variety and individuality. To relatively simple creatures whose teleological behavior is largely instinctive, we may not go wrong in ascribing a uniform purpose and good. But this picture is ill suited to creatures whose capacity for reflection upon their own lives makes them capable of culture. As the diversity of human cultural patterns comes to impress us as much as the uniformity of our evolutionary heritage, the sense in which we possess a common human nature becomes more and more attenuated.

A uniform conception of human nature has retained some credibility among those psychologists who rely on basic drives or instincts. It has been challenged largely by the rise of the social sciences, and especially by anthropology, sociology, and economics. If psychologists tend to see us as essentially similar within our apparent differences, anthropologists have been impressed by the enormous variety of cultural styles and the accompanying variety of conceptions of what constitutes a good or normal human life. Socialization theory has tended to reinforce this picture of cultural relativity. Sociologists treat individuals as cultural artifacts, with the most fundamental aspects of their personalities shaped by the group. An individual's identity is thus determined by affiliation with a particular community, and not merely by membership in the species. But it is economists who have carried an individualist conception of human nature to its extreme. Consumers, in economic theory, are conceived as centers of subjective preferences that determine their demands in the market. No limits are placed on the objects of these preferences or the contents of these demands; individuals can, in principle seek anything at all. Such isolated economic units have no history, no culture, and no nature. They also have no common good.

Economics is merely the most extreme form in which modern science has eroded the ancient conception of a uniform human nature. One need not go so far in order to suggest that the world view that supports an ideal theory is now beyond recovery. It has been replaced by a pluralism that, at least in its better moments, recognizes that different cultural patterns, styles of life, and conceptions of the good may all be equally worthwhile—that this is not a matter of truth and error. There may, of course, be some elements that are constant over cultural and individual variations; sociobiologists are these days attempting to identify just such elements and to explain their presence by means of natural selection.[13] Some good, therefore, may be common to all human beings. This fact, if it is one, need not tempt us back to an objective view. To the extent that certain goods are necessary for the pursuit of any plan of life, they will turn up as basic goods on a subjective account of human welfare. Subjectivists can therefore account for what objectivists have called basic needs: good food, clean air, unpolluted water, secure shelter, and so forth. It is a mistake to contrast objective needs with subjective preferences or aims. Basic needs are just those goods that are *needed for* the pursuit of a person's basic aims, whatever these may be. They manifest the residual uniformity of our nature underlying the diversity of our culture.

The conflict between ideal and discretionry theories is the conflict between ancient and modern conceptions of human nature. It is also the conflict between childhood and adulthood.

13. See, for example, Wilson (1978).

When we deal with children we do not hesitate to override their own aims and desires on the basis that we know better than they what is good for them. Even in these cases, however, the confirmation that we are right is the later acknowledgment of that fact by the subjects themselves; our intervention must turn out sooner or later to have furthered their own mature conception of their good. This paternalism that is appropriate when dealing with children is offensive and demeaning when applied to competent adults. To mature is to develop the capacity to choose one's own directions. An ideal theory is suited to the closed world of the ancients and to the equally closed world of the child.

Those who favor objective accounts of welfare generally direct their criticisms against subjective analyses that employ the desire or preference model, and which thus attempt to connect enhancing individual good with satisfying wants.[14] It is true that no simple analysis along these lines will suffice, for instances are ready to hand in which persons' getting what they want is manifestly harmful for them. Simple analyses also threaten to erase the distinction between selfish and selfless motivation by rendering into a truism the proposition that individuals always seek their own good. But if simple desire theories are inadequate, we should be wary of assuming that more sophisticated accounts will also fail. Various devices are available to one who would define well-being or interest in terms of wants or preferences: instead of single, isolated desires, the entire hierarchy of an individual's preferences can be invoked; instead of actual preferences, the analysis can appeal to "rectified" (rational, informed) preferences; the self-interested/altruistic dichotomy can be reintroduced at the level of objects of desire, and so on. It may, however, be true that the desire model is inadequate to explicate the

14. This was the strategy adopted in a paper (thus far unpublished) presented by Thomas Schwartz to the 1978 conference on The Limits of Utilitarianism at Virginia Polytechnic Institute.

notion of interest or welfare. If so, its failings need not lead one to embrace an objective theory. The desire model is merely one species of subjective analysis of welfare, and not the most promising.

There is one decisive objection to any objective theory of good or well-being. A thing is not in *my* interest, does not promote *my* welfare, unless it somehow makes *me* better off. Suppose that I am given some commodity for which I have no taste, which does not tend to satisfy any desire or aim (present or future) of mine, and which does not foster any experiences that I welcome or enjoy. If it is claimed, on some objective ground, that this commodity is nonetheless good for me, the question must be: what reason is there for thinking that it is good for *me?* It may well enhance the well-being of others, but what is its connection with *me?* My welfare is *my* welfare. What could explain how something is good for me except some essential reference to me, and what could that reference involve if not some subjective state of mine? Nothing but a subjective model can make sense of *individual* welfare.[15]

The price we pay for embracing an ideal theory is the loss of one form of individuality: respect for persons as beings who are competent to determine for themselves what their interests are. All ideal theories, whether natural-law or utilitarian, subject the private lives of individuals to some external conception of the good. This denial of individual sovereignty is quite in place in the public realm where the interests of others require protection. But to import it into the private realm is to externalize the individual's relation to his/her own welfare. And this is to neglect the essential difference between self and others: I am related internally to my own interest but externally to yours. What affects your welfare may or may not affect me as well, but what affects

---

15. Objective analyses of welfare thus suffer from the same defect as "nonnaturalist" analyses of goodness: they make it impossible to explain why an agent should *care* about his welfare.

my welfare necessarily affects me. This is why I am sovereign over the conception of my own good and not over yours.

The absolute form of a discretionary theory is a libertarian (or lexical) theory of rights. If such a theory is defective, any absolute theory is defective. At stake beween absolute and qualified theories is another form of individuality. The exceptionless rules of a libertarian theory are meant to protect individuals' autonomy over their private lives. Such a theory conceives the moral world as consisting of separate persons each leading a unique and distinct life. The boundaries between these lives are the most significant features of the moral landscape. Prudence may require individuals to trade off a smaller loss for a greater gain within their own lives; in such cases the same individual suffers the loss and is compensated by the gain. Morality, however, forbids trading off losses and gains across different lives, for in such cases the loser is being exploited for the benefit of the gainer. Trade-offs that flow across the boundaries between separate lives (and which are not consented to) fail to respect individuality by treating some persons as means for advantaging others. The proper focus for balancing costs and benefits is within a single life and not over different lives.

In a libertarian theory the protection of individuality takes the form of absolute liberty-rights. Such rights preserve autonomy by prohibiting the crossing of personal boundaries (except by consent). They leave individuals unencumbered in deciding what to do with their own lives, except for the provision that they may not violate anyone else's rights. On such a theory liberty has absolute weight against every other good: an individual's liberty may not be infringed for the sake of any quantity of any such good for that individual or for others. But liberty also has absolute weight against itself: an individual's liberty may not be infringed for the sake of any quantity of liberty for that individual or for others. Once the theory has defined what counts as violation of personal autonomy, such violation becomes a kind of act that it is never permissible to perform, whatever the circumstances.

Most moral theories require some respect for individual autonomy; indeed, such a requirement is a condition of adequacy for a moral theory. At issue here is not whether individuality ought to be respected, but only whether it ought to be respected absolutely. A moral theory that holds liberty or autonomy absolute is vulnerable to two different kinds of objection. The first is directed against the absolute weight assigned to liberty against all other goods. Conflicts can occur between a person's liberty and his/her own welfare or that of others. If liberty is absolute against welfare, no (compulsory) loss of liberty (however small) can be compensated by any gain in welfare (however great). Thus if a dime from you right now will enable me to make a telephone call that will avert massive loss of life (including yours) from some natural disaster, and if you have your own plans for that dime, I may not take it from you (it is, after all, *your* dime) even if there is no other way to avert the loss of life. Holding liberty (or any other good) absolute may render us powerless to avert moral catastrophes. Absolute rules may respond well to ordinary cases and enable us to conduct the common day-to-day business of morality quite successfully. But their strict prohibition of compulsory trade-offs can produce disastrous results in moral emergencies. When the stakes are dramatically raised we are justified in suspending some of the protections we commonly accord to individuals; as lawyers and judges know well, a rule that works perfectly well for ordinary cases may generate absurdity when applied to extraordinary ones. Insistence that the rule be observed whatever the consequences is the mark of the moral fanatic.

A set of absolute rules is too inflexible to cope with the exigencies of the moral life. A qualified theory will be more complex and less certain in its treatment of hard cases. Because it will hold no good absolute, its rules will always admit of exceptions in some conceivable circumstances. Goods must now be weighed against competing goods, and there must be some way of determining when the ordinary rules are to be set aside. Although none of this moral balancing is easy, confronting its necessity is a mark of maturity. A code of strict and inflexible rules is stuck at an infantile stage of moral development.

The other objection to a libertarian theory is directed against the absolute weight liberty has against itself. Conflicts can occur between a person's liberty and his/her own (long-range) liberty or that of others. If liberty is absolute against liberty, no violation of liberty (however slight) can be compensated by any preservation of liberty (however extensive). Thus, if some mad scientist has released into the atmosphere a gas that will destroy respect for autonomy for the next century, and I must violate your autonomy now to prevent everyone's autonomy (including yours) from being violated repeatedly in the future, a libertarian theory of rights will still forbid me to do so. How can such a theory claim to value autonomy? Why should it assign infinite (negative) weight to present violations of autonomy against future violations? If autonomy is sufficiently important to be assigned absolute weight against all other goods, is more of it not better than less? On the issue of intracommodity trade-offs, an absolute theory is not merely counterintuitive—it is irrational.

A libertarian (or lexical) rights theory holds liberty absolute against all other goods and against itself. A theory that assigns this status to any other good will suffer from the same defects. There is no alternative but to abandon absolute theories. Weakening the protection of individuality need not mean eroding it entirely. If we think of rights as the means of such protection, rights may be taken seriously without being held inviolable. Further, qualified protection of individual liberty is not inconsistent with a subjective and individualist conception of welfare. The two forms of individuality are different: one can both treat individuals as the sources of their own conceptions of the good and also hold that in some circumstances different goods (and the goods of different persons) may be traded off. Qualified discretionary theories therefore may respect individual taste without absolutely respecting individual liberty.

21. *Classical Utilitarianism*

A satisfactory moral theory will be both discretionary and qualified. These specifications do not define a unique theory; they are satisfied both by an intuitionism of rights and by classical utilitarianism. These theories differ in two principal respects. First, intuitionist theories lack a mechanism for ordering and balancing specific rights and duties; their implications for particular cases may therefore be indeterminate. By contrast, the principle of utility is (in theory at least) always capable of adjudicating conflicts among moral rules, thus generating a determinate result. Second, an intuitionism of rights treats rights as basic moral facts. Although utilitarianism can accommodate rights and duties, it derives them from the principle of utility. An intuitionism of rights differs from classical utilitarianism, therefore, both in being intuitionist and in being a theory of rights.

Intuitionist moral theories are closely modeled on the morality of common sense with its loose collection of potentially conflicting rights and duties and its lack of a higher-order procedure for resolving conflicts. What is at issue between intuitionist and utilitarian theories is whether the disorder of common-sense morality can be rationalized, and whether the principle of utility is the proper vehicle for such rationalization. A theory that generates determinate solutions to moral problems is preferable ceteris paribus to one that does not. Intuitionism is the concession that the moral life is incapable of unification around any central principle or value. It is therefore a theory of last resort to be embraced only when all others have been discredited. If a case can be made for the principle of utility as an ordering mechanism for moral rights and duties, then the superiority of utilitarianism over intuitionism will have been established. Such a result will

show both that we can do better than an unordered plurality of
specific rules and that rights and duties are not fundamental
moral categories. The way will then be open to a moral theory
that, besides being qualified and discretionary, is also unified.

Classical utilitarianism is the name of a family of related
theories that may differ from one another in significant respects.
They may be thought of as possible specifications of a more
primitive theory that we will call *proto-utilitarianism,* and which
is defined by the following conditions:

> (1) *Purity.* Whatever the objects of moral evaluation, their
> moral value is determined entirely by social utility.
> (2) *Utility.* Individual utility is a measure of individual welfare;
> social utility is an increasing function of individual utilities.
> (3) *Impartiality.* In measuring social utility (a) all individual
> utilities affected are to be counted, and (b) equal utilities are to be
> counted equally.

The first condition ensures that utilitarianism is a homogeneous
theory constructed around a single measure of moral value. The
second condition imposes some constraints on that measure.
However individual utility is defined, it must capture the notion
of individual interest or well-being. We know already that this
will require a subjective analysis. Social utility must be defined in
terms of individual utilities. Utilitarianism is thus individualist
both in adopting a subjective analysis of welfare and in reducing
social utility to individual utilities. The ultimate locations of
utility for the theory are individual sentient beings. Any function adopted for defining social utility must be increasing: a gain
in individual utility must entail a gain in social utility (at least
as long as the number of persons is constant). The simple case is
that in which social utility is just the sum of individual utilities.
However, there are other possibilities: social utility may be the
average of individual utilities, and so forth. The third condition
imposes further constraints on social utility by defining the utilitarian interpretation of the impartiality that constitutes the

moral point of view. If a sentient being is affected by an action, that being's utility must be included in a measure of the social utility of the action, and equal amounts of utility must be counted equally regardless of their owners. This impartiality condition distinguishes utilitarianism from narrower normative theories that either exclude some individual utilities entirely or count them for less than others. One limiting case of such a theory is egoism.

A particular version of utilitarianism is defined by a particular formulation of the principle of utility. We shall focus on two respects in which versions of the theory often diverge: the definition of individual utility, and the choice of objects of moral evaluation and categories of moral value. It will be assumed that for the classical theory social utility is the sum of individual utilities. Since "utility" is an entirely artificial term, the only constraint on an analysis of individual utility it that it must adequately capture the notion of individual interest or welfare. The concept of individual utility is the joint property of utilitarians and egoists, the latter urging the promotion of (some unique) individual utility and the former the promotion of social utility. A definition of utility that serves egoists will therefore also serve utilitarians.

When we limit ourselves to subjective accounts, we have two alternatives available: the desire model and the experience model.[16] The former defines welfare in terms of the satisfaction of wants or aims. Individuals are here construed as teleological systems possessing ends they strive to realize.[17] Wants are usually

16. There are brief comparisons of the two models in Grice (1967), pp. 10-12, and Glover (1977) pp. 63-65. I have also profited by reading unpublished discussions of these alternatives by Peter Singer and Richard Brandt.

17. Such an account will need to decide whether the realization of unconscious ends counts as utility. This decision will determine whether only sentient beings have utilities.

interpreted propositionally; thus, wanting the inflation rate to decline is wanting the proposition "The inflation rate declines" to be true. A want is satisfied when the corresponding proposition is true. An individual's well-being is, then, taken to depend on the extent to which his/her wants are satisfied or aims realized. Because wants are comparative, it is common to cast the desire model in terms of preferences. With respect to a given context of choice, an individual's preferences may, in principle at least, be ranked or ordered; the extent to which the individual's well-being is enhanced is directly proportional to the rank order of the preference that is satisfied. Individuals may be conceived of as possessing preference rankings for different objects and contexts with these rankings themselves ordered into some larger hierarchy of ends. However complex the picture, an individual's interest remains always a function of the extent to which his/her wants have been satisfied.

The experience model defines individual welfare in terms of states of mind that the subject likes, enjoys, or finds agreeable. For most persons such states of mind are likely to include pleasure, but they need not be restricted to sensations or feelings. An individual may enjoy feeling very little, or nothing at all; indeed, on some conceptions, the good life consists in the uninterrupted duration of just such neutral or "empty" states of consciousness. The model must permit considerable variation of personal style and make room both for those who value turbulence and intensity and those who prefer tranquillity and the subtler shadings of mood. However the model is developed, an individual's interest remains always a function of the extent to which the individual has gained experiences that he/she finds satisfying or enjoyable.

Both models are subjective: the desire model permits individuals to determine their own objects of desire, and the experience model permits them to determine their own sources of enjoyment. The classical utilitarians (Bentham, Mill, Sidgwick) tended toward the experience model, though they did not maintain a clear distinction between the two accounts.[18] In their theories, utility was first identified with happiness and then happiness was in turn defined in terms of pleasure. However, in order to support this connection between pleasure and happiness, pleasure had to be interpreted broadly as any feeling that the individual enjoys and wishes to have prolonged (a similarly broad construal was given to pain).[19] "Pleasure" thus came to function as a technical term covering a much wider range of experience than the sensations principally associated with sex and food. Neoclassical utilitarians (modern utility theorists) have decisively settled on the desire model, defining utility in terms of preference. The older view was found by philosophers, and especially by economists, to be offensively mentalistic. Because experiences are states of mind private to their owners, it was difficult to see how any public, interpersonal measure of individual utility was possible. Desires and preferences have the advantage of being susceptible of a behavioristic analysis. What persons prefer can, in principle at least, be ascertained by observing what they choose. A sophisticated theory has since been constructed around the logic of preference and the structure of preference rankings; but its presupposition is still that there is some intimate connection between welfare and the satisfaction of preference.

The important differences between the desire and experience models are obscured by the ambiguity of the term "satisfaction." On the one hand a person's desire is satisfied when the appropriate proposition is true. On the other hand a person is satisfied when he/she is content or pleased. My having a desire satisfied is no guarantee that I will be satisfied; the contrary is an everyday occurrence. Talk of individual satisfaction wanders freely back

18. The lines were blurred for Bentham and Mill by the psychological thesis that pleasure is the only thing people desire as an end. Even so, getting what one wants may not entail getting the pleasure one expects.

19. See, for example, Sidgwick (1962), p. 127.

and forth across the desire/experience boundary. It is easy to assume that an adequate explication of one sense of satisfaction is also an adequate explication of the other.

Although the desire model now furnishes the orthodox view, it is hopeless as an analysis of interest or welfare. Having a want satisfied is neither necessary nor sufficient for having one's interest furthered. It is not necessary since we may enjoy things we do not desire. If I stumble across something accidentally or am persuaded to try it by friends and then find myself liking it, my good fortune cannot be a matter of my desire for the thing being satisfied, for I had no such desire. If I subsequently come to desire the thing, then its having enhanced my well-being is the cause of its being desired; the former cannot therefore be analyzed in terms of the latter. Many (not all) of our desires have just this origin: we come to want things because we have found them agreeable or advantageous. This seems particularly the case for infants and nonhuman animals, to whom we would hesitate to attribute propositional desires. If something can be good for (promote the welfare of) such beings, then welfare cannot be a function of want satisfaction.

It is even clearer that having a want satisfied is not sufficient for having one's interest furthered. The counterpart of a pleasant surprise is the disappointment we experience on attaining an object of desire and finding that it does not measure up to our expectations. On the desire model our welfare has nevertheless been promoted, but how is this consistent with the regret we feel? At the extreme we may be actually harmed by having some desire satisfied, as when I want to stroll in a meadow that I fail to realize is inhabited by an irascible bull. Those who favor the desire model usually attempt to accommodate these cases by connecting welfare with informed rather than actual desires, or by invoking the full hierarchy of desires (including my desire not to be chased by bulls). But disappointment or harm is possible even under ideal conditions, where all that remains concealed from me is the fact that I will detest the object of my pursuit once I have attained it. To require *that* information to be in-cluded is simply to trim the desire model so that it coincides with the experience model.

Individual welfare is tied to particular persons: if my welfare is served, *I* am better off. Desires are tied to particular persons by ownership (my desires are the desires that *I* have) but not by object. I can in principle desire anything, including objects and states of affairs that have no connection with me and would not affect me if realized. Desires can range beyond the lives of their owners both spatially and temporally. Some objects of desire (a change of government, an end to whaling) may or may not af-fect me if achieved, depending on the circumstances. Others (new forms of energy for the twenty-second century) cannot af-fect me, in principle, since they can come to exist only after my demise. It is not odd that people should want things that cannot come about until after their deaths (at least it is not odd unless one assumes that people can want only what they think will promote their own welfare). When these wants are satisfied, how can they promote the welfare of their owners? There may have been countless people who died before the present century and who wanted some human being to fly or run a four-minute mile; have the Wright brothers and Roger Bannister made them all better off?

The desire model is particularly inept at distinguishing selfish from selfless desires.[20] It is a truism that we sometimes willingly subordinate our own well-being to that of others, as when you generously offer me the last space in the lifeboat. On the desire model my welfare is identical with the satisfaction of my desires. It does not follow that I always aim at my own welfare, but it does follow that I always achieve it when I get what I aim at, however altruistic my aim may be. Self-sacrificial behavior thus

20. It has been criticized on this ground by Richard Brandt (and defended by Mark Overvold) in papers delivered at the 1978 Virginia Polytechnic Institute conference on utilitarianism.

becomes a conceptual impossibility. The difference between a self-interested and an altruistic desire lies in the impact upon the agent of having the desire satisfied. Perhaps the desire model can manage to draw this distinction. One means is ready to hand: self-interested desires are those whose object, immediate or long-range, is some state of mind valued by the agent. But choosing this route reduces the desire model to the experience model by limiting the objects of desires to experiences found agreeable by the subject.

If something enhances my welfare, it must, directly or indirectly, immediately or in the long run, either produce states of mind I find agreeable or prevent states of mind I find disagreeable. A good or worthwhile life is one in which experiences of the first sort outnumber or outweigh experiences of the second sort. Individuals will determine their own sources of enjoyment or satisfaction and they will also determine their own ordering of these sources—these are matters of individual taste and here we should expect both uniformity and diversity. We are so constituted that certain things are likely to please us and others likely to displease us; further, there are some objects that promise to be indispensable to virtually any schedule of personal satisfactions. But beyond the core of primary goods generated by our common humanity, all of us will seek our own sources of meaning and enrichment. The good life can be only a life experienced as fulfilling by its subject. There is thus no unique pattern for the good life; there are merely good or worthwhile lives.

A mentalistic account of welfare, and thus of individual utility, raises questions about the measurement of utility. It is important to remember that these are questions as much for egoism as for utilitarianism—except for the additional demand that the measure be interpersonal. It seems foolhardy to expect that utility, construed as the having of agreeable experiences, can be reckoned in cardinal units. But any agent who is conducting a life knows a great deal about what will and what will not bring enjoyment or satisfaction. Past experience is not an infallible guide, but it does enable us to size up alternative directions open to us and make reasonable choices among them. There is in this nothing that all of us do not manage every day; the process is essentially unmysterious, though it is often complex and uncertain. It can seem mysterious only when more precision, and more quantification, are demanded than the nature of the problem allows. If I can know what is likely to please me, I can also know what is likely to please you; indeed I may be a better judge on some occasions of your welfare than of my own for I have less at stake. If we wish to know what will cause others joy or suffering, we may rely to a considerable extent on what they want for themselves; self-interested wants, though not constitutive of welfare, may serve as rough guides to welfare. Sometimes, however, we may need to override these wants, for we may occupy a better vantage point than the agents themselves. In such cases they are still sovereign over what counts as their own welfare— they must come to acknowledge that they are better off in their own terms—but they are not infallible authorities on the best means of promoting that welfare.

An egoist (or a tuist) must be able to trade off goods against evils within the boundaries of a single life. For these trade-offs, intrapersonal comparisons of agreeable and disagreeable states of mind suffice. Utilitarianism requires the additional step of trading off goods and evils across personal boundaries; it thus requires interpersonal comparisons of agreeable and disagreeable states of mind. The additional step does not raise new issues of principle, for we often know enough about the sensibilities of individuals to compare effects upon their well-being. Only the sceptical dogma that each individual has privileged access to his own experiences and can know nothing of the minds of others could make this process seem inexplicable. Some interpersonal comparisons will be better grounded than most intrapersonal ones: the reliability of our estimates in particular cases vary with the complexity of the alternatives available, the ambivalence of those affected by them, the uncertainty of our information, and so on. In large-scale social decision-making we must rely on standard assumptions about individual wants and needs; here there is no opportunity for finer tuning. On a more personal level, however, we often know enough to strike more delicate balances. The notion of summing individual utilities is thus misleading in suggesting that we literally add units of welfare for different persons. But when we choose a course of action on the ground that the balance of its benefits (to those who gain by it) over its costs (to those who lose) is more favorable than that produced by any alternative, we are aiming at the greatest net social utility. And that is all that utilitarianism requires that we be able to do.

22. *The Good and the Right*

A qualified moral theory weakens absolute individualist constraints on interpersonal conduct. Classical utilitarianism has been criticized on the ground that it abandons such constraints entirely. Social utility is the sum of the goods of distinct individuals. If the treatment of individuals is regulated only by this aggregative calculus, then it seems that in principle any course of action, however exploitive, can be justified by a sufficient social payoff. Utilitarianism thus appears to its critics to place no individualist limit on permissible interpersonal trade-offs of welfare. Individuals are simply so many locations for gains and losses on the social balance sheet and the maximization of utility pays little heed to the boundaries between their lives. As John Rawls has put it, "utilitarianism does not take seriously the distinction between persons."[21]

Whether this complaint is justified depends on the place utilitarians find in their theory for specific rights and duties—and thus for specific moral rules. Although utilitarianism is not a

21. Rawls (1972), p. 27.

rights theory, it does not follow that it assigns no weight to individual rights. All versions of the classical theory are committed to social utility as the basic measure of the moral value of the objects they evaluate. If we fix the content of utility by adopting the experience model, formulations of the principle of utility (and thus versions of the theory) will still vary in at least two respects: the category of moral value they employ and the objects they evaluate. The moral concepts available to the utilitarian may be divided into those that admit of a comparative form (thus possessing degrees) and those that do not. The former include "desirable," "valuable," "worthwhile," and so forth, and their negative counterparts; their paradigm is "good" (and "bad" or "evil"). The latter include the familiar deontic concepts "duty" and "obligation" and their negative counterparts; their paradigm is "right" (and "wrong"). Moral principles may be principles of good or principles of right. Individualist constraints are formulated as individual duties and rights, and thus as rules of right. Their status within a version of classical utilitarianism is determined by their relation to the principle of utility.

Principles of good order the alternatives open to agents in terms of some natural property that admits of degrees. This ordering enables agents to determine what it is best for them to do. Principles of right assign the alternatives open to agents to some set of mutually exclusive and exhaustive categories (right/wrong, required/permissible/prohibited, etc.). This assignment enables agents to determine what it is right for them to do or what they have a duty to do. Social utility is a natural property that admits of degrees. If there is to be a fit between the natural properties of objects and their moral value, the principle of utility must employ some comparative moral concept. The principle of utility must therefore be a principle of good, and utilitarianism must at bottom be a theory of the good. Utilitarians commonly assume that the alternatives available for choice can be ordered in terms of their utility, and that the alternative that will produce most utility (the maximal alternative) is best (has the highest moral value). Given that utility is comparative and that deontic moral notions are not, the problem is to generate rules of right from the principle of utility.

Utilitarians may opt for either a direct or an indirect theory of the right. On a direct theory the deontic status of an object is entirely determined by the utility of that very object, and thus by its position in the utility ranking of alternatives open to the agent. The deontic status of members of a set of alternatives can thus be read off their ranking, and there is a direct correlation between an object's goodness and its rightness. The familiar forms of act-utilitarian theory are all direct theories.[22] Maximizing theories require agents always to do the best thing open to them.[23] It is also possible to devise nonmaximizing direct theories. On an indirect theory the deontic status of an object is wholly or partly determined by the utilities of some other objects. Because of the independent role of these further utilities, the deontic status of members of a set of alternatives cannot be read off their ranking, and there is no direct correlation between an object's goodness and its rightness. The familiar forms of rule-utilitarian theory are all indirect theories. The best known is the generalized counterpart of a maximizing act-utilitarianism on which a particular act is right if and only if the general practice of acts of that kind maximizes utility and is otherwise wrong. It is also possible to devise nonmaximizing indirect theories.

It has usually been assumed that classical utilitarianism is a direct maximizing theory.[24] Although there is some support for

22. For the standard distinction between act-utilitarian and rule-utilitarian theories, see Lyons (1965).

23. Moore's version of ideal utilitarianism is a maximizing direct theory. See Moore (1903), chap. 5 and (1912), chap. 2.

24. This reputation is largely due to the influence of Moore's critique of Mill in (1903), chap. 3.

this assumption in the writings of the classical utilitarians,[25] a maximizing theory can make little sense of the social function of rules of right. Deontic concepts express requirements and prohibitions (absolute or qualified). They tell us, not what it is good or nice or generous to do, but what it is callous or indecent not to do. Rules of right formulate those minimal standards of mutual respect whose shared acknowledgment is a prerequisite for the very possibility of a society and whose social enforcement is therefore appropriate. For this reason rules of right are primarily both interpersonal and negative: they forbid us to threaten the liberty, integrity, or well-being of others. The duties they enjoin thus typically correlate with individual rights. The rules leave room for overachieving (supererogation), since we can generally do more for others than merely respect their rights, but they leave no room for underachieving. Rules that require us always to do the best thing open to us cannot play this minimalist role. Their enforcement would be appropriate in a community of saints, but they are too demanding for human societies. Utility maximization may be a plausible moral ideal, but it cannot serve as a standard of duty.

The failure of a maximizing theory could motivate utilitarians to explore other forms of direct theory. But indirect theories have greater promise, especially those that model the status of moral rules on the status of positive laws. The formal counterparts of conventional moral rules, laws are distinguished chiefly by the special institutions devised for their adoption and enforcement. Like moral rules, they impose duties and assign rights. Like moral rules, they are largely concerned with regulating interpersonal conduct, and especially with protecting individual security and integrity. A utilitarian theory of law has two distinct levels. At the design level we aim at devising the system of rules

25. Chiefly in Sidgwick (1962); see, e.g., pp. 411, 492. Bentham is less clearly committed to a direct theory, and Mill is clearly not committed to one. For the interpretation of Mill's theory, see Brown (1972, 1973), Lyons (1976, 1977, 1979), Copp (1979), Sumner (1979).

and sanctions whose enforcement will maximize utility over the long run for a given society. That system then defines individuals' legal rights and duties. At the level of application direct appeal to utility (to what is best) is suppressed, since a system of rules will operate more efficiently (generate more social utility) if it defines offenses, sanctions, excuses, defenses, and so forth in a narrower and more specific manner. There will therefore be no blanket utilitarian defense available for committing offenses. There will, however, be some room for a defense of necessity, since general rules cannot provide in advance for all possible contingencies. But the primary role for the principle of utility lies in the design of the system, which then operates with an internal logic of its own.

Moral rules are the products of social convention rather than legislative decision. Their sanctions are generally milder, taking the form of social pressure and appeal to conscience, and their enforcement is informal and unofficial. But they play a social role similar in many respects to law, and they share much of the content of a legal system. A utilitarian derivation of moral rights and duties should therefore be patterned after its derivation of legal rights and duties. A social morality will contain (but will not be restricted to) rules of right. If such a morality is to be generally acknowledged in a pluralistic society, its requirements must focus on the public sphere, imposing standards of respect for others. A utilitarian will support that social morality whose adoption (by convention) and enforcement (by informal sanctions) will in the long run maximize utility. The rules of such a system will determine the content of moral rights and duties. Such rules will discourage direct appeal to utility (to what is best), since the system will operate more efficiently (generate more utility) if individuals make most of their moral decisions by simply applying the rules to particular cases. Some such appeal must, however, be available for moral emergencies, since rules that are straightforward enough to be learned and used cannot anticipate highly unusual circumstances. In a well-designed system it should be necessary to violate the rules on direct utilitarian grounds only in genuine cases of necessity, where observing them will lead to disaster.

Legal rights and duties are defined by the laws actually in force, regardless of their justification. Moral rights and duties, by contrast, are defined by those moral rules whose enforcement will maximize utility. The deontic status of a particular act is thus determined by the utility of a rule requiring (or forbidding) the performance of acts of that kind. For a particular act to be right (to have a duty to do it), the use of sanctions to encourage doing acts of that kind must maximize utility. For a particular act to be wrong (to have a duty not to do it) the use of sanctions to discourage doing acts of that kind must maximize utility. Given the costs involved in resorting to sanctions, our moral duties will be mostly negative, forbidding various forms of threat to the integrity of others. We may in addition have some duties to confer benefits upon others or at least to save them from harms, but these are likely to be limited. Moral duties, therefore, will largely correlate with individual rights. An indirect theory thus promises to derive rules of right, including rules safeguarding rights, which have a minimalist social function.[26]

An indirect theory of the right is a formula for the design of a social morality. Given the limited sympathies of individuals and the complexities of moral contexts, our interpersonal affairs will be better conducted if they are regulated by some shared set of specific rules. The enforcement of those rules will be partly a

---

26. On the utilitarian derivation of individual rights, see Lyons (1977). My views on the place of specific moral rules within a utilitarian framework owe much to Lyons (1976); however, I depart from Lyons in certain important respects. For a similar account, see Sartorius (1975), chap. 4, which, however, presupposes an act-utilitarian theory. The contractarian analogue of a utilitarian derivation of moral rules is attempted in Mackie (1977), chap. 7. Both contractarian and utilitarian theories have the virtue of grounding rights and duties in welfare (individual or social).

matter of bringing negative sanctions to bear on particular violations. But this piecemeal procedure is itself inefficient. A better
alternative is the internalization of the rules by members of society, so that conformity comes to be free and unforced, regulated primarily by conscience and especially by the internal controls of guilt and shame. This internalization is learned in the
course of moral education, which is in turn but a part of the
wider process of socialization. A well-ordered social morality is
one that answers to the requirements of utility, and which has
won for itself a high degree of voluntary conformity, with minimal reliance on external sanctions and, perforce, upon the
harsher penalties of the law.

An indirect theory of the right coupled with a direct theory of
the good is neither act-utilitarian nor rule-utilitarian. Like an
act-utilitarian theory it permits direct appeal to utility, but only
in assessing the goodness of acts. Its theory of the good, furthermore, is not tied to evaluating only acts; it can in principle measure the goodness of any object, and there is obviously a great
deal of emphasis placed upon the utility of rules and of an entire
system of social morality. The aim of the theory of the good is
the long-range maximization of social utility, and this aim may
lead it to focus on the macro level of social design rather than
the micro level of the evaluation of individual acts. Its theory of
the right requires us to take account of the utility of establishing
and securing conformity to moral rules; indeed it grounds the
deontic status of a particular act not strictly in the utility of the
corresponding rule but in the utility of a system of morality that
contains that rule.

Even an ideal system of moral rules whose enforcement maximizes utility cannot avoid conflicts between the good and the
right. There are limits to the extent to which general rules can
be finely tuned to particular circumstances. Rules are formulated
for standard cases. In nonstandard cases the rule may demand a
course of action that will clearly go badly, or may forbid doing

what will clearly be best. Where what is best conflicts with what is right, which part of the theory takes precedence? We must remember that we are here dealing with a system of rules designed to generate a maximum of social utility in the long run. It is an essential component of such a system that direct appeal to utility in particular cases be constrained. A system that permits each individual agent to aim at maximizing utility in each individual case will not itself maximize utility in the long run. Utilitarians therefore have a prima facie reason for abiding by the rules even when doing so may cost utility in the particular case, for they therefore contribute to the strengthening of an efficient system. If the system has been well designed, then the clear cases of divergence between the good and the right will occur in moral emergencies in which abiding by the rules will lead to catastrophe. In genuine cases of necessity utilitarians must violate the rules of right in order to do what is best. Rights and duties are thus doubly qualified by utility. In the first place, absolute rules are unlikely to be efficient since they do not adapt well to nonstandard circumstances.[27] Any rule can therefore be overridden in some cases by another rule. A utility-maximizing social morality will contain no absolute duties and no absolute rights. And in the second place, there will be utilitarian justification for violating even these loose and qualified rules in some particular cases.

The moral rules contained within an indirect theory of the right function as individualist constraints (though not strict ones) on interpersonal conduct. By limiting direct appeal to utility they provide immunities for individuals against exploitation by others, immunities that are expressed as (defeasible) rights. Since these rights are ultimately derived from a theory of the good, utilitarianism also supplies a principle for ordering rights

27. Mackie likewise argues that rational contractors will not settle on absolute rules; see (1977), chap. 7.

and duties and for deciding hard cases. An indirect utilitarian theory of right thus promises to avoid both the rigidity of absolutism and the indeterminancy of intuitionism without sacrificing essential protection of the integrity of individuals. Rights can be taken seriously without being treated as morally basic.

CHAPTER SIX

Life and Death

A direct utilitarian theory of the good conjoined with an indirect theory of the right can serve as the deep structure for moral rules that allocate particular rights and duties. The remaining task is to show that it can also serve as the deep structure of a moderate view of abortion. Abortion is a difficult moral issue largely because it challenges us to decide whose rights or welfare we are to acknowledge in our moral decision-making. It is not a simple matter, therefore, to derive conclusions about abortion from a moral theory. If utilitarianism is the foundation for a moderate view of abortion, it must support both a sentience criterion of moral standing and a differential moral evaluation of prethreshold and postthreshold abortions.

The route from classical utilitarianism to a sentience criterion is broad and plain. The case for a differential treatment of abortions is, however, more complex. Abortion lies at the intersection of two different kinds of moral problem: homicide and reproduction. The implications of utilitarianism for the morality of abortion will not emerge until its treatment of both problems has been explored.

23. *Moral Standing Revisited*

Moral standing was defined in Section 5 in terms of the right to life. This definition was adequate as long as attention was confined to theories in which rights are basic moral facts. Now that such theories have been discarded the definition must be generalized. A moral theory consists of a set of norms to guide moral agents in their conduct toward themselves and (especially) others. In any such theory three elements may be distinguished:

(1) *Moral subjects:* the class of beings who are to regulate their conduct by the norms of the theory.

(2) *Moral objects:* the class of beings whose treatment by moral subjects is regulated by the norms of the theory.

(3) *Content:* the kind of treatment that the theory's norms stipulate must be accorded moral objects by moral subjects.

The first two elements jointly specify the *scope* of a theory: the classes of entities that it recognizes either as agents or patients. Moral objects may be subdivided into primary and secondary. A primary object is one to which the theory grants standing or significance in its own right. These are the entities for which the theory requires some special form of consideration or respect. To be designated a primary object is to be morally privileged. A secondary object is one that is not granted this intrinsic significance. The appropriate treatment of secondary objects will be derivative from the norms for primary objects. To be designated a secondary object is to be morally underprivileged.

The primary/secondary distinction separates the two categories of moral status. To be a primary object is to have moral standing; to be a secondary object is to lack standing.[1] Every moral theory implicitly or explicitly divides entities into those with standing and those without it. The content of a theory determines its interpretation of moral standing. Although the concept of having standing (being a primary object) is the common property of all theories, interpretations of that concept are theory-specific. In a rights theory moral subjects are those individuals capable of having duties. Primary moral objects are those entities that possess rights (in particular, the right to life), and secondary objects are those entities that lack rights. The content of a particular rights theory will determine the kinds of rights

1. That a theory's scope displays a subject/object division should remind us again that an appropriate criterion for counting as a subject (being a moral agent) may be an inappropriate criterion for counting as a primary object (having moral standing). Any application of a subject criterion to the context of primary objects must be justified.

owned by primary objects and the kinds of duties borne by subjects. The earlier narrow definition of moral standing is thus its interpretation in a theory in which rights are basic moral facts.

That interpretation is obviously unsuited to classical utilitarianism, which does not treat rights as basic. The theory determines the moral value of objects by reference to social utility, which is an aggregate of individual utilities. The primary/secondary distinction for utilitarians must be drawn in terms of this calculus. To have moral standing is to have one's utility included in the calculation of social utility; to lack moral standing is to have one's utility (if any) excluded. As befits a theory whose principle of good contains no individualist constraints, utilitarianism gives the notion of moral standing a purely aggregative interpretation.

A criterion of moral standing determines a division of objects into primary and secondary. A moral theory must provide some grounding for its own criterion of moral standing. Since a particular theory is partly defined by its scope, and thus by its division of primary and secondary objects, any derivation of a criterion of moral standing may appear trivial (since the whole entails each of its parts). However, this need not be so, for a theory's content may point the way toward its scope. In a rights theory the content of its rights may suggest the kind of entities that are appropriate bearers of those rights. Thus a theory of inviolable liberty-rights may draw the circle narrowly around autonomous, rational creatures—competent adult human beings, say, and their equals.[2] A theory that includes weaker rights may settle on a weaker criterion, one that distributes moral standing more widely.[3] Since rights protect autonomy, we should expect some degree of capacity for autonomous behavior to figure in any criterion grounded in a rights theory. Rights theories may be

2. As does Nozick (1974), pp. 33ff. Nozick also urges some (undefined) weaker moral standing for nonhuman animals (and children, the incompetent, etc.?).

3. As do Feinberg (1974) and Regan (1975).

viewed as so many possible specifications of a rights proto-theory whose basic commitment is to the protection and promotion of liberty and autonomy.[4] It may be that the requirements of this proto-theory will themselves uniquely fix a criterion of moral standing. If not, then different criteria will be appropriate for different species of the genus.

Utilitarianism has a proto-theory that uniquely fixes its criterion of moral standing. Social utility is a compound of individual utilities. Individual utility is a measure of individual welfare that is in turn defined in terms of experiences found agreeable or disagreeable by their subject. Utilitarian impartiality requires that the utilities of all creatures affected by an action be included in calculating the social utility of that action, and that equal utility count equally regardless of its location. All and only sentient beings are capable of having experiences that they like or dislike. All and only sentient beings, therefore, have utilities. If having moral standing means having one's utility included in the calculus, sentience must be the criterion of moral standing. A criterion that included any nonsentient beings would be redundant, and a criterion that excluded any sentient beings would be discriminatory.

Utilitarians are therefore committed to acknowledging the moral relevance of enjoyment and suffering regardless of its spatial and temporal location and the kind of creature who is its subject. They are at liberty to deny standing only to creatures who have no utilities to be included. They must therefore extend moral standing to many nonhuman animals.[5] Furthermore, the impartiality condition prohibits degrees of standing, since the equal utilities of all beings must count equally. The only form of standing in a utilitarian morality is full standing. This does not entail that all creatures must be accorded identical treatment. The treatment appropriate for any given individual will be determined by an impartial reckoning of the utilities of

4. In Nozick's terms, such a theory would be the common parent of both side-constraint and end-state theories of autonomy.

5. As does Singer (1975), chap. 1.

all affected creatures. Different creatures may not be equally af-fected; their utilities are then unequal. If equal utilities count equally, unequal utilities count unequally. This is easiest to see if we conceive of utility as measurable in interpersonal units. To accord moral standing to you and me is to count each unit of your utility for precisely as much as each unit of mine. However, if giving you a new pair of shoes will increase your utility by more units than giving me the shoes will increase mine, then that is a justification for extending favorable treatment to you. Equal counting of the equal utility of all sentient creatures does not require precisely the same treatment of all sentient creatures.

What is true for individuals is also true for species.[6] Utilitari-ans are committed to interspecific as well as interpersonal com-parisons of utility. Sentient nonhuman animals have the same moral standing as human beings: their equal utilities still count equally (and unequal utilities unequally). When adjusting trade-offs between species, account must be taken of both the sensitivity and the sensibility of the creatures involved. In some respects nonhuman animals suffer more easily and more keenly than we do; impartiality may then require stricter protection of their interests than of ours. But by and large more developed creatures have greater capacities for enjoyment and suffering than less developed ones. The life of the average human being is richer and fuller than that of the average trout or baboon. Human beings have a greater range of responsiveness than other animals and are thus affected by a greater variety of stimuli. Though human and nonhuman animals may have the same moral status, in many cases human utilities will simply outweigh nonhuman ones.[7] Equal consideration of utility again does not imply equal treatment.

6. See Singer (1975), pp. 17ff.

7. But not in all cases, nor even in the ones we most take for granted: the use of animals for food and as experimental subjects (see Singer 1975). Extending utilitarian impartiality to animals requires that we become vegetarians (at least as long as intensive farming practices persist) and that

This is not the place to work out the implications of utilitarianism for our treatment of nonhuman animals. It is enough that the theory supports a sentience criterion and thus ascribes moral significance to the threshold of sentience in the phylogenetic order. What must also be shown is that it ascribes moral significance to the threshold of sentience in the ontogenetic order.

24. Causing Death

On a differential view abortion straddles the boundary between two different categories of act: not creating a human being (with moral standing) and destroying such a being once it has been created. Early (prethreshold) abortions share the former category with the use of contraceptives, whereas late (postthreshold) abortions share the latter category with infanticide and other forms of homicide. Common-sense morality treats this boundary as highly significant: if agents choose not to reproduce and take steps (such as contraception) to carry out that choice, what they do is morally innocuous; whereas, if they choose to kill and take steps to carry out that choice, what they do is morally serious. It is the common acceptance of this boundary that underlies the intuitive plausibility of a differential view of abortion; the only additional ingredient needed is a sentience criterion of moral standing. Whether utilitarians can provide a foundation for a differential view will depend in part on how their theory treats the boundary. We need, therefore, to trace out the implications of the classical theory for causing death and preventing life.

Both kinds of act strain the resources of the theory. A utilitarian decision procedure is designed for contexts in which the existence (and therefore the number) of persons is not itself to be determined. In contexts with a fixed pool of persons it is possible in principle to calculate the way in which each available

---

we boycott inessential consumer goods whose testing inflicts suffering on animals.

course of action will affect the utility of each individual involved. This procedure is less straightforward when some courses of action will either reduce or expand the pool. In either of these cases utility calculations seem to require comparing the utility of existence to that of nonexistence. Moral problems of killing and reproduction are thus awkward for the theory.[8]

Of the two problematic kinds of act, killing is the easier for utilitarians to accommodate, since here a determinate individual has continued to exist up to the point of his/her demise. We therefore have no difficulty identifying the victim of a killing. Most of us regard homicide normally as a grave offense. The standard case is that in which the victim was a paradigm bearer of moral standing (a competent adult) and in which there were no special exculpating circumstances: the victim wished to live and faced the prospect of a satisfying life, the killing was intentional and undertaken for no proportionate cause (such as saving greater numbers of lives), the killing was unprovoked, and so forth. In the standard case homicide is murder, and murder (we all believe) is wrong. If a utilitarian is to explain why it is wrong he must begin by looking to its consequences. We may here distinguish two kinds of consequences a killing may have: its *central effects* are its consequences for the victim; its *side effects* are its consequences for others. Side effects are usually incurred by persons who continue to exist after the killing; they are not, therefore, problematic in principle for the theory. But the central effect of murder for the victim is his/her (subsequent) nonexistence. Common-sense morality plainly regards murder as wrong principally because of its central effects rather than its side effects (though the latter are not irrelevant). If murder is to be classified as an evil act by a utilitarian morality, then it must cause its victim some form of harm. But harm is interpreted by a utilitar-

8. The problems utilitarians encounter in dealing with the morality of killing have been emphasized in Henson (1971). I have discussed these issues at greater length in Sumner (1976).

ian in terms of experiences found disagreeable by their subject. If the dead can have no experiences, how can they be harmed by being killed? And if they are not harmed, then how can murder be evil?

Unraveling this puzzle requires showing how death can be a misfortune. To die is to cease to exist (permanently). For sentient beings the relevant mode of nonexistence is the extinction of consciousness; death, therefore, is a permanent end to consciousness.[9] Since death is (literally) nothing in itself, the misfortune of death must be sought in that of which it is the loss, namely, life. We have already a (rough) account of what makes a life good or worthwhile—states of mind valued by the person whose life it is. The alternative to death is (more) life. Death is a misfortune therefore, to the extent that further life would be a benefit.

Most harms are (literally) suffered and so presuppose the continued existence of their subject. But some are not. Losses or deprivations can be of two sorts. One can lose particular goods, in which case the subject of the loss continues to exist. But one can also lose all of life's goods at a blow and irrevocably, and then the subject of the loss ceases to exist. Consciousness is the condition of possessing any goods. To be permanently deprived of consciousness is to lose the possibility of any goods. But that is what it is like to die.[10] Death is ordinarily a great misfortune because ordinarily a great loss; its only peculiarity is that after it occurs there is no longer a subject of the loss. But there was, and that is the person upon whom the loss has been inflicted. To kill someone is therefore normally to cause that person a great loss and so a great harm.

The evil of murder is therefore located by utilitarians primarily

9. Which suggests the appropriateness of using cerebral, and especially cortical, criteria for determining death; see Veatch (1976), chaps. 1, 2.

10. An afterlife, whatever its peculiarities, presupposes the continuation of personal consciousness. If there is an afterlife, therefore, we do not really die (though if the afterlife is disembodied, our bodies are clearly mortal).

in its central utilities, as it ought to be. The side utilities of murder, however, are normally also not negligible. The life of an adult human being is generally deeply embedded in the lives of others: family, friends, associates, and so forth. The extinction of that life is a great loss (of the ordinary sort) for them as well. The side effects of murder thus confirm its evil. Utilitarianism is not unique in locating the evil of murder in its harmful consequences. Nor is it unique in allowing the costs of homicide to be compensated in cases of necessity by its benefits. But that justification cannot, ex hypothesi, apply to the standard case of murder.

That murder is evil can thus be shown by direct appeal to its utility. For an indirect deontic theory this is not sufficient to show that murder is wrong. For it to be wrong the existence of a law or conventional moral rule prohibiting it, reinforced by formal or informal sanctions, must maximize utility within a society. It is not difficult to see that this condition is satisfied. The most important function of both laws and moral rules is to require respect for the personal integrity of others; social life without this security quickly becomes intolerable.[11] Since security of life is the most basic form of protection needed for individuals to conduct their affairs, a legal system and a moral code must both condemn murder. On an indirect utilitarian theory, murder is therefore wrong.

The full dimensions of a utilitarian treatment of homicide are not exhausted by focusing on the standard case. Homicides may be nonstandard in two ways: either their victim is someone other than the paradigm bearer of moral standing (postthreshold abortion, infanticide, some cases of euthanasia) or their context is special in some respect (self-defense, negligence, insanity, necessity, some cases of euthanasia). A complete utilitarian treatment

11. The best demonstration of the utility of rules protecting personal security is still Mill (1969), chap. 5.

of nonstandard cases of homicide cannot be undertaken here. But it will be worthwhile to look at two special contexts: euthanasia and self-defense.

In cases of euthanasia the standard presumption that the victim has a worthwhile life to live may fail. When euthanasia can be justified, death is not a misfortune for the victim, and thus the harmful central effects of murder are nonexistent. Under the appropriate circumstances, then, utilitarians will not regard euthanasia as evil. Defining "appropriate circumstances" requires the notion of a life not worth living.[12] The value of a life is to be assessed from the point of view of its owner and in terms of its contents. Individuals will be able to order the possible lives open to them, at least roughly, in terms of the extent to which they find them desirable. Somewhere on that ordering there will be a balance point, such that lives above the point are found worth living and lives below the point found not worth living. To be worth living a life must be better than no life at all—better than not existing. Lives not worth living are therefore worse than nonexistence. In the context of homicide it is not entire possible lives whose worth in this sense must be compared, but only possible continuations of a life already under-way. Thus in most cases the individual whose life it is furnishes us with a point of view from which possible futures can be compared. But not in all cases; sometimes individuals are too immature or disordered to provide that point of view. In such cases we must resort to standard assumptions: the sorts of lives that a normal or reasonable person would find worth living, or not worth living.[13] Where individuals can furnish their own point of view then, since they are most intimately acquainted with their own tastes and preferences, they are normally the best judges of whether the future facing them is one worth enduring. The subjectivity of welfare and the sovereignty of taste make it inappropriate for

12. See Glover (1977), chap. 3.
13. Ibid., pp. 161–162.

others to impose their preferences. Thus individuals may quite rationally choose to lead lives filled with pain, if those lives also contain goods that *for them* compensate for this suffering.

Individuals may find themselves confronted with an unavoidable future that they know they will find intolerable. When this is the case (further) life ceases to be a benefit and death ceases to be a misfortune. Suicide may then be the prudent course of action, and if suicide is impractical, the assistance of others may be invoked. In these circumstances, voluntary euthanasia may be for the best.[14] Whether it is morally permissible is a further question. Both laws and moral rules are designed for standard cases; there are limits to the exceptions and qualifications that they can embody without becoming too complex to serve their regulatory purpose. There are good reasons for making the fewest possible inroads on the prohibition of homicide, since every exception may provide a loophole to be exploited by the unscrupulous and thus may reduce the general level of security of life. On the other hand a blanket prohibition of euthanasia will force some unlucky individuals to endure avoidable misery. Some balance must be struck between the protection of life and the prevention of needless suffering. One possibility is that victims be allowed to die but that no active steps may be taken to kill them. But this distinction between passive and active euthanasia is crude and provides no remedy for some of the most pressing cases.[15] Where euthanasia is concerned, no simple rule will respond to all possible exigencies and we may do better to aim at an appropriate mechanism for deciding particular cases—a mechanism rigorous enough to prevent abuses but also flexible enough to respond to immediate needs. The deontic status of euthanasia is thus not easy to determine, although there are surely some cases in which even active eauthanasia would be permitted by any set of rules for which there is a utilitarian justification.

14. Ibid., chaps. 13–14.
15. Ibid., chap. 7.

Some lives are so miserable that no rational person could want to live them, and it cannot then be wrong to end them.

Self-defense defines a category of justifiable homicide. If I kill you in order to repel your murderous attack upon me, it is your life or mine. In either case one of us dies, and it might seem that utilitarians ought to be indifferent between us. In terms of central utilities this is so, assuming that your life means as much to you as mine does to me. But this narrow approach neglects the side effects of our acts. If you succeed in your attack, the security of others is thereby diminished; if I succeed in my defense, that security is thereby enhanced. Since utilitarians have good reason for wishing to secure widespread protection of life, they also have good reason for regarding killing in self-defense (under the appropriate circumstances) as justifiable homicide. The same considerations determine its deontic status. Building no exception for self-defense into the prohibition of homicide will render victims defenseless against attack, whereas a too generous exception will furnish pretexts for murder. The proper venue for deciding hard cases is a court of law. There is thus reason for imposing a high standard on killing in self-defense. It is appropriate for such a standard to require a clear and present threat to some basic personal good (life, bodily integrity, liberty) that cannot be effectively repelled by any means short of killing. Homicides that satisfy this standard will be permissible, and those that violate it will be wrong. Others will simply be hard cases.

An indirect utilitarian theory of the right will thus permit some acts of euthanasia and some homicides in self-defense. This result has an obvious application to postthreshold abortions, since eugenic and therapeutic grounds are the only ones on which such abortions could be performed under a differential policy. Meanwhile, however, there is a more puzzling nonstandard case of homicide to ponder. Victims may deviate from the paradigm bearer of moral standing in a number of respects. One of these respects is age. The evil of death is directly proportional to the value of life. Where all other factors are equal, the value of life is directly proportional to its length. This is, presumably, why we regard it as more tragic that someone should die at twenty than at eighty: the less life already lived the more is left and so the more is lost. But then it seems to follow that, ceteris paribus, the younger the victim the worse it is for him/her to die. Infanticide is then a greater evil than the killing of older children or adolescents or adults—and (postthreshold) abortion is a greater evil still.

Some of our responses to the deaths of children do indeed follow this pattern. Thus we are especially horrified by child murder and by the butchery of infants and children by terrorists or soldiers. But our outrage in these cases seems to stem largely from the innocence and defenselessness of the victims (the fact they could not have *deserved* to die). The killing of children in such circumstances is an atrocity because it is cowardly and needless. If we strip away these sources of moral passion, then we certainly regard the death of a child as tragic; it is a waste that anyone should die so young. But do we regard the death of a younger child as a greater tragedy than that of an older child or an adolescent or an adult? Why do we regard the killing of children by their parents as a lesser evil than their murder by strangers? There are certainly mitigating circumstances on which we may fasten: infanticide by parents is generally less cold-blooded and often the product of stress or anxiety. But again if we set these factors aside, do we really believe that the death of an infant is a greater loss than the death of someone more mature, just because the infant was younger and had more life still to come?

In such cases we seem to be responding in part to defects of knowledge. An infant's or child's life has not yet developed to the point where its ultimate course is visible. We know little, therefore, of whether it will be long or short, blissful or miserable. Where we are ignorant of what the child has lost we are also ignorant of the cost of death for it. The life of a child is not yet fully formed, does not yet possess a determinate shape. The death of a child is a statistical loss, since in all likelihood the child's life would otherwise have been worth living. But it is more difficult to see it as a loss for a particular determinate person, since this particular person is not yet fully determinate. But how much do we want to rest on these epistemic factors? If we could foresee accurately the future course of a life, would our attitude alter?

Central effects would lead us to expect that, other factors equal, the evil of death is directly proportional to the remaining duration of life. If our evaluations depart from this pattern, we are probably attending to side effects. As a life develops and acquires a determinate form it becomes more thoroughly and intricately woven into the lives of other persons. A developed life has individuality: it is the life of just this person with just these idiosyncrasies, habits, interests, tastes, ambitions, roles, bonds of affection, dependencies, and so on. A developed life is a concrete reality that can become a unique and irreplaceable part of the lives of others. There is no one quite like you for parents to dote on, friends to enjoy, lovers to treasure. When such a life vanishes a vacuum remains in the lives of those who have been intimately connected with it. Undeveloped lives, which lack this rich fabric of connections, are more easily replaced. A mature fetus or a young infant is still largely a potential individual. Its death is a loss, but the vacuum is more readily filled—even for the parents, who can set about having another child.[16]

It is largely side utilities such as these which seem to explain why our intuitive measure of the tragedy of death is not linear with the age of the victim. Perhaps we find the death of persons

16. One reason that abortion has traditionally been treated as a less serious offense than infanticide is that we cannot know the victim, both because it is hidden from us and also because there is at this stage little to know and to support bonds of affection. This is also the reason that quickening has often been selected as the point at which protection of life begins; when the fetus can be felt, then we have some contact with it as a particular individual.

in the prime of life the most tragic of all, partly because they tend to have the most complex networks of associations with others. Another reason we are inclined to regard (postthreshold) abortion and infanticide as morally less serious than murder lies in the fact that social rules forbidding these acts cannot play quite the same role as rules prohibiting murder. Such rules can, if they are effective, protect the lives of fetuses and infants, but they cannot save their beneficiaries from fear or anxiety. Laws and moral rules are principally designed so that members of society can set about their own projects secure from the fear of aggression. The very young have no projects and also no sense of being threatened by others. One of the justifying aims of homicide laws thus cannot apply to either abortion or infanticide.

25. *Preventing Life*

Homicide is more easily accommodated within a utilitarian framework than is reproduction. When a person is killed we can identify both the subject and the nature of the harm done. Killing a person deprives that person of further existence but it does not alter the fact that he/she once existed. To reproduce is to create a unique new life; if *that* act of reproduction had not occurred, *that* life would never have existed. Reproduction thus affects the number of persons who *ever exist*. And so, therefore, does electing not to reproduce (e.g., by the use of contraceptives).

When a particular agent is faced with a moral decision, we may distinguish between two categories of persons who may be affected by the outcome of that decision. *Independent persons* are all those who will exist (at some time) regardless of the course of action chosen by the agent. *Dependent persons* are all those who will exist (at some time) only if some particular course of action is chosen by the agent.[17] The (timeless) existence of indepen-

17. Or some member of a subset of the available alternatives, if there is more than one way of bringing a particular person into existence.

dent persons is thus causally unaffected by this agent's decision in this context, whereas the existence of dependent persons is not. All persons extant either before or at the time of decision are independent, for it is not within the agent's power to bring it about that they never exist. Only future persons can be dependent persons. In most decision contexts all affected persons are independent, for we are not usually deciding whether to create new persons. But when individuals are deciding whether to have children, one person (the child they will have if they so decide) is dependent.[18] We may now adapt to the reproductive context the distinction between central effects and side effects drawn in the previous section. The central effects of reproduction are its effects for its dependent person—the new life that is thereby created. Its side effects are its effects for all independent persons—parents, family, acquaintances, other members of society, and (independent) future generations. That side utilities must be included by utilitarians in evaluating the morality of reproduction is obvious; the problem is what to do with central utilities.

Moral questions of reproduction (like questions of abortion) can arise in a personal context in which individuals (or couples) are deciding whether to have children, or in a political context in which societies are choosing population policies; the theoretical problems for utilitarians are the same in both contexts. Because the personal context is the simpler, we will focus on it.[19] Let us assume that a woman is deciding whether to have a child.[20] The project she envisages is both the bearing and rearing of the child, the latter part of the project either alone or with the

18. For convenience, I shall assume that what is at stake is whether to have a child now (rather than, say, three children over the next six years) and that the birth will not be multiple.

19. I have discussed these issues in the social context in Sumner (1978).

20. Again for convenience, I shall treat the reproductive decision as though it is being made unilaterally by a woman (men cannot make such unilateral decisions). We might imagine a single woman choosing to become pregnant by artificial insemination. Alternatively, a couple may be considered as a unitary agent.

participation of others. This project will consume a great deal of her time, energy, and resources for the next twenty years or so. There are also other projects open to her (hobbies, adventures, careers, etc.) that could fill roughly the same space in her life over that period. Selecting one of these possible projects imposes opportunity costs in restricting her ability to pursue the others.[21] Reproduction is unique among her options in increasing the number of persons; it alone affects a dependent person and has central effects. All of the other options are therefore so many possible ways of not reproducing.

A utilitarian must treat her decision as possessing a moral dimension. Moral issues arise when an agent's decision will affect the welfare of others. Even if we leave the dependent person out of the account, the addition of further individuals in a world of finite resources cannot fail to affect the well-being of at least some independent persons. In such a world, having a child is an act that must be considered from the moral point of view. Of course, it may also be considered from nonmoral points of view. The woman may simply think of it as a project that would enrich (or impoverish) her life, just as other projects might. But she must not neglect its impact on others. How, then, are utilitarians to compare reproduction with the nonreproductive possibilities open to her? What, in particular, are they to do with its central utilities?

Different answers to this question have generated different versions of utilitarianism. Two kinds of revision of the classical theory have been proposed. The first alters the definition of social utility from the sum of individual utilities to the average (per capita) of individual utilities. The classical theory is a *total* theory, the revision an *average* theory.[22] The second imposes re-

21. The options are exclusive alternatives only if each is construed as filling all of the available space in her life. Combinations of partial projects are of course possible.

22. See Rawls (1971), pp. 161ff., and Sikora (1975). Of the classical utilitarians only Sidgwick explicitly considered (and rejected) the average theory; see Sidgwick (1962), pp. 415–416. See also Sumner (1978), note 8.

strictions on the inclusion of central utilities in the calculation of social utility. The classical theory is an *open* theory, the revision a *restricted* theory. Though the two kinds of revision differ in nature and implications, they are motivated by a common conviction that the classical theory handles moral problems of population ineptly. Its alleged ineptness is rooted in its inclusion of central utilities on the same footing as side utilities. Both the revisions abandon this casual acceptance of central utilities, either by redefining social utility or by placing constraints on the counting of central utilities.

The classical and the average theory are extensionally equivalent for all cases in which no dependent persons are involved, for in those cases the average utility of each course of action open to the agent is its total utility divided by a constant (the number of independent persons). The theories diverge, however, in their treatment of reproduction. If the dependent person will have a life that is worth living (one with positive utility) but whose utility will be below the average for all independent persons, creating that person will produce a gain in total utility (other factors equal) but a loss in average utility. This difference will alter the ranking of reproduction against nonreproductive projects, and thus will alter its moral value. The average theory is more conservative about adding new persons than the classical theory. If reproduction is to generate an increase in social utility, the central utility it contributes must be greater than the existing average.

There is more than one form of restricted theory. A *discount* theory gives the utilities of dependent persons a lesser weight than the equal utilities of independent persons. No one seems to have proposed a discount theory only for central utilities, though some have favored discounting the utilities of all future persons.[23] An *asymmetrical* theory counts negative central utility (a dependent life not worth living) against reproduction but does not count positive central utility (a dependent life worth

23. See Williams (1978).

living) in favor of reproduction.[24] Finally, a *closed* theory simply excludes central utilities altogether.[25]

If we think of the classical (total, open) theory, the average theory, and the varieties of restricted theory as so many possible specifications of proto-utilitarianism, there is an initial presumption in favor of the classical theory. Utility consists in the having by a subject of experiences which that subject likes or enjoys. Utility is thus an occurrence or state of affairs. The organizing idea of utilitarianism is that this state of affairs is a good thing in itself, whenever and wherever it occurs. It is because this state of affairs is intrinsically valuable that its production is the appropriate measure of the moral value of actions. It is because more of it is better than less that social utility is an increasing aggregative function of individual utilities. Agents have available to them a variety of means for realizing this state of affairs. For the purpose of moral decision these means are to be compared solely in terms of their efficiency; one means is superior to another in a given context if (all things considered) it will produce more utility. Sometimes agents will be able to choose between producing only side utilities—making (independent) people happy—and producing both side utilities and central utilities—making happy (dependent) people. When making this choice their stan-

24. Jan Narveson has advocated an asymmetrical theory in Narveson (1967b, 1973, 1978). See also Govier (1979). It is sometimes difficult to distinguish between those who advocate an asymmetrical counting of central utilities and those who merely wish to preserve the deontic asymmetry of common sense: that one can be obligated not to have a child because its life will be horrible, but one cannot be obligated to have a child because its life will be happy. The latter is not in dispute; I argue below that the classical theory will support this asymmetry.

25. See Narveson (1967b, 1973, 1978), Singer (1976), Bennett (1978), and Govier (1979). The open/closed issue is also discussed (in other terminology) by Derek Parfit in Parfit (1976a, 1976b) and in an unpublished paper entitled "Overpopulation"; see also Glover (1977), chap. 4. A closed theory is of course inconsistent with an asymmetrical theory, a fact that leads me to wonder whether Narveson and Govier really mean to embrace both.

dard again ought to be efficiency: the more utility (all things considered) the better. But only the classical theory employs this standard.

Any version of a restricted theory obviously violates utilitarian impartiality by counting the utilities of dependent persons (in one way or another) for less than the utilities of independent persons. It is precisely the point of restricted theories to violate impartiality in the case of central utilities. The average theory also violates impartiality, though less blatantly.[26] If an agent has the choice of producing a certain quantity of central utility and the same quantity of side utility, then the average theory will favor the latter, since it returns a higher average. The average theory counts the utilities of dependent persons for less than the equal utilities of independent persons. All of the revisions of the classical theory thus violate the impartiality rule in one way or another. One of the attractions of utilitarianism is precisely its rigorous impartiality, its commitment to counting utilities without distinction of their owners' race, gender, species, or spatiotemporal location. Dependent persons differ from independent persons only in the fact that their very existence is causally dependent on a given agent's decision in a given context. If no other distinction will justify partiality, why should this one?

The straight route from proto-utilitarianism thus leads to the classical theory. Some counterbalancing reason is needed to incline one toward revisionism. Two such reasons are commonly offered: that there is something odd about counting central utilities on a par with side utilities, and that the classical theory has unacceptable implications for moral problems of reproduction. If these allegations fail, there is no impediment to retaining the classical theory.

The oddity that some find in including central utilities can take a variety of forms. For one thing, such utilities seem to resist being captured in the format of benefits and harms, whereas

26. See Sumner (1978), pp. 101–103.

side utilities do not.[27] Both benefits and harms are comparative:
I benefit you when I make you better off than you would otherwise have been, and I harm you when I make you worse off.
Benefits and harms thus presuppose the possibility of comparing
the implications for your welfare of different ways in which I
could affect you. If a woman has a child, her decision has affected that child (it has caused the child to exist). But how
could she thereby either benefit or harm the child, since the only
alternative is that the child never exist? The child has been benefited only if otherwise it would have been worse off, and harmed
if otherwise it would have been better off. But in this case it
would not otherwise have *been*.

It is certainly true that creating a person cannot be benefiting
or harming the person in the usual way—the way, that is, in
which we benefit or harm independent persons. But why should
we tailor our model for benefits and harms exclusively to independent persons? We have already seen that death is a harm for a
person when the remainder of the person's life would have been
worth living, and is a benefit when the remainder of that life
would not have been worth living. In these cases the alternative
to (continued) existence is (subsequent) nonexistence, and so
we compare the utility of existing to that of not existing. Why
cannot we do the same for entire lives? If a woman has a happy
child (one with a life worth living) then she has benefited that
child, since its life is better for it than never having existed at all.
Likewise, if she has a miserable child (one with a life not worth
living) then she has harmed that child. Nothing prevents our
comparing life with the alternative of nonexistence. But then
nothing prevents our construing central utilities as benefits or
harms.[28]

The emphasis placed by some utilitarians on benefits and
harms (utility increments and decrements) may result from their

27. Narveson (1967), pp. 65ff.
28. As has been recognized by Parfit (1976b).

unconscious flirtation with rights theories. If you have a right, it must be possible both for that right to be respected and for it to be violated. Either respecting your right or violating it requires your existence (at some time). You cannot therefore have a right to come into existence (which could not be violated) or a right not to come into existence (which could not be respected). The act of creating you can neither respect nor violate your rights. In evaluating reproduction, a rights theory must exclude (its version of) central effects, namely, the rights of the dependent person. Rights can find no grip until a person has begun to exist. Benefits and harms can appear to have the same logic, and thus also to have a place only within people's lives. If they did have that logic, they would be inadequate vehicles for the interpretation of utility. Rights theories embody individualist constraints in ways in which a utilitarian theory of the good does not. Rights theories are preoccupied with how individual (existing) persons fare, whereas utilitarianism is preoccupied with the production of utility, regardless of where, when, or how it occurs.[29] Rights theorists have good reason for confining their attentions to independent persons. Utilitarians do not, and if it seems to them that they do, they are a little in love with a theory of rights.[30]

The classical theory may also seem odd in its inclusion of the utilities of "merely possible persons."[31] Consider again a woman deliberating among alternative projects. The classical theory requires that she forecast the utility of each, and thus that she include the welfare of the child in estimating the utility of reproduction. She cannot of course know in advance just which particular person her child will be, but she does know that if she opts for reproduction the resulting child will be *some* particular person, and she can also know that *any* child she will have is

29. As Parfit has put it, "a gain, a loss, another gain. . . ." (Parfit 1973, p. 157).

30. As Narveson has come to suspect; see Narveson (1978), p. 56.

31. Govier (1979).

likely to lead a worthwhile life. She makes her utility comparison and then elects to become an airline pilot instead of a mother. The central utility that was one of the factors leading her to that decision was the utility of a possible person who will never in fact exist—a *merely* possible person. Counting the utilities of actual persons is straightforward, but is it not strange to count the utilities of merely possible persons?

A utilitarian procedure for ranking courses of action in terms of their utility (and thus in terms of their moral value) necessarily involves counting merely possible utilities. Of a set of exclusive alternatives at most one can be chosen. The procedure requires predicting the utility each alternative would have if chosen. Before a choice is made, all of these are possible utilities; each could be actual *if* the appropriate choice were made. After a choice is made, one utility *is* actual (if the prediction is accurate); all of the others are now *merely* possible. Even in contexts involving no dependent persons the theory routinely requires reckoning merely possible utilities. What difference can it make, in contexts involving dependent persons, if some of these are also the utilities of merely possible persons? Of course only actual utilities determine in retrospect whether the best choice was made, and only actual persons have actual utilities. But this remains so if central utilities are included.

The counterintuitive results that the classical theory allegedly generates all concern duties. On the one hand the theory threatens to entail that individuals (or couples) have the duty to have children, as long as doing so will increase total utility.[32] Further, the theory also threatens to violate a deontic asymmetry that is deeply embedded in common-sense morality: that individuals can have a duty not to have a miserable child (whose life will not be worth living), but they cannot have a duty to have a happy child (whose life will be worth living). Both of these ob-

32. Avoiding this outcome seems to have been the principal motive of virtually every proponent of a revisionist theory.

jections presuppose a duty to do whatever will increase utility.[33]
But even a maximizing direct theory of the right is more selective in its distribution of duties, requiring that a course of action
generate more utility than any other available alternative. It is
doubtful that having a child is often a more efficient way of producing utility than all possible projects for improving the lot of
independent persons, and it becomes more doubtful as the world
becomes more overpopulated. Even on the crudest utilitarian
theory of duty prospective parents will not often have a duty to
have children, however happy those children might be.

In any case, an indirect theory of the right readily avoids these
unwelcome results. Having children can be a duty only if a law
or moral rule requiring women (or couples) to have children,
and imposing penalities on them if they fail, would maximize
utility. Any rule allocating such long-range projects to individuals would far transcend the minimalist function of social rules.
In deciding to remain childless, a woman harms no one. She
does refrain from conferring a benefit (upon a dependent person), but social rules backed by sanctions do not usually require
individuals to confer benefits. A society may need to maintain
population at a certain level (it may be important, for instance,
for the present generation to replace itself) but this collective
need does not readily factor into individual duties. To this point
in human history reproduction has been an area best left to the
free choice of individuals (or couples). Enough are normally inclined to have children to render the use of sanctions needless.

---

33. They also presuppose that having a child typically has a high utility
yield, so that reproduction always looks like a good utilitarian bet as
compared with other projects. A happy life no doubt contains a great deal of
utility, but it is not clear that all of this utility is to be reckoned as a
consequence of the act of creating that life (what about the later
contributions of other persons?). Determining how much utility a reproductive act has requires solving some difficult problems about the joint
production of utilities. Meanwhile the assumption that having a child is
most people's best bet for utility production must not stand unchallenged.

Should these numbers decline, incentives may be appropriate (such pronatalist incentives already exist in most countries), but penalties would be justifiable only in some repopulation emergency. There are possible worlds in which an indirect utilitarianism could entail a duty to have children, but ours is not one of them. (In the actual world we are more likely someday to have a duty not to have children). Thus the mere fact that a woman could have a child who would lead a worthwhile life can lead to no duty on her part to do so.

The case in which a child if conceived and born would lead a life of horrible suffering is different. Suppose that genetic screening or prenatal diagnosis reveals that a woman, unless she takes steps to prevent it, will certainly (or very probably) have a child that will suffer from some painful, incurable, and debilitating disease that will end its life before the age of five. Not taking the necessary steps (whether contraception or abortion) will harm that child, since it will inflict upon the child a life worse than no life at all. Social rules are principally designed to prevent interpersonal harms, and there is no reason not to extend their protection to dependent persons. A woman may, therefore, have a duty not to have a child that will lead a miserable life. But then the classical theory supports the deontic asymmetry of common sense: there is no duty to have a happy child but there may be a duty not to have a miserable child. And it does so without imposing any restrictions on how utilities are to be counted, and thus without violating utilitarian impartiality.

The implications of the classical theory for reproduction are thus common-sensical after all. Taking steps to prevent a new life from being created (e.g., by the use of contraceptives) is morally innocuous since there is no moral duty to reproduce. But then there is also no reason for embracing any form of revisionist theory. Such theories are worse than redundant. When one tinkers with a theory in order to force some desired result from it, one runs the risk of also producing unexpected and unwanted results. The average theory is conservative about population increase but not about population decrease. Since average utility is less responsive to the numbers of persons than is total utility, the best population policy for the average theory would be one of contraction to that pool (however small) whose numbers would enjoy the highest possible average.[34] The pressure for a contractionist social policy would have its analogue in the personal context, since the best choice for most couples would be to remain childless (unless they were certain of having a child whose happiness would be well above average). Meanwhile, an asymmetrical theory is blatantly inconsistent in including negative and excluding positive central utility. It could be advanced as a special case of a negative form of utilitarianism, but that theory is inconsistent for the same reason. In any case, an indirect theory of the right provides a better account of the connection between duty and harm to others.

A closed theory has particularly unpalatable results.[35] It cannot, of course, support a duty not to have a child whose life will be intolerable, for it cannot include the child's suffering as a reason not to conceive it. It can support a duty to have a (post-threshold) abortion or to commit infanticide in such a case, for the child is then an independent person whose utility is to be counted. But what plausibility is there in a theory that gives a woman no moral reason to avoid creating a child whose life will

34. Sumner (1978), pp. 104–106. My claim, however, that the average theory would lead us to approach this pool by killing off individuals whose lives were of below-average utility, is mistaken. Since such individuals would clearly be affected by such a policy, they must be included in the denominator when calculating average utility. I owe this realization to Jan Narveson. The original mistake was made by Henson (1971), p. 325. There is also an additional problem for average utilitarianism. Comparing courses of action in terms of their total utility does not literally require adding cardinal units of utility; it is enough if we can make certain kinds of interpersonal comparisons (Sen 1970, chap. 7). Computing average utility, on the other hand, requires cardinal units. But that might be a stronger measure of individual utility than is available.

35. See Parfit (1976a, 1976b).

be intolerable but does give her a reason to kill such a child once
it has been created? The theory also has the somewhat alarming
consequence that from the moral point of view it would be a
matter of utter indifference if this generation were to produce no
future generations at all—as long as our extinction did not injure the interests of those already living.[36]

26. *Utilitarianism and Abortion*

Classical utilitarianism implies a sentience criterion of moral
standing. It also supports the common-sense moral distinction
between preventing life and causing death, treating the former as
(normally) innocuous and the latter as (normally) serious. The
theory thus distinguishes the morality of contraception from the
morality of infanticide. Applying a sentience criterion to human
development leads to the threshold dividing early from late abortions. Early abortion, like contraception, prevents the emergence
of a human being with moral standing. Late abortion, like infanticide, causes the death of a human being with moral standing. If the classical theory distinguishes the morality of contraception from the morality of infanticide, it must also distinguish
the morality of prethreshold abortion from that of postthreshold
abortion. But then it explains and underscores the moral significance of the threshold and grounds a differential view of abortion.

The matter, however, is not as straightforward as it may seem.
The basic idea of a differential view is to extend the morality of
contraception forward across the frontier of conception, and also
to extend the morality of infanticide backward across the frontier of birth. The junction of the two categories is the threshold
at which the fetus becomes sentient; this is the crossover in
human ontogenesis between preventing the life and causing the
death of a being with moral standing. Of course abortions just

36. Bennett (1978), pp. 65ff.; compare Glover (1977), pp. 69–70, and
Kavka (1978), pp. 195–198.

on either side of the threshold (in the earlier weeks and in the later weeks of the second trimester) are not dramatically different, since fetal development is gradual. But the hypothesis is that they nonetheless belong to different moral categories and should be treated differently by an abortion policy. Distinct categories of acts often contain members that are close neighbors; that is not a problem. But there is a problem in showing that classical utilitarianism acknowledges the significance of the threshold separating the categories.

The problem can be exposed by attending exclusively to the central effects of contraception and early abortion on the one hand, and infanticide and late abortion on the other.[37] Electing the former has the result that the life of some being with moral standing does not occur; electing the latter has the result that such a life does not continue. Assuming that this life would be worth living, the outcome in both cases is so much foregone (central) utility. Thus the outcome in both cases, from the point of view of an open classical theory, is the same: *that* utility is prevented from occurring. The alternatives simply intervene at different stages in the process leading to a new life. If the central utility of all these acts is the same, how can the classical theory assign them to different moral categories? And if it cannot so assign them, how can it acknowledge the moral significance of the threshold of sentience?

The classical theory easily supports the application of a sentience criterion to the phylogenetic order because animal species do not move through time from presentience to sentience; the division of species into those with and those without standing is static. But the life history of a human being is (normally) just such a transition. A prethreshold fetus, unlike an oyster or a radish, has sentience in its future (if it is allowed to develop). For utilitarians the future matters; indeed it is all that matters. Thus

37. See Glover (1977), chaps. 11 and 12, for discussion of essentially the same problem.

intervening at various stages of the reproductive process, whether this involves preventing conception, killing a fetus, or killing an infant, all comes in the end to the same thing: all or almost all of the life of a being with moral standing never happens.

This problem weighs especially heavily on the classical theory. A closed theory that does not count central utilities has no difficulty explaining the moral importance of the threshold. If it adopts (as it should) a sentience criterion of moral standing, it can identify the threshold as the stage at which a new person (in the morally relevant sense) first begins to exist. Contraception and prethreshold abortion will have no negative central utilities (or rather, their negative central utilities will not be counted against them). But postthreshold abortion and infanticide will have such utilities. Thus the threshold will divide morally innocuous from morally serious acts.

But a closed theory is not a satisfactory theory, and so the question is how the threshold can be embedded in an open theory. The materials for answering this question are all at hand. First we must again separate issues of moral value from issues of deontic status. Thus we can ask of each of contraception, abortion, and infanticide either whether it is best (under the circumstances) or whether it is permissible. An answer to the one question, for an indirect utilitarian theory of the right, is not an answer to the other.

Let us begin with the issue of the good. The moral value of a course of action is determined by its position on a utility ranking of the alternatives open to the agent. It is important, therefore, to identify the alternatives properly. Having a child is a project whose alternatives are other comparable projects. *Not* having a child is not a project; it merely clears space for a project. Contraception, abortion, and infanticide are all means of ensuring that one does not have (i.e., bear and rear) a child. Thus they too are not projects; they are at best parts of (nonreproductive) projects. If we are to compare having a child with its alternatives, we need to know what else is open to the agent to do instead. The moral value of contraception, abortion, or infanticide will depend on the nature and value of these alternative projects. If having a child is the worst thing a woman could do (counting in both central and side utilities), one or another of these acts may be part of a best option. If having a child is the best thing a woman could do, none of them will be part of a best option. Since the ordering of projects will vary from person to person, and from context to context, we should not expect any uniformity in the moral ranking of these courses of action. Each of them will always have its cost in central utility, but this deficit can be made up in a great many other ways.[38]

Because contraception, abortion, and infanticide intervene at different stages in the reproductive process, they are employed in different contexts. Infanticide is unique in being (usually) unnecessary; if the aim is simply not to rear a child, then there are ways of accomplishing that compatible with the life of the child. Except in special circumstances, such as severe neonatal abnormalities, infanticide is a needless waste; the central utility of the child's life can be preserved and the side utility of the woman's autonomy gained as well. Contraception, on the other hand, is the least costly in side utilities. Because it is typically cheaper, easier, and safer than abortion, it is generally a better option. Abortion occupies a middle ground. Although in most of its forms it is inferior in side utilities to contraception, it is also the only means of terminating a pregnancy before term. Fetuses, unlike infants, cannot be transferred to those who will welcome them. Once an unwanted pregnancy is under way, abortion is indispensable for generating side utilities for the pregnant

38. Roupas (1978), who argues correctly that abortion involves a loss of (central) utility, then makes the astonishing claim that a woman can compensate this loss only by having more children and thus that "the only thing that really matters is how many children a woman bears in her life" (p. 180). This is to treat women as reproductive machines whose only possible contributions to social welfare take the form of having children.

woman. Consideration of side utilities thus leads us to the familiar conclusion that, other factors equal, contraception is better than abortion and abortion better than infanticide.[39]

The contextual differences among the three acts do not, however, expose the moral significance of the threshold. The context of a prethreshold abortion is much the same as the context of a postthreshold abortion; at both stages the fetus is nontransferable and abortion is the only means of avoiding the bearing of a child. The central effects of the two acts, moreover, are essentially the same. It is true that side effects render early abortion preferable to late, but the moral significance of the threshold is not rooted in this fact. If classical utilitarianism can explain that significance it must do so at the level of its theory of the right.

It is in this level that the boundary between preventing life and causing death is embedded. Rules of right formulate individualist constraints (rights and duties). Their primary purpose is protection of individual security, and their primary vehicle is individual rights. Positive laws and conventional moral rules do not normally require that we confer positive benefits on others, especially where doing so requires self-sacrifice. It is the essentially negative content of moral rules (their prohibition of causing harm) that explains why infanticide is (normally) wrong and contraception is (normally) not. Infanticide terminates the life of a being with moral standing; it therefore (normally) harms its victim. Contraception forestalls the life of a being with moral standing. If that life would have been a benefit for that person, contraception avoids conferring a benefit, but it does no

---

39. The reasons given in the preceding section for thinking that infanticide is less serious than other forms of homicide also apply here. At the stage of contraception the lives that are being prevented are complete ciphers who cannot, as particulars, have any connections with the lives of actual persons. At the stage of abortion, especially early abortion, this is also true; the loss for others is thus more easily remedied. Other factors equal, the earlier one intervenes in the reproductive process the better, so far as side effects are concerned.

one harm. Thus infanticide, but not contraception, can violate a right to life. Laws and moral rules (backed by sanctions) that prohibit killing will maximize utility, since agents generally have better courses of action open to them than killing; avoiding killing does not normally require self-sacrifice. Such rules are designed to redirect action into more productive channels. Laws and moral rules (backed by sanctions) that require the having of children will not maximize utility, since, for many agents, having a child will not be one of the better courses of action open to them. Given normal variation in the desire to reproduce, no rules are here required to redirect action into more productive channels.

Moral rules create moral categories, and these categories are most effective if they have reasonably distinct boundaries. Some boundary is needed between homicide (which normally causes harm and violates a right to life) and nonreproduction (which merely avoids conferring a benefit and cannot violate a right to life). A morality that draws this boundary in some clear and salient fashion will be more efficient than one that does not. The criterion of sentience furnishes the needed boundary. In its applications outside the abortion context (to inanimate objects, living things, extraterrestial life forms, artificial intelligences, the severely abnormal, and the irreversibly comatose), it tells us when our actions are capable of causing harm and violating rights. Indeed, the criterion defines for us what is to count as harm. Building a sentience criterion into our system of moral rules alerts us to the fact that our actions have a moral dimension when they affect sentient beings, regardless of how those beings may otherwise differ. Such a system is more intelligible and more coherent when its rules governing homicide are built around the same criterion. Those rules then become special cases of the more general rule that causing harm to sentient beings is morally serious (a violation of our duty and their rights). But we are dealing with a sentient being only after the threshold. Thus if the rules governing homicide are to have a utilitarian justification, they will distinguish the deontic status of pre and postthreshold abortions. We draw the most salient and defensible distinction available to us if we classify early abortion with contraception and late abortion with infanticide.

The future awaiting a human fetus is not relevant to its moral status; that status is based on what it has already achieved. The threshold is a moral quantum leap, for it is the stage at which the fetus joins the class of beings whose rights are secured by our network of positive laws and conventional moral rules. But once it is capable of being harmed, the future awaiting a human fetus is highly relevant to the extent to which it can be harmed. Before the threshold there is (in the deontically relevant sense) no creature to harm and no right to life to be violated. After the threshold there is such a creature, and its normal future is a rich and full life. To lose that life is to sustain an enormous loss. It is for this reason that postthreshold abortion (like infanticide) is morally more serious (other factors equal) than, say, killing nonhuman animals. The greater potential of human fetuses determines, not whether they have moral standing, but how strict the rules protecting their lives ought to be once they have gained that standing.[40]

Those rules ought to offer postthreshold fetuses and infants protection of life comparable to that normally accorded adults. Thus killing in these cases will be justified only by the familiar kinds of considerations, including self-defense and euthanasia. Self-defense cannot apply to infanticide, but both justifying grounds can apply to postthreshold abortions. The moral rules and the social policy regulating such abortions ought therefore to allow exceptions for these two contingencies. For prethreshold abortions, which cannot cause harm, no such regulation is required. Here abortion, like contraception, must be treated as a private act, one requiring no special justifying conditions. But then we have indirect utilitarian support for all of the

40. See Carrier (1975) for a similar view.

main features of a differential view of abortion: early abortions to be permitted at will, late abortions to be permitted only on therapeutic and eugenic grounds, and a boundary between the two located at the threshold of sentience.

As in the case of contraception, one need not resort to a gimmicked revision of classical utilitarianism in order to generate an intuitively acceptable view of the morality of abortion and support an attractive abortion policy. A classical theory with an indirect account of moral rules, and thus of moral rights and duties, is the deep structure of a moderate, differential view of abortion. To the extent that such a view is independently attractive, the classical theory is thereby strengthened. To the extent that the theory is independently attractive, a differential view is thereby strengthened. Their symbiotic relationship permits each to borrow from the virtues of the other.

List of Works Cited

ANSCOMBE, G. E. M.
  1968   "Modern Moral Philosophy," in Judith J. Thomson and
         Gerald Dworkin, eds., *Ethics*. New York: Harper & Row.
BADGLEY, Robin F., et al.
  1977   *Report of the Committee on the Operation of the Abortion Law.*
         Ottawa: Supply and Services Canada.
BEAUVOIR, Simone de
  1953   *The Second Sex.* New York: Bantam Books.
BENNETT, Jonathan
  1966   "Whatever the Consequences," *Analysis* 26, 3 (January).
  1978   "On Maximizing Happiness," in R. I. Sikora and Brian
         Barry, eds., *Obligations to Future Generations*. Philadelphia:
         Temple University Press.
BOURKE, Vernon J.
  1951   *Ethics.* New York: Macmillan.
BRODY, Baruch
  1972   "Thomson on Abortion," *Philosophy and Public Affairs* 1, 3
         (Spring).
  1974   "On the Humanity of the Fetus," in Robert L. Perkins, ed.,
         Abortion: Pro and Con. Cambridge, Mass.: Schenkman Pub-
         lishing Company.
  1975   *Abortion and the Sanctity of Human Life: A Philosophical
         View.* Cambridge, Mass.: MIT Press.
BROWN, D. G.
  1972   "Mill on Liberty and Morality," *Philosophical Review* 81, 2
         (April).
  1973   "What is Mill's Principle of Utility?," *Canadian Journal of
         Philosophy* 3, 1 (September).
CALLAHAN, Daniel
  1970   *Abortion: Law, Choice and Morality.* New York: Macmillan
         Company.
CARRIER, L. S.
  1975   "Abortion and the Right to Life," *Social Theory and Practice,*
         3, 4 (Fall).

CATES, Willard, Jr., et al.

1977 "Legal Abortion Mortality in the United States: Epidemiologic Surveillance, 1972–1974," *Journal of the American Medical Association* 237 (January 31).

CISLER, Lucinda

1970 "Unfinished Business: Birth Control and Women's Liberation," in Robin Morgan, ed., *Sisterhood is Powerful*. New York: Random House.

COPP, David

1979 "The Iterated-Utilitarianism of J. S. Mill," in Wesley E. Cooper et al., eds., *New Essays on John Stuart Mill and Utilitarianism*. Guelph: Canadian Association for Publishing in Philosophy.

DANIELS, Charles B.

1979 "Abortion and Potential," *Dialogue* 18, 2 (June).

DEVINE, Philip E.

1978 *The Ethics of Homicide*. Ithaca and London: Cornell University Press.

DONAGAN, Alan

1977 *The Theory of Morality*. Chicago and London: University of Chicago Press.

DONCEEL, Joseph F.

1970 "Immediate Animation and Delayed Hominization," *Theological Studies* 31, 1 (March).

DONNER, Wendy

1978 *John Stuart Mill's Concept of Utility*. Ph.D. Dissertation, University of Toronto.

DRINAN, Robert F.

1967 "The Inviolability of the Right to be Born," in David T. Smith, ed., *Abortion and the Law*. Cleveland: Western Reserve University Press.

1967– "The Right of the Fetus to be Born," *Dublin Review* 514
1968 (Winter).

ENGELHARDT, H. Tristram, Jr.

1974 "The Ontology of Abortion," *Ethics* 84, 3 (April).

ENGLISH, Jane

1975 "Abortion and the Concept of a Person," *Canadian Journal of Philosophy* 5, 2 (October).

FEINBERG, Joel
   1973   *Social Philosophy.* Englewood Cliffs: Prentice-Hall.
   1974   "The Rights of Animals and Unborn Generations," in
          William T. Blackstone, ed., *Philosophy and Environmental
          Crisis.* Athens, Ga.: University of Georgia Press.
   1978   "Voluntary Euthanasia and the Inalienable Right to Life,"
          Philosophy and Public Affairs 7, 2 (Winter).

FINNIS, John
   1974   "The Rights and Wrongs of Abortion," in Marshall Cohen
          et al., eds., *The Rights and Wrongs of Abortion.* Princeton:
          Princeton University Press.

FIRESTONE, Shulamith
   1972   *The Dialectic of Sex: The Case for Feminist Revolution.* New
          York: Bantam Books.

FOOT, Philippa
   1967   "The Problem of Abortion and the Doctine of the Double
          Effect," *Oxford Review* 5 (Trinity).

FOX, Michael
   1978   " 'Animal Liberation': A Critique," *Ethics* 88, 2 (January).

GLOVER, Jonathan
   1977   *Causing Death and Saving Lives.* Harmondsworth: Penguin.

GOLDING, Martin P.
   1968   "Towards a Theory of Human Rights," *The Monist* 52, 4
          (October).

GOODPASTER, Kenneth E.
   1978   "On Being Morally Considerable," *Journal of Philosophy* 75,
          6 (June).

GOVIER, Trudy
   1979   "What Should We Do About Future People?," *American
          Philosophical Quarterly* 16, 2 (April).

GRANFIELD, David
   1969   *The Abortion Decision.* Garden City: Doubleday and Com-
          pany.

GREENGLASS, Esther
   1976   *After Abortion.* Toronto: Longman Canada Limited.

GRICE, Russell
   1967   *The Grounds of Moral Judgement.* Cambridge: Cambridge
          University Press.

GRISEZ, Germain

1970a *Abortion: The Myths, the Realities, and the Arguments.* New York and Cleveland: Corpus Books.

1970b "Toward a Consistent Natural-Law Ethics of Killing," *American Journal of Jurisprudence* 15.

GROSS, Hyman

1974 *A Theory of Criminal Justice.* New York: Oxford University Press.

GUTTMACHER, Alan F., ed.,

1967 *The Case for Legalized Abortion Now.* Berkeley: Diablo Press.

HARDIN, Garrett

1971 "Abortion—or Compulsory Pregnancy?," in Martin Ebon, ed., *Everywoman's Guide to Abortion.* Richmond Hill, Ontario: Simon and Schuster of Canada, Ltd.

HÄRING, Bernard

1973 *Medical Ethics.* Edited by Gabrielle L. Jean. Notre Dame: Fides Publishers.

Harvard Medical School, Ad Hoc Committee to Examine the Definition of Brain Death

1968 "A Definition of Irreversible Coma," *Journal of the American Medical Association* 205 (August 5).

HENSON, Richard G.

1971 "Utilitarianism and the Wrongness of Killing," *Philosophical Review* 80, 3 (July).

HOWELL, Robert

1973 "Correspondence," *Philosophy and Public Affairs* 2, 4 (Summer).

KAVKA, Gregory

1978 "The Futurity Problem," in R. I. Sikora and Brian Barry, eds., *Obligations to Future Generations.* Philadelphia: Temple University Press.

KEETON, G. W.

1949 *The Elementary Principles of Jurisprudence,* second edition. London: Sir Isaac Pitman and Sons, Ltd.

KELLY, Gerald

1958 *Medico-Moral Problems.* St. Louis: Catholic Hospital Association.

KENNY, John P.
  1962 *Principles of Medical Ethics,* second edition. Tenbury Wells:
        Thomas More Books.

KREMER, Elmar J.
  1974 "Abortion and Pluralism," in E. J. Kremer and E. A. Synan,
        eds., *Death Before Birth.* Toronto: Griffin House.

LADER, Lawrence
  1966 *Abortion.* Indianapolis: Bobbs-Merrill.

LANE, The Hon. Mrs. Justice, et al.
  1974 *Report of the Committee on the Working of the Abortion Act.*
        London: Her Majesty's Stationery Office.

LOUISELL, David W., and John T. NOONAN, Jr.
  1970 "Constitutional Balance," in Noonan, ed., *The Morality of
        Abortion: Legal and Historical Perspectives.* Cambridge, Mass.:
        Harvard University Press.

LYONS, David
  1965 *Forms and Limits of Utilitarianism.* Oxford: Clarendon Press.
  1976 "Mill's Theory of Morality," *Nous* 10, 2 (May).
  1977 "Human Rights and the General Welfare," *Philosophy and
        Public Affairs* 6, 2 (Winter).
  1979 "Liberty and Harm to Others," in Wesley E. Cooper et al.,
        eds., *New Essays on John Stuart Mill and Utilitarianism.*
        Guelph: Canadian Association for Publishing in Philoso-
        phy.

MACKIE, J. L.
  1977 *Ethics.* Harmondsworth: Penguin.

MANNES, Marya
  1971 "A Woman Views Abortion," in Martin Ebon, ed.,
        Everywoman's Guide to Abortion. Richmond Hill, Ontario:
        Simon and Schuster of Canada, Ltd.

MCFADDEN, Charles J.
  1967 *Medical Ethics,* sixth edition. Philadelphia: F. A. Davis Co.

MELDEN, A. I.
  1977 *Rights and Persons.* Oxford: Basil Blackwell.

MELZACK, Ronald
  1973 *The Puzzle of Pain.* Harmondsworth: Penguin.

MILL, John Stuart

1969 "Utilitarianism," in *Essays on Ethics, Religion and Society.* Edited by J. M. Robson. Toronto: University of Toronto Press.

1977 "On Liberty," in *Essays on Politics and Society.* Edited by J. M. Robson. Toronto: University of Toronto Press.

MOORE, G. E.

1903 *Principia Ethica.* Cambridge: Cambridge University Press.

1912 *Ethics.* London: Oxford University Press.

MORGAN, Robin, ed.

1970 *Sisterhood is Powerful.* New York: Random House.

NAGEL, Thomas

1974 "War and Massacre," in Marshall Cohen et al., eds., *War and Moral Responsibility.* Princeton: Princeton University Press.

NARVESON, Jan

1967a *Morality and Utility.* Baltimore: Johns Hopkins Press.

1967b "Utilitarianism and New Generations," *Mind* 76, 301 (January).

1973 "Moral Problems of Population," *The Monist* 57, 1 (January).

1978 "Future People and Us," in R. I. Sikora and Brian Barry, eds., *Obligations to Future Generations.* Philadelphia: Temple University Press.

NEWTON, Lisa

1975 "Humans and Persons: A Reply to Tristram Engelhardt," *Ethics* 85, 4 (July).

NICHOLSON, Susan Teft

1978 *Abortion and the Roman Catholic Church.* Knoxville, Tenn.: Religious Ethics.

NOONAN, John T., Jr.

1965 *Contraception.* Cambridge, Mass.: Harvard University Press.

1968 "Deciding Who is Human," *Natural Law Forum* 13.

1970 "An Almost Absolute Value in History," in Noonan, ed., *The Morality of Abortion: Legal and Historical Perspectives.* Cambridge, Mass.: Harvard University Press.

NOZICK, Robert

  1969   "Coercion," in S. Morganbesser et al., eds., *Philosophy, Science and Method*. New York: St. Martin's Press.

  1974   *Anarchy, State, and Utopia*. New York: Basic Books.

PARFIT, Derek

  1973   "Later Selves and Moral Principles," in Alan Montefiore, ed., *Philosophy and Personal Relations*. London: Routledge and Kegan Paul.

  1976a   "On doing the Best for our Children," in Michael D. Bayles, ed., *Ethics and Population*. Cambridge, Mass.: Schenkman Publishing Company.

  1976b   "Rights, Interests, and Possible People," in Samuel Gorovitz et al., eds., *Moral Problems in Medicine*. Englewood Cliffs: Prentice-Hall.

PATTEN, Bradley M., and Bruce M. CARLSON

  1974   *Foundations of Embryology*, third edition. New York: McGraw-Hill Book Company.

PAUL VI

  1968   *Humanae Vitae*. Kingston: Canadian Register.

PEFFER, Rodney

  1978   "A Defense of Rights to Well-Being," *Philosophy and Public Affairs* 8, 1 (Fall).

PELRINE, Eleanor Wright

  1971   *Abortion in Canada*. Toronto: New Press.

PIUS XI

  1939   *Casti Connubii*, in *Five Great Encyclicals*. New York: Paulist Press.

PLUHAR, Werner S.

  1977   "Abortion and Simple Consciousness," *Journal of Philosophy* 74, 3 (March).

POTTS, Malcolm, et al.

  1977   *Abortion*. Cambridge: Cambridge University Press.

PRICE, Richard

  1974   *A Review of the Principal Questions in Morals*. Edited by D. D. Raphael. Oxford: Clarendon Press.

PURDY, Laura, and Michael TOOLEY

  1974   "Is Abortion Murder?," in Robert L. Perkins, ed., *Abortion:*

Pro and Con. Cambridge, Mass.: Schenkman Publishing Company.

RASHDALL, Hastings

1924   *The Theory of Good and Evil,* second edition. London: Oxford University Press.

RAWLS, John

1971   *A Theory of Justice.* Cambridge, Mass.: Harvard University Press.

REGAN, Tom

1975   "The Moral Basis of Vegetarianism," *Canadian Journal of Philosophy* 5, 2 (October).

1976   "Feinberg on What Sorts of Beings can have Rights," *Southern Journal of Philosophy* 14, 4 (Winter).

ROSE, Steven

1976   *The Conscious Brain.* Harmondsworth: Penguin.

ROSS, Sir David

1930   *The Right and the Good.* Oxford: Clarendon Press.

1939   *Foundations of Ethics.* Oxford: Clarendon Press.

ROUPAS, T. G.

1978   "The Value of Life," *Philosophy and Public Affairs* 7, 2 (Winter).

SARTORIUS, Rolf E.

1975   *Individual Conduct and Social Norms.* Encino and Belmont, California: Dickenson.

SARVIS, Betty, and Hyman RODMAN

1974   *The Abortion Controversy,* second edition. New York and London: Columbia University Press.

SEN, Amartya K.

1970   *Collective Choice and Social Welfare.* San Francisco: Holden-Day.

SIDGWICK, Henry

1962   *The Methods of Ethics,* seventh edition. Chicago: University of Chicago Press.

SIKORA, R. I.

1975   "Utilitarianism: The Classical Principle and the Average Principle," *Canadian Journal of Philosophy* 5, 3 (November).

SINGER, Peter
  1975   *Animal Liberation.* New York: New York Review.
  1976   "A Utilitarian Population Principle," in Michael D. Bayles, ed., *Ethics and Population.* Cambridge, Mass.: Schenkman Publishing Company.
SMART, J. J. C.
  1956   "Extreme and Restricted Utilitarianism," *Philosophical Quarterly* 6, 25 (October).
SNYDER, Soloman H.
  1977   "Opiate Receptors and Internal Opiates," *Scientific American* 236, 3 (March).
ST. JOHN-STEVAS, Norman
  1967–   "Abortion and the Law: The English Experience," *Dublin*
  1968   *Review* 514 (Winter).
STONE, Christopher D.
  1975   *Should Trees Have Standing?* New York: Avon Books.
SUMNER, L. W.
  1974   "Toward a Credible View of Abortion," *Canadian Journal of Philosophy* 4, 1 (September).
  1976   "A Matter of Life and Death," *Nous* 10, 2 (May).
  1978   "Classical Utilitarianism and the Population Optimum," in R. I. Sikora and Brian Barry, eds., *Obligations to Future Generations.* Philadelphia: Temple University Press.
  1979   "The Good and the Right," in Wesley E. Cooper et al., eds. *New Essays on John Stuart Mill and Utilitarianism.* Guelph: Canadian Association for Publishing in Philosophy.
SZASZ, Thomas S.
  1971   "The Ethics of Abortion," in Martin Ebon, ed., *Everywoman's Guide to Abortion.* Richmond Hill, Ontario: Simon & Schuster of Canada, Ltd.
THOMSON, Judith Jarvis
  1974a   "A Defense of Abortion," in Marshall Cohen et al., eds., *The Rights and Wrongs of Abortion.* Princeton: Princeton University Press.
  1974b   "Rights and Deaths," in Marshall Cohen et al., eds., *The Rights and Wrongs of Abortion.* Princeton: Princeton University Press.

TOOLEY, Michael

    1972   "Abortion and Infanticide," *Philosophy and Public Affairs* 2, 1 (Fall).

    1973   "A Defense of Abortion and Infanticide," in Joel Feinberg, ed., *The Problem of Abortion.* Belmont, Calif.: Wadsworth Publishing Company.

TORREY, Theodore W., and Alan FEDUCCIA

    1979   *Morphogenesis of the Vertebrates,* fourth edition. New York: John Wiley and Sons.

VEATCH, Robert M.

    1976   *Death, Dying, and the Biological Revolution.* New Haven and London: Yale University Press.

WADE, Francis C.

    1975   "Potentiality in the Abortion Discussion," *Review of Metaphysics* 29, 2 (December).

WARNOCK, G. J.

    1971   *The Object of Morality.* London: Methuen and Co., Ltd.

WARREN, Mary Anne

    1978   "On the Moral and Legal Status of Abortion," in Tom L. Beauchamp and LeRoy Walters, eds., *Contemporary Issues in Bioethics.* Encino and Belmont, Calif.: Dickenson Publishing Company, Inc.

WATTERS, Wendell W.

    1976   *Compulsory Parenthood: The Truth About Abortion.* Toronto: McClelland and Stewart.

WERTHEIMER, Roger

    1974   "Understanding the Abortion Argument," in Marshall Cohen et al., eds., *The Rights and Wrongs of Abortion.* Princeton: Princeton University Press.

WILLIAMS, Glanville

    1957   *Salmond on Jurisprudence,* eleventh edition. London: Sweet and Maxwell, Limited.

    1974   *The Sanctity of Life and the Criminal Law.* New York: Alfred A. Knopf.

WILLIAMS, Mary B.

    1978   "Discounting Versus Maximum Sustainable Yield," in R. I. Sikora and Brian Barry, eds., *Obligations to Future Generations.* Philadelphia: Temple University Press.

WILSON, Edward O.

   1978 *On Human Nature.* Cambridge, Mass. and London: Harvard
        University Press.

Women's Liberation Movement

   1972 "Brief to the House of Commons," in *Women Unite!* To-
        ronto: Canadian Women's Educational Press.

World Health Organization

   1971 *Abortion Laws.* Geneva: World Health Organization.

Index